THE TROUBLESHOOTER'S GUIDE TO DO-IT-YOUR-SELF GENEALOGY

Advanced Techniques for Overcoming Obstacles, Removing Roadblocks & Unlocking Your Family History!

www.essentialgenealogy.com

"W. Daniel Quillen's *Secrets of Tracing Your Ancestors* shows those new to the hobby how to begin their genealogy, while showing seasoned family historians some new tricks. Covering the basics such as organization, the best genealogical websites and how to do family group sheets, Quillen approaches his subject with passion and a touch of humor. The book also looks at features of advanced genealogy such as using professionals and writing your personal history. Most chapters feature additional resources pointing readers toward other resources." – *Family Chronicle magazine*

"*The Troubleshooter's Guide to Do-It-Yourself Genealogy* is a fantastic guide that answered a lot of my questions about doing your family history. I could not put this book down and I love all of the websites that he lists, websites I didn't even know existed!" – *Kisetta's roundup of genealogy books on amazon.com*

"Thanks for your help and for writing your excellent book!" – *Laura Johnson*

"I have enjoyed reading your book and I've found excellent leads for finding ancestors." – *Donna Mann*

"... It is not only informative but entertaining. Incorporating your own experiences in brought the book to life. Again, thank you for helping me to understand the many aspects of genealogy and for supplying a roadmap to finding more information about our ancestors." – *Dana L. Hager*

"Of all the books I have looked at yours is the best...and you write with your heart and soul. Thanks for writing such a great book." – *Karen Dredge*

"I got this book out of the library, but before I was half-way through it, I decided I had to have my own copy. Lots of helpful suggestions! I'd recommend it for all new and experienced family historians." – *Margaret Combs*

"I am embarking on the family history journey and have found your book to be very helpful ... thanks for putting together an easy to follow guide." – *Suzanne Adams*

"I started working on my family tree and was given your two books about tracing ancestors for Christmas this year. They are a gold mine of information! And the examples you give from your research experience are wonderfully helpful."
– *Jan McIntosh*

About the Author

For the past twenty-plus years, W. Daniel Quillen has been a professional writer specializing in travel and technical subjects. He has taught beginning genealogy courses to university students and working adults, is a frequent lecturer in beginning and intermediate genealogy classes in Colorado and speaks at national genealogy conferences. He has compiled his years of genealogical training and research into eight Cold Spring Press genealogy books, with more on the way. He lives in Centennial, Colorado with his wife and children. If you would like to contact him about anything in this book, his e-mail address is: wdanielquillen@gmail.com. For more information about all our books and our genealogy services, visit **www.essentialgenealogy.com**.

THE TROUBLESHOOTER'S GUIDE TO DO-IT-YOUR-SELF GENEALOGY

W. Daniel Quillen

Cold Spring Press

COLD SPRING PRESS

www.essentialgenealogy.com

ISBN 13: 978-1-59360-188-1
Library of Congress Control Number: 2014931249

Notice: FamilySearch is a registered trademark of Intellectual Reserve, Inc.

PHOTO CREDITS
Front cover photo: Gilles Dubois from flickr.com. Top back cover photo: HA!
Designs-ArtbyHeather from flickr.com. Second from top back cover photo:
T"eresa from flickr.com. Second from bottom back cover photo: Annes Place
from flickr.com. Bottom back cover photo: Library of Congress.
Page 7: yhoitink from flickr.com. Page 124: W. Daniel Quillen.

TABLE OF CONTENTS

Sidebars, Samples, & Tables

As I sit here pondering beneath my family tree

I think about the many souls whose roots sprang up as me.

My thoughts are turned to mother and her chosen path in life

And how it may have differed had she not become dad's wife.

I wonder what the options were back in her time and place.

What forces were her barriers? What dreams were hers to chase?

What were my father's interests? What did the future store

For one whose health made him unfit to fight a world war?

How far back does one have to go through father's pedigree

To find the one whose heart defect was passed along to me?

Perhaps I'll find some nobleman or magistrate or scholar

Or that the family's fame rests on an enterprising brawler.

I'd really like to find the source of grandma's flaming hair.

There's more to genealogy than who, what, when and where.

Strong trees and family legends are anchored by deep roots

And from the trunk that I've become will spring forth tender shoots.

The shoots will grow to branches, the branches will extend

Through countless generations toward the journey's end.

As I learn about our past, I'll add unto the store

Of histories and legends that make up my family lore.

— *Wendell Tolman*

1. INTRODUCTION

"If you don't know where you're going, any road will get you there."
—*The Cheshire Cat, Alice In Wonderland (Lewis Carroll)*

Welcome to the continuing world of genealogy! Perhaps you have started your genealogical journey with my beginner's guide to genealogy – *Secrets of Tracing Your Ancestors*, now in its sixth edition – or perhaps from some other source. Regardless, you're here, you're ready to go, so let's get started!

One of the things you've probably already learned in your quest to expand your genealogical knowledge and skills is that the more you know, the more you know how much you don't know. And yet, as you learn more skills and further your work, you stumble across new areas, new resources, new tools to assist you at every turn. Indeed, with the proliferation of information accessible on the Internet, information that was once available only by personal visits to distant cities is now available at your very fingertips. And countless records that today are accessible only in person are nearing the time when they too will be available by the click of a mouse.

In my own genealogical research through the years, I have reached more than the occasional dead end – or so it seemed. But as I learned more about the genealogical craft, I learned new ways to find information that had once eluded me. I have gathered a number of those methods in this book – sort of your *Troubleshooters* guide to help you get around those faux dead ends and find the information you are looking for, the information that is keeping you from reaching further back into your genealogical past.

We live in an exciting technological time, a time that brings our ancestors ever closer and closer. Whether through vital records, family and county histories or photographs, or other means, we are able to learn more than we have ever been able to learn and in a shorter timeframe.

While this book is targeted at genealogists with intermediate skill levels, those who have more advanced skills should also be able to glean more than a few nuggets. Those who are beginning genealogists will also benefit from information in this book, although in order to build a strong foundation for your genealogical research, you may wish to also seek out a book more focused on learning the genealogical ropes from the ground up, a book like *Secrets of Tracing Your Ancestors*, for example!

As I did in *Secrets*, I will introduce my family to you, as I will use several of them to illustrate research techniques and sources. As we progress through the book, you'll get to know my family better, as I will use many of them to illustrate various aspects and methods of genealogical research.

I am William Daniel Quillen, and I am married to the lovely Bonita Blau. We have six children.

My parents are:
• William Edgar Quillen and Versie Lee Lowrance

My grandparents were:
• Helon Edgar Quillen and Vivian Iris Cunningham
• Elzie Lee Lowrance and Alma Hudson

My great grandparents were:
• Edgar Estil Quillen and Theodora Charity McCollough
• William Edward Cunningham and Emma Adelia Sellers
• Thomas Newton Lowrance and Margaret Ann McClure
• Francis Marion Hudson and Margaret Ellen Turpin

My 2nd great grandparents were:
• Jonathan Baldwin Quillen and Sarah Minerva Burke
• William Lindsay McCollough and Lucy Arabella Phillips
• William Huston Cunningham and Amanda Stunkard
• John Thomas Sellers and Celeste Elizabeth Horney
• Alpheus Marion Lowrance and Catherine Gemima Reece
• Jeremiah Hudson and Frances Duvall

My 3rd great grandparents were:
• Charles Franklin Quillen and Susan or Susannah _____
• Samuel McCollough and Elizabeth Throckmorton
• Oliver Sayers Phillips and Charity Graham

- Joseph Cunningham and Sarah Rogers
- Matthew Stunkard and Margaret Peoples
- John T. Sellers and Elizabeth Ritchey
- Leonidas Horney and Jane Crawford
- Isaac Lowrance and Anna Witherspoon
- Francis Marion Hudson and Mary Magdalene Yates
- John E. Duvall, Jr. and Elizabeth _____

As you progress in your genealogical research, you may wish to pick up some of my other books on genealogy. We recently launched the series *Quillen's Essentials of Genealogy*, with books that focus more directly on the following topics:

- *Mastering Online Genealogy*
- *Mastering Immigration and Naturalization Records*
- *Mastering Census and Military Records*
- *Researching Your European Roots*
- *Researching your Irish and British Roots*
- *Mastering Family, Library & Church Records*

So, strap on your genealogical seatbelt and let's begin our journey together. I guarantee it will be a journey of joy and satisfaction, tempered with frustration and disappointment, replaced by triumph and excitement.

2. GENERATIONAL ASSISTS

"I find that the harder I work, the more luck I seem to have."
— Thomas Jefferson

As I have done my own genealogical research through the years, I have come to realize that different resources are available to me depending on the generation on which I am working. For (a silly) example, it's obvious to anyone, whether an experienced genealogist or not, that if I am looking for information on an ancestor that lived in the 1700s, I won't be using as a resource the personal memories and information possessed by anyone alive today! Likewise, the Social Security Death Index will not provide much assistance when seeking information about an ancestor who may have fought in the War of 1812. Common sense comes into play, of course, but also understanding the records that are available generation by generation will assist in your research. This section introduces you to records you may want to consider using for various generations of your ancestors. Following are short descriptions of some multi-generational sources; we'll discuss them more in-depth in later chapters of the book.

Numerous Eras
There are a variety of resources that will yield important genealogical information about your ancestors, almost without regard to their generation. Following are a few:

Censuses – One of the first acts of Congress of the newly formed United States was to establish the requirement for an official census of the citizenry of the nation every ten years. Starting in 1790 and extending to present day, censuses prove a valuable tool for genealogists. States got into the act too, and often conducted their own censuses – population, agriculture, industrial, etc.

Church records – Through the centuries, Churches have been inveterate record keepers, especially of births, deaths and marriages. During certain periods, they may be some of the only records available for some individuals.

Family Bibles – influenced, perhaps by all those *begats* in the Bible, generations of people have studiously completed the center sections of their family Bibles with information about births, deaths and marriages. Family Bibles may have genealogical information hidden within their pages, information that was often written at the time of the event.

Message Boards – Stalking message boards of various genealogy websites will often yield clues to unraveling research riddles.

Newspapers – Newspapers can be rich sources of information – genealogical and otherwise – about your ancestors. As the Internet proliferates, more and more newspapers are putting their earliest editions online in searchable databases. Currently there are a number of newspapers online from 1785 to present. Most online sources have search capabilities (better in some than others), and these assist you in pinpointing an article about your ancestor.

Obituaries – Obits are often wonderful sources of information. Of course they provide death dates, but they often supply other genealogical information, such as birth dates and places, names of living relatives, sometimes even the names of deceased parents, often the married names of daughters and sisters, and the places where children and siblings lived at the time of the deceased's death. Sometimes the cause of death is listed, which might be especially helpful if there is a history of health afflictions in your family. If the obituary of your direct-line ancestor doesn't yield the information you're hoping to glean, a good practice is to search for the obituaries of their siblings. While your direct ancestor's obituary may omit important information, his or her sibling's obituary may not.

Wills – The official documents called wills came into being around the time of the Norman Conquest – late in the 11th century – and have been providing rich genealogical information for nearly 1,000 years. In addition to real property, the names of spouses, children (often including the married names of daughters and sisters), even parents and siblings can be determined from wills.

In addition to the resources listed above, the following are resources and tools that may be of particular use in the indicated timeframes:

1930s to current day
For ancestors that lived during this time period, here are a few sources that may be of value in your search:

Living relatives – living relatives are always a wonderful source of information – but always a starting point, owing to dimming memories.

1930 and 1940 Censuses – The 1930 and 1940 censuses may provide first steps in your research as you search for relatives from the not-too-distant past. A number of genealogy-related questions help your research.

Social Security Death Index (SSDI) – The Social Security Act was signed into law by Franklin Delano Roosevelt on August 14, 1935. It provided an old-age pension for Americans. It is a database that holds over 80 million names of individuals who have been issued social security numbers. Genealogical information associated with the SSDI includes full name, dates of birth and death, and state and/or county of residence at time of death.

The person themselves – Don't overlook this important, living genealogical resource. You don't have to wait until they die to begin learning about their lives (but also try to learn a little about their ancestors too)!

Wills – These are great sources of information, often containing a great deal of genealogical information.

ENJOY ME WHILE I'M HERE!

Even as a child and teenager, I was interested in learning more about my grandmother's family, in particular her parents. Through the years, I asked numerous times, and she usually provided perfunctory, if any, information about them.

Finally, after I had asked yet again, my grandmother, with a little frustration in her voice, said, "Oh leave them be – they're dead and gone. Enjoy me while I'm here!"

A good point – while these aging progenitors of ours are a rich source of genealogical information about their family, don't forget to enjoy them while they are here!

1880 to 1930
Cemetery records – tombstones and sexton's records
Censuses – state and federal
Church records
Funeral home records
Immigration and naturalization papers
Living relatives (older, of course)!
Military records – draft and enlistment records
Mortality schedules (1880)
Passenger lists
Passport applications
Wills and other probate records
Vital statistics records

1830 to 1880
Cemetery records – tombstones and sexton's records
Censuses – state and federal
Church records
County histories
Funeral home records
Immigration and naturalization papers
Land records
Mortality schedules (1850, 1860, 1870)
Passenger lists
Passport applications
Service / Civil War records
Wills and other probate records
Vital statistics records

1780 to 1830
Cemetery records – tombstones and sexton's records
Censuses – colonial, state and federal
Church records
County histories
Funeral home records
Immigration and naturalization papers (1790 on)
Land records
Military pensions and other records
Passenger lists

Passport applications
Wills and other probate records
Vital statistics records

Generational Assists Checklist

____ Recognize that certain records will be more helpful than others based on the timing of the event (birth, life, death, military service, etc.) you are searching.

____ Familiarize yourself with the records available for certain timeframes.

____ Identify the timeframe in which you are researching, determine which resources will be of the most assistance.

Additional Resources

Steven Fisher (editor), *Archival Information (How to Find It, How to Use It)*, (Greenwood Press, 2004).

Sharon DeBartalo Carmack, *The Genealogy Sourcebook*, (McGraw-Hill, 1998)

Loretto Dennis Szucs and Sandra Hargreaves Luebking (editors), *The Source – A Guidebook to American Genealogy*, 3rd Edition, (Ancestry Publishing, 2006).

3. USING THE LDS CHURCH

"To raise society to a higher level is the chief business of the Church."
– A. P. Gouthey

In *Secrets of Tracing Your Ancestors*, I devote a chapter to using the genealogical resources available from the LDS Church. As this book is targeted at more experienced genealogists than the audience for *Secrets*, I am assuming you already know what an enormous assist the LDS Church is to genealogists, and the value of their extensive genealogical collection. I will address some of the resources of the LDS Church in this chapter, but not nearly in the depth I did in *Secrets*.

The Genealogical Society of Utah is an affiliated entity of the LDS Church and has been collecting genealogical data for a century and a half. They have been microfilming church and government vital statistics records almost since the technique was developed. To date, they have microfilmed records in over 132 countries, and they have made access to those records available to anyone who wishes to see them, regardless of their religious affiliation.

As you begin working with the LDS Church, there are three areas you'll want to learn about and get very familiar with:

• Family History Library
• Family History Centers
• FamilySearch™ website

Following is an overview about each one of these resources:

The Family History Library
The Family History Library is a massive building (nearly 150,000 square feet) that is located in downtown Salt Lake City at 35 North West Temple (Tel. 801/240-2331). In addition to millions of names of the world's people in books, microfilm and microfiche and every other conceivable type of

storage, there are hundreds of volunteer, part-time and full-time workers that are there to assist the nearly 2,000 visitors that visit each day.

I mentioned the library was the gateway to millions of names, and I wasn't using the term millions euphemistically! It is estimated that the various collections of the library contain the names of over three quarters of a billion names! And they add approximately 50,000 rolls of microfilm each year. The principal collections contain the names of individuals from the United States, Canada, Europe, the British Isles, Latin America, Asia and Africa. The majority of the information they have is for people who died prior to 1920.

Family History Centers
If you don't live in Utah or within driving distance of the Family History Library, don't be disappointed – you can still access most of the names that have been collected. The LDS Church has established over 4,500 branches of the Family History Library, called Family History Centers (FHC). These FHCs are located literally throughout the world, almost always located in a room or rooms of a local LDS meetinghouse. They are located throughout the United States and in over 110 countries. They are used quite frequently – over 100,000 rolls of microfilm are sent to FHCs monthly – over 1 million a year! Like the Family History Library, individuals do not have to be LDS to visit or use their resources.

To find the FHC nearest to you, go to www.familysearch.org, and at the top of the page, click on Family Search Centers. Enter either your city and state or your postal code and you'll be provided with the address and location of the Family History Centers closest to you. Included will be the address, phone number and telephone number of the center, as well as the days and hours the center is open. In the FHCs that serve smaller population areas, the hours are by appointment. If you do not have Internet access, call 800/346-6044 and representatives there will help identify the closest Family History Center to you.

The FHCs are staffed by volunteers; some are seasoned genealogists, many are not. But they should know about the resources available at the library, how to order microfilms, fiche and other records, and generally be able to help you navigate the waters at the FHC.

Many of the Family History Library's records are available at the FHCs. Visit your local FHC and order whatever microfilm or information you're looking for, and within a week or two they will arrive. They will remain in the center for six weeks, so you should have ample time to review them. If for some reason that isn't enough time, you can extend them for six more weeks. There is a small cost to cover shipping — $5.50 for each roll of microfilm and $.15 for each microfiche page.

The FHCs are equipped with microfilm and microfiche readers to make your life easier. Many FHCs also have subscriptions to such search companies as Ancestry.com, Fold3.com and HeritageQuest.com, and individuals can use them without charge while at one of the FHCs.

In some cases, your state library may also be able to order microfilm and microfiche from the Family History Library for you. If that's the case, check with your state library or local Family History Center.

FamilySearch.org

To assist genealogists worldwide, the LDS Church has developed an extensive genealogy website (*www.familysearch.org*) and database that allows individuals to gain access to the genealogical resources that the LDS Church has gathered through the years. It is called **FamilySearch**. Millions of records are available online for researchers, including birth, death, marriage records, military records and census data, family histories, and much more. Like all other genealogical resources provided by the LDS Church, FamilySearch is available to anyone regardless of religious affiliation.

The FamilySearch website was launched on May 24, 1999. From Day 1 it has been immensely popular – and incredibly busy. It gets roughly 14.5 million hits *each day*. Through the first decade-plus of its existence, it has garnered nearly **18 billion hits** and is still going strong. It has definitely positioned itself as one of the premier websites available to genealogists.

Records in FamilySearch come from a variety of areas. Over 40 million names were contributed from 1979 to 1999 by members of the Church of Jesus Christ of Latter-day Saints. These names represent members of their families whose records and information has been researched through the years.

Over 700 million names are included in the FamilySearch archives through partnerships with governments, churches and other records from over 130 countries. Most of the records are for individuals who were born between the 16th and early 20th centuries, although many records extend back beyond that period, especially church records.

In addition to these records, other records are available, such as the Social Security Death Index, Vital Records Indexes (a collection that contains birth, christening and marriage records from selected countries throughout the world), and censuses from the United States, Britain and other countries.

Education
One of my favorite areas of FamilySearch, and one of I have used extensively, is their fabulous *Education* section. This section provides articles, online courses and research helps to assist you in thousands of areas of research. These easy-to-follow resources have been produced for many states and countries, and provide research hints and assists on how to do research in the areas of the world you are searching. From the FamilySearch home page, click on *Get Help,* then click on *Help* and *Learn Home* and you'll be taken to a page that lists several resources for you: *Research Wiki, Learning Center and Research Assistance.*

The *Research Wiki* is a treasure trove of articles on genealogy- and research-related topics. As of this writing, there are over 65,000 articles available on a tremendous number of topics. Are you looking for information on US military records? Type that into the Wiki Search box, and you'll be treated to thousands of articles about researching US military records. Wondering how to begin research in Germany? Type *German Research* into the Wiki Search box and find over 1,000 articles on doing research in Germany. This powerful tool, like everything on FamilySearch.org, is free.

The *Learning Center* consists of courses that provide bite-sized information bits on a variety of research topics. Thousands of five- to 60-minutes videos are available for viewing at your leisure, covering a multitude of topics. As I was writing this section, I went to this segment of FamilySearch.org, and the main page listed videos on the following topics:

Most Popular Courses
Ireland Beginning Research Series – Church Records – 39 minutes
Beginning Italian Research – 59 minutes

England Beginning Research – Research Overview – 33 minutes
Genealogy Bootcamp – 27 minutes
Getting Started with Family History Research – 12 minutes

New Courses
Finding and Using Historic Newspapers – Part 1 – 29 minutes
Irish Emigration to North America: Before, During and After the Famine – 47
    minutes
Messages from the Grave: Listening to Your Ancestor's Tombstone – 52 minutes
Scotland's Old Parish Registers – How to Access, Use, and Interpret – 46 minutes

Aren't those just enough to make your genealogical heart go pitter-patter? And when you realize that these courses are just the tip of the learning iceberg, you'll be doubly excited.

The *Blog*, like the *Research Wiki* and the *Learning Center* sections, is another great source of information. Experienced FamilySearch patrons have been asked to share their expertise about FamilySearch, how to get the most out of it, assist other users, etc. Recent discussions centered on locale-specific questions and answers, discussions on how to locate specific resources on FamilySearch, etc. Some of the questions were specific to an individual: "I am looking for information about John Carroll, who was born about 1805 in Cork and married Margaret Driscoll." A short time later, a seasoned re-searcher posted a link to the marriage records for John Caroll and Margaret Driscoll. Other questions were more generic in nature: asking how to find a country's marriage records at FamilySearch, why a particular resource listed information in a particular manner, etc.

Taken together, these segments of FamilySearch are a great boon to genealo-gists, beginners as well as more experienced researchers.

LDS Church Checklist
____ If you are able to go to Salt Lake City, Utah to go to the Family History Library, determine what information you are seeking before you go.

____ Before you go to Salt Lake City, gather all necessary genealogical in-formation you may need while you are at the library.

____ Familiarize yourself with the genealogical services offered by the LDS Church.

____ Understand the value of local Family History Centers and how to get the most out of them.

____ Prepare the names you are doing research on before you go to a Family History Center.

____ Call your local Family History Center to determine days and hours they are open.

____ Be patient with Family History Center volunteers.

____ Locate the website for FamilySearch (*www.familysearch.org*).

____ Familiarize yourself with the information that is available on the FamilySearch website.

Additional Resources

Parker, J. Carlyle, *Going to Salt Lake City to Do Family History Research*, Marietta Publishing Company. (January 1996)

Warren, Paula Stewart and James W. Warren, *Your Guide to the Family History Center*, Betterway Publications. (August 2001)

Warren, Paula Stewart and James W. Warren, *Making the Most of Your Research Trip to Salt Lake City*, Warren Research and Publishing.

4. THE UNITED STATES CENSUS

"The true test of civilization is, not the census, nor the size of the cities, nor the crops, but the kind of man that the country turns out."
– Ralph Waldo Emerson

Every decade from 1790 to the present, the United States government has conducted population censuses of each state in the United States. These censuses provide a rich source of genealogical data, sometimes the only information that can be found on certain people and families. It also provides information about family relationships and locale.

In 1787 Secretary of State Thomas Jefferson directed the US Marshals of each state to appoint enumerators who would be responsible for collecting the census information. Most states simply added this responsibility to the plates of tax assessors, seeing that they were already gathering essentially the same information for tax purposes. As the population grew, and as more and more information was requested with each subsequent census, additional census enumerators were added.

Who, What, When, Where, Why and How…

Perhaps you remember from your junior high or high school days the "5 Ws" of good journalism: telling the Who, What, When, Where, Why, and How of a given situation. That is exactly what the US Census does. The Constitution of the United States called for the enumeration (census) of all of its citizens beginning in 1790 and continuing every ten years after that. The earliest censuses were little more than tally marks of the population, gathered together under the head of a family. But as the years progressed, they evolved to the point that they gathered very discrete information about each family and each family member in the United States.

Following is how censuses addressed the 5 Ws (& an H):

Who. Censuses were concerned with finding out the names of every person who lived in a certain area at a certain time. The censuses between 1790 and 1840 listed heads of family only, with tallies of all other persons in the household by age and sex. For example, here is the census for one of my relatives in the 1830 census:

1830 Census — Tuscarora township, Mifflin County, Pennsylvania

Head of Family: Joseph Cunningham
2 males under 5 years, 0 females 5 to 10 years
2 males 5 to 10 years, 1 female 5 to 10 years
2 males 10 to 15 years, 0 females 10 to 15 years
0 males 15 to 20 years, 1 female 15 to 20 years
1 male 30 to 40 years, 1 female 30 to 40 years

Beginning in 1850, every succeeding census has included the names and ages of each and every person living at that location at that time.

What. As mentioned above, the earliest US censuses focused on counting people only. As time went by, Congress realized that enumerators could glean enormous amounts of information about the population by asking just a few additional questions. From its beginnings as a tallying system, it grew to provide such information as:

• Names, ages and sex of each person enumerated
• Race
• Occupation
• Real estate information (value, owned or rented)
• Birth place of the individual and his / her parents
• Literacy
• Relationship to the head of the household
• Marital status and how long couples had been married
• Number of children born to a mother, and how many were living at the
    time of the census
• Year they became a US citizen
• Language spoken
• Whether they had attended school in the last year
• Military status
• Disabilities

Imagine what a gold mine a census can be as you begin or continue your research! I like them because they often tell me more about the individuals than just their names (things like their birth place, occupation, infirmities, etc.). It also gathers the individuals together into families.

When. Each census took the enumeration for a given date. For example, the 1910 census captured information about every individual who was living in a particular household on April 15, 1910. Even if the enumerator didn't come by the house until May 1910, the question would be asked about those living in the house on April 15 of that year. (So – babies born after April 15 won't be included, while those who moved or died after April 15 will be included.) The enumeration date varied from census to census; sometimes it is on the census page, and other times you have to do a little digging to discover the date used for enumeration purposes.

Censuses were taken in the US every ten years between 1790 and today. Due to privacy laws, as of this writing, the latest census available for the public to view is the 1940 census. (By law, individual records cannot be released to the public until 72 years after the census in which they were collected.) All censuses between 1790 and 1940 are available to view and search, except the 1890 census. Tragically, the vast majority of the 1890 Census was destroyed in a fire (or by the water that was used to put out the fire!).

1890 CENSUS – ALL IS NOT LOST!

As a genealogist, the temptation is to sigh and just skip over the 1890 census while doing your research. That might be a mistake. The federal government, in concert with Ancestry.com and the Allen County Public Library (a well-known genealogical powerhouse) has done what they could to recreate elements of the 1890 census, from the scraps of the census that remain, veterans schedules, Native American Censuses, 1885 and 1895 state censuses, directories, and various and sundry other documents, they have cobbled together about 20 million names of Americans – about 30% of the US population at that time. Included is the Oklahoma territorial census, which was taken during the same time period as the federal census, but it was not lost in the fire that destroyed most of the federal census. Since Oklahoma was an Indian Territory at the time, it wasn't included in the federal census.

So if you are searching for someone and wish you had some records from 1890, take a look and see what is available in this collection.

Where. Each census is very specific about where the people lived. The earliest censuses included the county and / or city where the family lived; later censuses included that information as well as the street addresses of the individuals.

Why. The initial reason for censuses was to determine legislative representation and for tax purposes. But Congress soon realized that important demographic information could be compiled from the census. Hence questions about national origin, literacy and occupation gave them a snapshot of what the nation looked like.

How. Enumerators went from house to house carrying large binders or tablets with the census template. They asked whoever was at home (presumably the oldest person available – preferably the head of the household) information about each of the individuals residing in the household on a given date. Just think of the difficulty that must have been in the days before ball-point pens! From the hundreds of census pages I have looked at (all microfilmed), it appears that all enumerators were required to use pen and ink rather than pencil. Many is the time that I have imagined in my mind's eye a tired, dusty enumerator stopping at the way-out-in-the-middle-of-nowhere home of one of my ancestors and asking all those questions! (Thank you from the bottom of my heart, enumerators!)

Questions, Questions, Questions
As time went on, the census forms evolved, and additional questions that were of interest to the government were added. Following are the various questions that were asked for each census:

1790
- Head of family
- Free White Males
- 16 and up, including head of family
- Under 16
- Free white females
- Including head
- All other persons
- Slaves
- County
- City

SO YOU WANT TO BE A CENSUS ENUMERATOR?

"Mr. Harrington will have the appointment of about 140 enumerators in the district. He is now ready to receive all applications for appointments and will furnish application blanks to all who wish to apply to him for them.

The appointment of enumerators will be made with reference to physical activity and to aptness, neatness and accuracy in writing and in the use of figures. The census requires active, energetic persons of good address and readiness with the pen. Only such can do the work with satisfaction to the Government or profit to themselves.

Each person seeking appointment as census enumerator must make a written application to the supervisor for the district of which a resident, giving the Christian name and surname in full; whether a citizen of the Unites States or not; present legal residence, sex and color; age; place of birth; the principal facts of education and of professional or business experience, including a statement of all national, state, county or municipal offices held at any time; nature of present occupation, if any; previous experience in census work; physical condition and knowledge of English and other languages. This application must be made in handwriting of the applicant throughout, and must be certified as such.

The work of the enumerators will not commence until June 1 and will probably be finished by July 15.

The compensation to be paid to enumerators is fixed by section 16 of the Act of March 3, 1899, and a minimum rate of two cents for each living inhabitant, two cents for each death, fifteen cents for each farm, twenty cents for each establishment of productive industry is provided for all subdivisions where such allowance shall be deemed sufficient....The compensation allowed to enumerators will be not less than three nor more than six dollars per day of ten hours actual field work.

Any enumerator who, without justifiable cause, neglects or refuses to perform the duties of his position, after accepting an appointment and qualifying for the work, will be subject to a fine of five hundred dollars."

(From an article entitled <u>Work on The Census - How Appointments are Made</u> in The News, Frederick, Maryland, February 7, 1900)

Note: No schedules are known to exist for the 1790 Census for Delaware, Georgia, Kentucky, New Jersey, Tennessee, and Virginia. It is thought that they were destroyed during the War of 1812 when the British attacked Washington. Some Virginia records are available from state enumeration records taken in 1790.

1800
- Head of family
- Free white males
- Under 10
- 10-16
- 16-26
- 26 to 45
- 45 and over
- Free white females
- Under 10
- 10-16
- 16-26
- 26 to 45
- 45 and over
- All others
- Slaves
- Remarks

1810
(Same as 1800)

1820
- Head of family
- Free white males
- Under 10
- 10-16
- 16-18
- 16-26
- 26 to 45
- 45 and over
- Free white females
- Under 10
- 10-16

- 16-18
- 16-26
- 26 to 45
- 45 and over
- Foreigners not naturalized
- Agriculture
- Commerce
- Manufacturers
- Free coloreds
- Slaves
- Remarks

1830

- Head of family
- Free white males
- Under 5, 5 to 10, 10 to 15, 15 to 20, 20 to 30, 30 to 40, 40 to 50, 50 to 60, 60 to 70, 70 to 80, 80 to 90, 90 to 100, over 100
- Free white females
- Under 5, 5 to 10, 10 to 15, 15 to 20, 20 to 30, 30 to 40, 40 to 50, 50 to 60, 60 to 70, 70 to 80, 80 to 90, 90 to 100, over 100
- Slaves
- Free colored

1840

(Same as 1830)

1850

- Name
- Age
- Sex
- Color
- Occupation
- Value of real estate
- Birth place
- Married within year
- School within year
- Cannot read or write
- Enumeration date
- Remarks

1860
- Name
- Age
- Sex
- Color
- Occupation
- Value of real estate
- Value of personal property
- Birth place
- Married in year
- School in year
- Cannot read or write
- Enumeration date
- Remarks

1870
- Name
- Age
- Sex
- Color
- Occupation
- Value of real estate
- Value of personal property
- Birth place
- Father foreign born
- Mother foreign born
- Month born in census year
- School in census year
- Can't read or write
- Eligible to vote
- Date of enumeration

1880
- Name
- Color
- Sex
- Age June 1 in census year
- Relationship to head of house
- Single

- Married
- Widowed
- Divorced
- Married in census year
- Occupation
- Other information
- Can't read or write
- Place of birth
- Place of birth of father
- Place of birth of mother
- Enumeration date

1890
Note: the vast majority of the 1890 census was destroyed in a tragic fire. Only fragments remain.

1900
- Name of each person whose place of abode on June 1, 1900 was in this family
- Relation to head of family
- Sex
- Color
- Month of birth
- Year of birth
- Age
- Marital status
- Number of years married
- Mother of how many children
- Number of these children living
- Place of birth
- Place of birth of father
- Place of birth of mother
- Years of immigration to US
- Number of years in US
- Naturalization
- Occupation
- Number of months not employed
- Attended school (months)
- Can read

- Can write
- Can speak English
- Home owned or rented
- Home owned free or mortgaged
- Farm or house

1910
- Name of each person whose place of abode on April 15, 1910 was in this family
- Relation to head of family
- Sex
- Race
- Age
- Marital status
- Number of years married
- Mother of how many children
- Number of these children living
- Place of birth
- Place of birth of father
- Place of birth of mother
- Years of immigration to US
- Naturalized or alien
- Language spoken
- Occupation
- Nature of trade
- Employer, worker or own account
- Number of months not employed
- Can read and write
- Attending school
- Home owned or rented
- Home owned free or mortgaged
- Farm or house
- Civil War veteran
- Blind or deaf-mute

1920
- Name of each person whose place of abode on January 1, 1920 was in this family
- Relation to head of family

- Home owned or rented
- Home owned free or mortgaged
- Sex
- Color or race
- Age
- Marital status
- Years of immigration to US
- Naturalized or alien
- Year of naturalization
- Attending school
- Can read or write
- Place of birth
- Mother tongue
- Place of birth of father
- Mother tongue of father
- Place of birth of mother
- Mother tongue of mother
- Can speak English
- Occupation

1930

- Name of each person whose place of abode on April 1, 1930 was in this family.
- Relationship of this person to the head of the family.
- Home owned or rented
- Value of home, if owned, or monthly rental, if rented
- Radio set
- Does this family own a farm?
- Color or race
- Age at last birthday
- Marital condition
- Age at first marriage
- Attended school or college any time since Sept. 1, 1929
- Whether able to read or write
- Place of birth
- Place of birth of father
- Place of birth of mother
- Mother tongue (or native language) of foreign born
- Year of immigration into the United States
- Naturalization

- Whether able to speak English
- Trade, profession, or particular kind of work done
- Industry or business
- Class of worker
- Whether actually at work yesterday
- Whether a veteran of U.S. Military or naval forces
- What war or expedition
- Number of farm schedule

1940
- Name of each person whose usual place of residence on April 1, 1940, was in this household.
- Relationship of this person to the head of the household
- Sex — Male (M), Female (F)
- Color or race
- Age at last birthday
- Marital status — Single (S), Married (M), Widowed (Wd), Divorced (D)
- Attended school or college any time since March 1, 1940 (Yes or No)
- Highest grade of school completed
- Place of birth
- Citizenship of the foreign born
- Residence April 1, 1935: City, town, or village having 2,500 or more inhabitants
- Name
- Place of Birth of Father
- Place of Birth of Mother
- Mother Tongue (or Native Language)
- Veterans: Is this person a veteran of the United States military forces; If so, enter "Yes"
- Veterans: War or military service
- For all women who are or have been married: Has this woman been married more than once?
- For all women who are or have been married: Age at first marriage?
- For all women who are or have been married: Number of children ever born (Do not include stillbirths)

I have found it helpful to make copies of the census templates as I do research in censuses. There are a variety of places on the Internet where census templates can be round, such as *www.genealogygenius.com/pages/default.aspx* or on my website at *www.essentialgenealogy.com/form_records*.

GET INVOLVED!

One of the things that impresses me about most genealogists is their willingness to share their research, abilities and successes with others. Well, FamilySearch.org, the LDS Church genealogy website, provides you opportunities to do just that – to give back to the genealogical community. And it is easy to do.

From the home page of FamilySearch.org, look near the top right-hand side of the Home page for the label *Volunteer*. Once you click on that, you'll be taken to a page that lists a number of volunteer opportunities. At the time of this writing, FamilySearch was looking for individuals to volunteer in the following areas: indexing, being a live research assistant, and writing articles.

Here is a little information about each of those opportunities:

Indexing – this is an opportunity to provide indexes for a variety of different genealogy records, including state censuses, birth, death and marriage records from around the world, etc. At any given time, there are hundreds of indexing projects you can lend your time and talents to.

Being a live research assistant – if you are an expert in a particular area of genealogy – Germany, Illinois, Ireland, Ohio, England, Virginia, Canada, etc., you have the opportunity to use your skills to assist other genealogists who are doing research in those areas. The support you provide can be via the telephone or via chatting on the Internet.

Writing articles – as the title of this item implies, if you have expertise in a particular area of genealogy, you may be able to write an article or lesson that will help other in that particular area. (Note: the author of this book has been quoted in some of those articles!)

Much of the success the LDS Church has had in their genealogical efforts throughout the years has been because of the legions of volunteers they have had assisting them. So if you have skills that you can share – please consider signing up with FamilySearch as a volunteer.

Indexing

We are fortunate to be living at a time when all the United States federal censuses have been indexed. Most any place that has a collection of the US censuses also has indexes for each census. Believe me – in years' past I have searched more than one census without the aid of an index, and it's a pain and a half.

Indexes for the censuses are by year and by state within the census year, and they are immensely helpful in finding ancestors, either in the state you expect them, or occasionally even in a state where you least expect them!

As you deal with indexes, generally you'll be inputting information into a search engine for the service that is providing the census (Ancestry.com, Fold3, FamilySearch.org, etc.). Completing search engines is more of an art than a science. My recommendation is to NOT place every bit of information you have (or think you have) into the search engine. Doing so may gate the search engine too much, and you may not get hits for your search.

For example, if you put the state your ancestor was born in, the search engine may disregard someone with the same name but who shows on the census as having been born in another state. My great grandfather, for example, is listed in various censuses as having been born in Virginia and Tennessee. When entering their year of birth, be sure and select the drop-down box that allows you to indicate you are willing to receive hits for individuals whose birth date is within 1, 2 or even 5 years of the year you enter.

If you have used some of the extra data (birth year, birth place, middle name, middle initial, etc.,) and are not getting any hits, then try searching the index by providing less information.

Soundex

If you do much genealogical work at all with the US Census, you will sooner or later come across a term and tool called *Soundex*. A Soundex index is not your typical alphabetical index. Rather, the Soundex indexing system attempts to provide all the advantages of an alphabetic index, yet at the same time tries to eliminate the vagaries of spelling variations for names. More on that in a few paragraphs.

The Soundex method was created in 1935 as a means of determining birth information for the new Social Security system introduced by FDR. It also provided meaningful work for members of the WPA (Works Projects Administration) during the Great Depression. These WPA workers applied the principles of the Soundex indexing system to the 1880 and 1900 through 1930 censuses. Here is information about the years of the census for which the Soundex system was used:

1880 -- only families in the 1880 census that had children 10 years of age or younger were included (The FDR administration was looking for birth years for individuals potentially eligible for the Social Security program);

1900 – all states were Soundexed;

1910 – only 21 states were completed;

1920 – all states were Soundexed;

1930 – twelve southern states were Soundexed.

In the previous section, we discussed the fact that all the US Federal censuses have been indexed, so you may be asking yourself: "Why is Dan telling me about an alternative to the alphabetical index, if all the censuses have been indexed?" Good question!

Here's the deal – as thankful as I am for the legions of census enumerators through the years, they often misspelled family names. When they did that, sometimes it's difficult to find those names in the indexes of the censuses. Let me give you an example: for years, I was unable to find my third and fourth great grandfathers (and my second great grandfather as a youngster) in the 1860 census. Finally, quite by accident, I discovered them living next door to one another. The reason I had been unable to find them was that their names were so badly misspelled that the search engines I was using for the index didn't recognize them! Instead of Quillen, they were spelled Quline and Quilling. Had the Soundex system been used for the 1860 census, I would have been able to find them lickety-split.

For example, if you were researching the name Cronin, in a strictly alphabetic index you might miss some ancestors who spelled their name Chronin. In essence, the Soundex indexes by the sound of the surname, instead of the spelling. Once you learn how to use the Soundex system (which you'll learn if you continue reading), I think you'll agree it is a remarkably ingenious way of indexing.

Each surname is assigned a four-digit alphanumeric code. The first letter of the individual's surname is always the first letter of the Soundex code. From that point, you ignore all vowels (A, E, I, O, and U) as well as the letters H, W and Y. Then, you assign a numeric value to the next three consonants (see sidebar below).

SOUNDEX CODING RULES

Use the following coding scheme to determine the Soundex code for the names you are researching:

1 for the letters B, P, F, and V
2 for the letters C, S, K, G, J, Q, X and Z
3 for the letters D and T
4 for the letter L
5 for the letters M and N
6 for the letter R

Then follow these (relatively) easy Soundex rules:

1. Always use the first letter of the surname, regardless of whether it is a consonant or a vowel;
2. After the initial letter of a surname, ignore all vowels (A, E, I, O, and U) as well as the letters H, W and Y;
3. Double consonants (ll, nn, etc.) are counted as one letter;
4. Only code the first three consonants after the first letter of the name – ignore the remaining consonants;
5. If a surname does not have three consonants after the first letter of the name, the number 0 is used to fill in the rest of the code.
6. Side-by-side letters that have the same Soundex code should be counted as one letter. For example, ignore the K and S in Dickson, since C, K and S all have the same Soundex code. This applies to first and second letters in a surname also.
7. If a surname has a prefix (Van, D', Von, etc.), then code the name with and without the prefix – the indexer may have used either name for coding.

Let's do a few examples to get you used to the idea and to see how it all works:

The surname Hudson would be coded H-325:
- Ignoring the vowels, H, W, and Y, Hudson becomes Hdsn, and:
- H = the first letter of the surname
- 3 = the numeric code for the letter D
- 2 = the numeric code for the letter S
- 5 – the numeric code for the letter N

Note that when considering the consonants in the rest of the name, we ignore any letter H (Rule #2), but since it is the first letter of the surname, we use it in the code.

The surname Quillen would be coded Q-450:
- Ignoring the vowels and the double ll (Rules #2 and 3), Quillen becomes Qln;
- Q = the first letter of the surname;
- 4 = the numeric code for the letter L
- 5 = the numeric code for the letter N
- 0 = the numeric code when there are no other consonants (see Rule # 5)

Now I don't have to concern myself with whether the name in the census record was spelled Quillan, Quillen, Quillin, or Quillon. The Soundex code for each one is Q-450.

The surname Techmeyer would be coded T-256:
- Ignoring the vowels, the H and the Y (Rule #2), Techmeyer becomes Tcmr;
- T = the first letter of the surname;
- 2 = the numeric code for the letter C
- (We ignore the H – Rule #2)
- 5 = the numeric code for the letter M
- R = the numeric code for the letter R

The surname See would be coded S-000
- Ignoring the vowels, See becomes S:
- S = the first letter of the surname
- 0 = the numeric code for no additional consonants (see Rule #5)
- 0 = the numeric code for no additional consonants (see Rule #5)
- 0 = the numeric code for no additional consonants (see Rule #5)

The surname Van Brederode could be coded V-516 or B-636 (see Rule # 7):
- Ignoring the vowels (Rule #2), Van Brederode becomes Vnbrdrd;
- V = the first letter of the surname;
- 5 = the numeric code for the letter N
- 1 = the numeric code for the letter B
- 6 = the numeric code for the letter R

And we ignore the remaining consonants in the name (Rule #4)

OR

- Ignoring the vowels (Rule #2) and assuming the name was indexed under Brederode, Van Brederode becomes Brdrd;
- B = the first letter of the surname;
- 6 = the numeric code for the letter R
- 3 = the numeric code for the letter D
- 6 = the numeric code for the letter R

And we ignore the remaining consonant in the name (Rule #4)

Hopefully, you can begin to see the power and versatility of the Soundex system of indexing. It is not flawless, however. As seen in the above example of a name with a prefix, that can pose a problem. Native American names might also pose a problem: did the researcher assign a Soundex code for *Painted* or *Shirt* for Painted Shirt, *Sitting* or *Bull* for Sitting Bull, etc. In cases like that, just code the name both ways and search for each coding.

Once you have converted the surnames you are searching for into a Soundex code, it's time to take the next step: searching through the Soundex cards.

Soundex Cards
Armed with the Soundex code, you'll now search the Soundex rolls for a match. Indexers (WPA workers) used index cards for each name on the census, and these cards are now on one of over 2,300 microfilm rolls. Unless you want to search through every state and US territory, you need to have at least a general idea of where your ancestor lived at the time of the census you are searching. At a minimum, you'll need to know the state your ancestor is from.

Soundex cards are arranged by state, and alphabetically and numerically within each state. For example, the card for the Addams family (A-352)

YEAR: 1880 1900 1910 1920 (Circle Year) **SoundexCard**

| Head of Family | | E.D. | Sheet |

| COUNTY | | LOCALITY: City, Town or Municipal District |

| SOUNDEX CODE | NATURALIZED? Yes No | IMMIGRANT YEAR | NATURALIZED YEAR |

OTHER MEMBERS OF FAMILY

NAME	RELATIONSHIP	AGE	BIRTH PLACE

Soundex index only exists for 1880, 1900, 1910 and 1920 Census

Above is an image of a Soundex card

would follow the card for the Asher family (A-260), even though if we were indexing strictly alphabetically Addams would precede Asher.

Since there is genealogical information on this card, you may be tempted to stop here. But don't do that – you've come most of the way on your journey to discover your ancestor on the census, and your goal is just around the corner. In addition to the important genealogical information on the card (which helps you to determine whether or not this is the right person), you'll find (in the top right-hand corner of the card) the E.D. (Enumeration District), the census sheet, volume number, county and locality. These identification marks will enable you to go to the actual image of the census page wherein this family is listed. Also note the Soundex code in the left-center portion of the card.

Once you have found a card that seems to match the person or family you are searching for, examine it closely. If you are looking for your second great grandfather and you think he was born around 1850, then the person listed on this card should have his name, an approximate age of 30 (if you are looking at a card for the 1880 census), and correct color and sex.

Note that there are only seven lines for family members on this card. Often, this won't be enough space to include all individuals living with the person listed. In those instances, another card will follow this one with the additional individuals on it. It will have the head of the family's name on it, along with the additional individuals, but it will not have the ED, volume, sheet, etc. listed. If you believe this is the card for your ancestor, copy the information.

The Census
Using the information from the card, you should be able to locate the exact place in the census where your ancestor is found. Once you find the correct state, search for the county that is listed on the Soundex card. (Note: If your ancestor lived in a large city, it may be listed separately from the county the city is in.)

Write it Down!
Now that you've found your ancestor and his or her family, what next? First and foremost, write down the information exactly as it appears on the census. Writing the information down exactly is very important. For example, even though you KNOW that your great grandmother's name was Susan, if her name appears as Susannah on the census, resist the temptation to "correct" the entry when you copy the information. It may just be that

the family traditions about her name being Susan are incorrect, and that her real name was Susannah.

I had an interesting experience with that in my own family. Family tradition held that my great grandmother was born in Arkansas. Yet when I located her as a child on a census schedule, it listed Texas as her state of birth. Even though I knew that wasn't right, I wrote the information down exactly as it appeared. Years later, I learned from one of my great aunts that my great grandmother's birth place really was Texas...she only told people she was born in Arkansas because she was embarrassed to admit she was born in Texas! (Sorry to those from the Lone Star state!)

Back to writing exactly what appears: you can write the information on a piece of paper or use a census template. You can create your own census templates, or you can go to my website (*www.essentialgenealogy.com/ forms__records*) and download census templates for free.

What Next?
Okay, so now you have found your second great grandfather in the US Census. Now what do you do? Before you declare victory and move on – consider a caution. While the amount of information that is found in censuses is immense, remember that it is considered a secondary source of information – much of the information was written down many years after the event happened. Events like place of birth of parents, year and/or months of birth, etc. could be incorrect.

Finding the Censuses
Notwithstanding the lack of exact information, I heartily recommend that you use census records to assist you in finding families you are searching for. So, where do you find them? There are several places. If you live in the state where your ancestors lived, the genealogy section of the state library will have at least your state's census records, and they may have the records for other states. (See the Appendix for a listing of state libraries nationwide.)

If the state library doesn't have the census microfilms, then there are fourteen locations of the national archives, and each has all the states' censuses on microfilm. The addresses for the Regional National Archives Centers are located in the Appendix.

And finally, a number of subscription services such as Ancestry.com and Fold3.com and FamilySeaarch.org also have census records online.

Don't forget that your local Family History Center also allows you to order and view census microfilms from the Family History Library in Salt Lake City.

United States Census Checklist

___ Identify the state(s) your ancestor may have lived in during a certain timeframe.

___ Determine whether your ancestor will be a child or adult in the census.

___ Locate the appropriate census.

___ Learn how to use the Soundex system of indexing. Learn its strengths and limitations.

Additional Resources

Steven Fisher (editor), *Archival Information (How to Find It, How to Use It)*, (Greenwood Press, 2004).

5. STATE CENSUSES &
MORTALITY SCHEDULES

*"I just want to know how people with multiple personalities fill
out their census papers."* — Unknown

State Censuses

As helpful as the US Federal Censuses are, many of the states (and territories before statehood) conducted their own censuses. Often overlooked
by genealogists, these censuses provide yet another source for locating ancestors – seeing if they remained in the area they had been during the US
Census, identifying children who may not have been born at the time of
the Federal census, etc., etc.

The state and territorial censuses generally did not follow the federal practice
of enumeration in the first year of each decade. The state enumerations were
generally later in the decade. Some states did this frequently (in this regard,
you're lucky if your ancestors lived in Michigan, New Jersey or New York, for
example), and others only once (my home state of Colorado, for example).
Some didn't do them at all, especially those who entered the union later
than others. Sometimes these censuses were very similar in content to the
US Federal census, sometimes they were more extensive (New Jersey and
New York, for example), and other times they were much more abbreviated.
Regardless, these oft-forgotten records are another source of genealogical
information that may help you locate and/or pin down some elusive ancestors.

For those states that didn't conduct censuses, some conducted "censuses" of
tax payers, and while these tax lists don't list families, they do list heads of
household on a specific date at a specific place, and can serve as a substitute
for a state census. For example, say you have found your ancestor in the
1880 census. Being a keen and experienced genealogist, you know that the
vast majority of the 1890 census was destroyed by fire, so you look for your
ancestor in the 1900 census, but even though you find his family, he's not
there. Now – that represents a pretty wide span of time in which he could

have died – 20 years. But if the state has a tax list for any of the years in between 1880 and 1900, you may be able to narrow the timeframe. If, for example, he shows up in 1893, then the timeframe is down to seven years. If, however, you find his wife listed as the head of household in 1885, then the timeframe is five years. (Caution – it is possible that he may have simply abandoned his family, or divorced, and that accounts for his disappearance!)

Mortality Schedules

Another important record that was kept coincident with the US Census was the **Mortality Schedule** for the 1850 through 1880 censuses. These schedules listed everyone who had died between June 1 of the year before the census and May 31 of the census year. They listed the name, age, sex, marital status, race, occupation, birth place, cause of death and length of illness for each individual who passed away during that year.

Now, one year's worth of death information might not seem like a lot, but it represents 10% of the deaths in a decade, so you have the possibility of finding information about that elusive ancestor of yours. And – this before most states began requiring that deaths be recorded. The mortality schedule may in fact be the only place the death is recorded, outside the family's Bible!

Let me give you a simple example using a member of my family. I know that many generations of my family were born, lived and died in Scott County, Virginia. Using the mortality schedule of the 1880 US census, I searched for any Quillens in Scott County Virginia that might have died between June 1, 1879 and May 31, 1880. Sure enough, I found this listing in the mortality schedule:

James G. Quillin   1/12   Male White Month of death – January

I then searched to see if I could find the family to whom he belonged, and discovered this sad family:

Ewel H. Quillin   40 Male White
Elizabeth D. Quillin 40 Female White

As heartbroken as Ewell and Elizabeth were at the loss of their precious one-month old son James G., I believe they would have been doubly heart-broken not to have their little son with them, gathered together as a family in my records. Had I not checked the mortality schedule for 1880, I would likely have never known that James was a member of their family, because his name appeared in no other source that I have yet found. I would have missed this important family member.

Checking the mortality schedules and matching those you find there to their family is fairly straight forward. Here's how I found James G. Quillin, and was able to join him to his family:

1. I used my subscription to Ancestry.com to access the 1880 census.
2. To find the mortality schedules at Ancestry, I went to the *Search* tab, clicked on *Card Catalog*, then in the *Keyword Search* menu I typed *1880 Mortality Schedules*.
3. I searched the mortality schedule for 1880 using Quillen and Scott County, Virginia as delineators.
4. I found James G. Quillin (note the different spelling) listed on the mortality schedule in the Estilleville, Scott County, Virginia enumeration district. I noted that he was associated with family #104 of the enumeration district.
5. I then went to the 1880 US Census (not the mortality schedule) for the Estilleville, Scott County, Virginia enumeration district and found family #104 in the enumeration district – Ewell H. and Elizabeth D. Quillin.
6. Note: the census enumerators numbered each dwelling and family they found in each enumeration district. These numbers are usually the left-most columns on the census record. In this manner, I was able to match James G. Quillin with his family.

If you have an opportunity to search mortality schedules, you may find it interesting to note the ages of those who died. So many of them are children under age 10 — infant and young child mortality was very high in the mid-1800s. I guarantee it will tug at your heartstrings!

Generally speaking, you'll find each state's mortality schedules wherever you find their federal censuses. Those locations include each state's library and archives, several subscription-based services like Ancestry.com, Heritage Quest, FamilySearch.org, etc.

Following is state-by-state information about the existence (or not!) of and details about state censuses and mortality schedules:

Alabama

Alabama became a state in 1819. Territorial censuses were taken for Washington County, Mississippi Territory, which included present-day Alabama, for 1801, 1808, and 1810. State censuses were taken in Alabama in 1820, 1831, 1844, 1850, 1855, and 1866. The Alabama state censuses can be viewed at the Alabama Department of Archives and History, and several are available on microfilm through the Family History Library of the LDS Church.

1820 – Only eight counties are available, and none of them are indexed: Baldwin, Conecuh, Dallas, Franklin, Limestone, St. Clair, Shelby, Wilcox. The census provides the name of head of household; free white males and females in age categories; number of slaves and free persons of color in age categories.

1850 – There is no index. The census provides the name of head of household; free white males and females in age categories; number of slaves and free persons of color in age categories.

1855 – The 1855 state census is indexed (14 counties: Autauga, Baldwin, Blount, Coffee, Franklin, Henry, Lowndes, Macon, Mobile, Montgomery [on film, but not included in the index], Pickens, Sumter [not on microfilm and not included in the index], Tallapoosa, Tuscaloosa). The census provides the name of head of household; number of free white males and females in age categories; number of slaves and free persons of color in age categories.

1866 – There is no index. The census provides the name of head of household for African-Americans and whites; number of females and males in age categories.

There were also Confederate Veterans' Censuses taken in 1907, 1921, and 1927.

The 1890 federal population census for part of Perry County, Alabama, survived a fire in 1921. The remaining portion is for Perryville, beat number 11 and Severe, beat number 8.

Mortality schedules exist for the 1850, 1860, 1870, and 1880 censuses.

Alaska

Alaska became a territory in 1912 and a state in 1959. Miscellaneous censuses of parts of the Aleutian Islands have been indexed in *Alaska Census Records, 1870-1907* by Ronald Vern Jackson. This book is available on microfilm from the Family History Library of the LDS Church. It is also available online from Ancestry.com.

Mortality schedules do not exist for Alaska.

Arizona

Arizona became a state in 1912 - no state censuses. No formal, statewide censuses were conducted for Arizona. However, censuses covering specific demographics were conducted and may be helpful. Territorial censuses exist for 1864, 1866, 1867, 1869, 1871, 1872, and 1882 although they are not all complete. The Family History Library of the LDS Church has each of these available on microfilm, and has indexes for 1864, 1866, 1867, and 1869. Numerous are available through Ancestry.com, and all are available at the Arizona Department of Libraries, Archives and Public Records.

Mortality schedules exist for the 1850, 1860, 1870, and 1880 censuses.

Arkansas

Arkansas became a state in 1836. No state censuses were conducted. However, the Arkansas History Commission has sheriff's censuses for several counties in 1829 and Arkansas County in 1823. These are available on microfilm from the Family History Library of the LDS Church. They are also indexed in *Arkansas Sheriff's Censuses: 1823 and 1829*, written by Ronald Vern Jackson. Only the heads of households are listed in these censuses.

Mortality schedules exist for the 1870 and 1880 censuses.

California

California became a state in 1850. There is an 1852 state census. Before California became a state, censuses (called *padrones*) were taken of the Indian, Mexican and Spanish populations. They have been published in *The Quarterly (Historical Society of Southern California)*, vols. 15, 18, 41-43, 54, and are available at the Family History Library of the LDS Church. The 1852 state census is also available at the California State Archives. An index for the census is available.

There were also censuses taken of Los Angeles in 1790, 1836 and 1844. The Family History Library of the LDS Church has these censuses on microfilm. Especially helpful are the Los Angeles censuses of 1790, 1836, and 1844. The original records are scattered among various archives. The Family History Library has copies on microfilm.

Mortality schedules exist for the 1850, 1860, 1870, and 1880 censuses.

Colorado

Colorado became a state in 1876. No state censuses are available for Colorado; however, there is a special 1885 federal census in addition to the normal 1880 census. Colorado was formed from portions of four territories: Nebraska, Kansas, New Mexico and Utah. The Colorado portions of those territorial censuses have been gathered into an 1860 Colorado Territorial census. (Note – the portion of the Utah census was not enumerated since that part of the Colorado was not yet settled.) The Family History Library has copies on microfilm.

There is an 1870 Colorado Territorial census available at the Family History Library of the LDS Church and at the Colorado State Archives.

Mortality schedules exist for the 1860, 1870, and 1880 censuses.

Connecticut

Connecticut became a state in 1788. There are no state censuses, except for a 1917 military census available at the Connecticut State Library.

A 1670 census was researched and published by Jay Mack Holbrook in Connecticut 1670 Census, which lists over 2,300 heads of household as recorded in tax lists and other available records.

Mortality schedules exist for the 1850, 1860, 1870, and 1880 censuses.

Delaware

Delaware became a state in 1787. There are no state censuses. However, a census covering seven townships (a small percentage of the state's townships) has been combined with the tax lists for the state.

A Colonial census was taken in 1693 of the Swedes who were members of the

Swedish Lutheran Church and who were living in several eastern seaboard states, including Delaware. The information is contained in *The 1693 Census of the Swedes on the Delaware*, written by Peter Stebbins Craig (Winter Park, FL, SAG Publications, 1993). The book is available on microfilm from the Family History Library of the LDS Church.

Mortality schedules exist for the 1850, 1860, 1870, and 1880 censuses.

District of Columbia

The District of Columbia has district censuses for 1803, 1807, 1818, 1867, and 1878, which are at the Maryland State Archives. There are also police censuses for 1885 to 1919, which list heads of households.

A *Veterans Schedule* taken in 1890 is available on microfilm at the Family History Library of the LDS Church.

District censuses are available for 1803, 1807, 1818, 1867 and 1878. The first three give very little information, but the latter two are very detailed. These records can be found in the Maryland State Archives.

Police censuses were also taken in 1885, 1894, 1897, 1905, 1906, 1907, 1908, 1909, 1912, 1915, 1917, 1919, and 1925, although the 1925 census is missing. These police censuses were published in the *Annual Reports of the Commissioner of the District of Columbia*, and are available at the National Archives as well as at the District of Columbia Archives.

Mortality schedules exist for the 1850, 1860, 1870, and 1880 censuses.

Florida

Florida became a state in 1845. State censuses of Florida exist for 1845, 1855, 1865, 1868, 1875, 1885, 1895, 1935, and 1945.

Colonial and territorial censuses exist for 1783, 1786, 1790, 1793, 1814, 1825 and 1837. State censuses begin in 1845, and were conducted every ten years until 1945. Each of these records is available at the Florida State Archives.

Mortality schedules exist for the 1850, 1860, 1870, and 1880 censuses.

Georgia

Georgia became a state in 1788. State censuses of Georgia were taken in various years. These state censuses are available at the Georgia Department of Archives and History, and some county censuses between 1827 and 1890 are available at the Family History Center of the LDS Church.

Mortality schedules exist for the 1850, 1860, 1870, and 1880 censuses.

Hawaii

Hawaii was annexed by the United States in 1898 and became a state in 1959. No state censuses.

Censuses from Hawaii's colonial days are available for portions of Hawaii for 1866, 1878 (Hilo, Oahu, Maui and Hawaii only), 1890 (all islands except Niihau), and 1896 (Honolulu only). All are available at the Hawaii State Archives and the Family History Library of the LDS Church.

The Hawaii State Archives also has two census files which contain various and sundry records (school census, population lists etc.) covering the periods from 1840 to 1866 1847 to 1866.

There are no mortality schedules available for Hawaii.

Idaho

Idaho became a state in 1890. There are no state censuses. However, parts of Idaho were included in several Territorial censuses: 1850 Oregon, 1860 Washington and the 1870 and 1880 censuses for Idaho Territory. Parts of southern Idaho were included in the 1860 and 1870 censuses of Cache County, Utah.

There are several non-population censuses available for 1870 and 1880 in Idaho. These censuses covered agricultural and industrial topics. An online name index is available from the Idaho State Archives website. On the same website you'll find a census of the *Idaho State and Territorial Penitentiary Inmate Files* from 1864 to 1947, in case any of your ancestors were of the unsavory type.

Mortality schedules exist for the 1870 and 1880 censuses.

Illinois

Illinois became a state in 1818. State and Territorial censuses are available for 1810, 1818, 1820, 1825, 1830, 1835, 1840, 1845, 1855, and 1865. Indexes are available for the 1810, 1818 and 1820 at the Illinois State Archives, as well as the Family History Library of the LDS Church.

At the Illinois State Archives, there is a Name Index to Early Illinois Records, which provides a name index for most of the state, territorial and federal censuses.

Mortality schedules exist for the 1850, 1860, 1870, and 1880 censuses.

Indiana

Indiana became a state in 1816. Indiana has some state enumerations for 1853 to 1877.

Mortality schedules exist for the 1850, 1860, 1870, and 1880 censuses.

Iowa became a state in 1846. State censuses were taken from 1846 to 1925.

Mortality schedules exist for the 1850, 1860, 1870, and 1880 censuses.

Kansas became a state in 1861. Kansas has state censuses for 1865, 1875, 1885, 1895, 1905, 1915, and 1925.

Mortality schedules exist for the 1850, 1860, 1870, and 1880 censuses.

Kentucky became a state in 1792 - no state censuses.

Mortality schedules exist for the 1860, 1870, and 1880 censuses.

Louisiana became a state in 1812 and has state censuses for a few parishes: 1813 (St. Landry), 1833 (St. Tammany), 1837 (Ascension), 1856-57 (Carrollton).

Mortality schedules exist for the 1850, 1860, 1870, and 1880 censuses.

Maine became a state in 1820. There was a Maine state census in 1837, which is available for several cities and towns.

Mortality schedules exist for the 1850, 1860, 1870, and 1880 censuses.

Maryland

Maryland became a state in 1788, and conducted no state censuses.

However, during the Colonial period, several censuses were taken in Maryland. In 1776, a census was taken of those who took oaths of allegiance to America, and in 1778, a census was taken of those who opposed the Revolutionary War. Those opposed were primarily Mennonites and Quakers, as well as some Tories that still remained in America. There were others who refused to take an oath of allegiance to the new country. Information about both of these censuses is contained in books written by Bettie Stirling Carothers, available in the Family History Library of the LDS Church, as well as on microfilm. They are also available in the Maryland State Library. They are entitled simply *1776 Maryland Census* and *1778 Maryland Census*.

Censuses of Civil War veterans living in Maryland were conducted in 1890 – this is particularly of interest, since the vast majority of the 1890 US census was lost in a fire. The title of the book is *1890 Special Census of the Civil War Veterans of the State of Maryland*, by L. Tilden Moore, and it is available at the Maryland State Library.

A Colonial census was taken in 1693 of the Swedes who were members of the Swedish Lutheran Church and who were living in several eastern seaboard states, including Cecil County, Maryland. The information is contained in *The 1693 Census of the Swedes on the Delaware*, written by Peter Stebbins Craig (Winter Park, FL, SAG Publications, 1993).

Mortality schedules exist for the 1850, 1860, 1870, and 1880 censuses.

Massachusetts

Massachusetts became a state in 1788. There are state censuses for Massachusetts for 1855 and 1865.

Among other data gathered, the 1865 Massachusetts state census asked if males were legal voters or naturalized voters.

Mortality schedules exist for the 1850, 1860, 1870, and 1880 censuses.

Michigan

Michigan became a state in 1837. State censuses were taken in the years 1845, 1854, 1864, 1874, 1884, 1894, and 1904.

Mortality schedules exist for the 1850, 1860, 1870, and 1880 censuses.

Minnesota became a state in 1858. State censuses were taken in 1865, 1875, 1885, 1895, and 1905.

Mortality schedules exist for the 1850, 1860, 1870, and 1880 censuses.

Mississippi became a state in 1817. State censuses were taken in some counties in 1818, 1820, 1822, 1823, 1824, 1825, 1830, 1833, 1837, 1840, 1841, 1845, 1850, 1853, 1860, and 1866.

Mortality schedules exist for the 1850, 1860, 1870, and 1880 censuses.

Missouri became a state in 1821. There are Missouri state censuses for a few counties for 1844, 1857 through 1858, 1868, and 1876.

Mortality schedules exist for the 1850, 1860, 1870, and 1880 censuses.

Montana became a state in 1889 - no state censuses.

Mortality schedules exist for the 1870 and 1880 censuses.

Nebraska became a state in 1867. There are state censuses for 1869, 1885, and 1913 through 1914 (taken for German immigrants from Russia).

Mortality schedules exist for the 1860, 1870, and 1880 censuses.
Nevada became a state in 1864, and a state census was taken in 1875.

Mortality schedules exist for the 1870 and 1880 censuses.

New Hampshire became a state in 1788 - no state censuses.

Mortality schedules exist for the 1850, 1860, 1870, and 1880 censuses.

New Jersey
New Jersey became a state in 1787. There are state censuses for 1855, 1865, 1875, 1885, 1895, 1905, and 1915.

A Colonial census was taken in 1693 of the Swedes who were members of the Swedish Lutheran Church and who were living in several eastern seaboard states, including western New Jersey. The information is contained in *The 1693 Census of the Swedes on the Delaware*, written by Peter Stebbins Craig (Winter Park, FL, SAG Publications, 1993).

Mortality schedules exist for the 1850, 1860, 1870, and 1880 censuses.

New Mexico became a state in 1912 - no state censuses.

Mortality schedules exist for the 1850, 1860, 1870, and 1880 censuses.

New York became a state in 1788. State censuses were taken in 1825, 1835, 1845, 1855, 1865, 1875, 1892, 1905, 1915, and 1925. In 1855, every person in the household was listed. Prior to that, only heads of household were listed. The 1855, 1865 and 1875 censuses captured country of birth of those who were enumerated. In 1890, there was a police census taken of all individuals in New York City.

Mortality schedules exist for the 1850, 1860, 1870, and 1880 censuses.

North Carolina became a state in 1789 - no state censuses.

Mortality schedules exist for the 1850, 1860, 1870, and 1880 censuses.

North Dakota became a state in 1889. State censuses were taken in North Dakota in 1905, 1915, and 1925.

Mortality schedules exist for the 1870 and 1880 censuses.

Ohio became a state in 1803. All that remains of the 1810 census are the returns for Washington County. Some town or county enumerations were taken from 1803 to 1911.

Mortality schedules exist for the 1850, 1860 and 1880 censuses.

Oklahoma became a state in 1907 - no state censuses.

Oregon became a state in 1859. Oregon state censuses were taken in 1892 (Marion County) and 1905 (a few counties).

Mortality schedules exist for the 1850, 1860, 1870, and 1880 censuses.

Pennsylvania

Pennsylvania became a state in 1787. No state censuses. However, the Pennsylvania State Archives has "septennial censuses" (tax lists with the names of the taxable inhabitants), which were taken every seven years, and exist for these counties:

1779: Bedford, Berks, Chester, Lancaster.

1786: Bedford, Berks, Bucks, Chester, Dauphin, Fayette, Franklin, Lancaster, Montgomery, Northampton, Washington, Westmoreland, York.

1793: Berks, Cumberland, Delaware, Lancaster, Montgomery, Philadelphia City, Philadelphia County, York.

1800: Adams, Allegheny, Armstrong, Bedford, Berks, Bucks, Centre, Chester, Cumberland, Dauphin, Delaware, Fayette, Franklin, Greene, Huntingdon, Lancaster, Luzerne, Lycoming, Mifflin, Montgomery, Northampton, Northumberland, Philadelphia City, Somerset, Washington, Wayne, Westmoreland, York.

1807: Dauphin (Derry Township), Franklin, Montgomery, York.

1814: Franklin.

1821: Columbia, Franklin, Huntingdon, Mifflin.

1828: Franklin.

1835: Franklin.

1842: Franklin, Montgomery (Pottsgrove Township only).

1849: Wyoming County.

1863: Philadelphia City.

A Colonial census was taken in 1693 of the Swedes who were members of the Swedish Lutheran Church and who were living in several eastern seaboard states, including Pennsylvania. The information is contained in *The 1693 Census of the Swedes on the Delaware*, written by Peter Stebbins Craig (Winter Park, FL, SAG Publications, 1993).

Mortality schedules exist for the 1850, 1860, 1870, and 1880 censuses.

Rhode Island

Rhode Island became a state in 1790. Rhode Island has state censuses for 1865, 1875, 1885, 1915, 1925, and 1936.

The 1865 Rhode Island census lists the town of birth for those born in that state – a great genealogical find if you are fortunate enough to have an ancestor born and living in Rhode Island in 1865!

Mortality schedules exist for the 1850, 1860, 1870, and 1880 censuses.

South Carolina

South Carolina became a state in 1788. South Carolina has state census records for some counties for 1829, 1839, 1848, 1869, and 1875. The original records are at the South Carolina Department of Archives and History. Some of them have been published in South Carolina periodicals. The 1848 census of Charleston city has been published and is at the Family History Library.

South Dakota became a state in 1889. State censuses were taken in South Dakota in 1895, 1905, 1915, 1925, 1935, and 1945.

Mortality schedules exist for the 1860, 1870, and 1880 censuses.

Tennessee became a state in 1796 - no state censuses.

Mortality schedules exist for the 1850, 1860, 1870, and 1880 censuses.

Texas became a state in 1845 - no state censuses.

Mortality schedules exist for the 1850, 1860, 1870, and 1880 censuses.

Utah became a state in 1896 - no state censuses.

Mortality schedules exist for the 1850, 1860, 1870, and 1880 censuses.

Vermont became a state in 1791 - no state censuses.

Mortality schedules exist for the 1850, 1860, 1870, and 1880 censuses.

Virginia became a state in 1788 — no state censuses for Virginia. However, tax lists, available for most counties from about 1782 to 1850, are valuable census substitutes.

Mortality schedules exist for the 1850, 1860, 1870, and 1880 censuses.

Washington became a state in 1889. A state census of Washington was taken in 1892.

Mortality schedules exist for the 1860, 1870, and 1880 censuses.

West Virginia became a state in 1863 - no state censuses.

Mortality schedules exist for the 1850, 1860, 1870, and 1880 censuses.

Wisconsin became a state in 1848, and Wisconsin state censuses were taken in 1855, 1865, 1875, 1885, 1895, and 1905.

Mortality schedules exist for the 1850, 1860, 1870, and 1880 censuses.

Wyoming became a state in 1890. A 1905 Wyoming state census is at the Wyoming State Archives.

Mortality schedules exist for the 1870 and 1880 censuses.

Okay – so now you understand the value of state censuses and US Census mortality schedules, what next? Where do you find these treasures to assist you in your search for your ancestors? An excellent resource that captures much of the foregoing information about state censuses and provides much more was written by Ann S. Lainhart in her *State Census Records* (Baltimore Genealogical Publishing Co, 1992). If you are serious about researching state census records, this would be an excellent book for you to obtain. Among other places, it is available from Amazon.com.

Many state censuses and mortality records have been published online as well as in book format. The books may be available through inter-library loan, or may be available as microfilmed copies through the LDS Church website www.familysearch.org.

Ancestry.com, Heritage Quest, Fold3.com, and FamilySearch.org also offer many of the censuses and mortality schedules online. Mortality schedules are also available through the Family History Library of the LDS Church, the Daughters of the American Revolution organization, and the state archives of the various states. Numerous free websites have popped up in recent years that also offer access to mortality schedules. While their collections aren't usually as extensive as some of the subscription services, they are free, so you may want to try them out first. Several I have found helpful include Mortality Schedules.com at *www.mortalityschedules.com* and New Horizons Genealogy at *www.newhorizonsgenealogicalservices.com*. As new sites are added all the time, just google *Mortality Schedules* and see what comes up. I'll caution you, though: most will lead you straight to subscription services like Ancestry.com.

State Censuses & Mortality Schedules Checklist

____ Identify the state(s) your ancestor may have lived in during a certain timeframe.

____ Determine if the state in which your ancestor lived conducted a state or territorial census.

____ Locate the appropriate state census.

____ Search the mortality records of the Federal Census.

____ If you find an ancestor on the mortality schedule, match them up with their family on the US Census of the same year.

Additional Resources

Lainhart, Ann S: *State Census Records* (Baltimore Genealogical Publishing Co, 1992)

Loretto Dennis Szucs and Sandra Hargreaves Luebking (editors), *The Source – A Guidebook to American Genealogy*, 3rd Edition, edited by Ancestry Publishing, 2006.

The website below is helpful for your examination of state census records and mortality schedules:

www.progenealogists.com/statecensus.htm — the website for Pro Genealogists is very helpful for researching state censuses as well as for providing a host of other helpful information.

6. PROBATE RECORDS & WILLS

"The report of my death was an exaggeration." – Mark Twain

A rich and often overlooked source of genealogical information is found in probate records and wills left by your ancestors. These great sources are frequently overlooked because they are sometimes more difficult to find – few wills are online, especially when compared to many other online sources that are available at the click of a mouse.

Although not as easily accessible online as many other genealogical resources, probate records and wills often yield nuggets of genealogical information. Many probate records and wills can be found online, but the vast majority, at least at this writing, may require a visit to the area where your ancestor lived or possibly an inter-library loan of a microfilm or book. The LDS Family History Library in Salt Lake City, Utah, has a large collection of wills and probate records on microfilm, which is available at many local family history centers in communities throughout the world.

Every state has laws that require that the estates of deceased persons must be handled through the courts, whether the person left a will or not. The titles of the officials who oversee the probate process vary by jurisdiction, and may be called probate judges, city, county or district judges, town or county clerks or registrars of wills.

Generally speaking, there are three levels of information available for wills:

•The original will (depending on the era, it may be handwritten);
•A copy of the transcribed will that is bound in a will book for the jurisdiction;
•An abstract (summary) — of a will.

While each has its benefits, the latter two offer the opportunity for the introduction of errors, either through carelessness or an effort to economize. For example, an original will may include the names of all a deceased person's children, but the transcription or abstract may leave them out if they did not receive any personal or real property in the will. Perhaps they were too young to receive property, or perhaps they had already received their inheritance – in the form of a dowry for a married daughter, or a homestead for a married son, etc. Of course, it is possible that the missing child(ren) was/were disinherited!

On the other hand, the latter two sources may well be indexed. Often the indexes for probate records and wills include every name mentioned in the records and wills the index covers – so all you need is the name of one of your ancestors to locate a will. He or she may appear as a person named to receive property, or as a witness, executor / personal representative, etc. If they are not the testator or named in the will, their designation as a witness or executor may indicate a familial relationship to the deceased, and is certainly worth additional research.

Following are a few websites I have had success in using to find online probate records and wills:

- *www.CyndisList.com/wills.htm*
- *genealogy.about.com/hobbies/genealogy/msubwills.htm?rnk=r&terms= wills*

When searching for wills and probate records, don't only look for those of direct-line ancestors. Aunts and uncles have been known to be very generous as they neared death. Often, they will name nieces and nephews in their wills, and their inclusion can again provide genealogical data: "To my brother John's son Tommy, I leave…." I have read many wills from aunts and uncles, especially those not married, or who were married and had no children, where a great number of relatives received property, and were specifically mentioned in the will. In a personal instance, I had a great uncle who left me 5% of some lands he owned – along with a host of other cousins, aunts and uncles, each of whom received a portion of his property ranging from 5% to 25%! The will itself is a rich genealogical source, if a pain and a half to administer!

Let's put my family to work again, and use a document from their past to illustrate the genealogical value of wills. Below are excerpts from a will that was set down by my fifth great uncle, John Lowrance, in 1781 in Rowan

---

PROBATE RECORDS & WILLS – TERMS TO KNOW

Abstract – a term commonly used with wills and deeds, where the critical information in an original document is summarized.

Executor – the person who will be responsible for seeing that the instructions in a will are carried out. Also called a personal representative. If a woman, she may be called an executrix.

Intestate – a person who dies without a will is said to have died intestate.

Moveables – a term typically found in wills, indicating possessions other than land (clothing, farm implements, livestock, money, etc.).

Probate records – Court records that represent the final disposal of a person's personal and real property after s/he dies. Probate records are a summary that provides information about the person who has died – their name, birth date, death date, individuals who received property and where they lived.

Testate – an estate where a legal will has been made.

Testator – the maker of a will; the person whose personal and real property will be disbursed as a result of the will.

Will – A legal document witnessed by several others that represents an individual's wishes for the disbursement of his/her property after their death. It often contains information about family members.

County, North Carolina. (Note: I have not forgotten how to use my spell-checker – I have preserved the original spellings throughout this will.)

John Lowrance will recorded in Rowan County, North Carolina, Superior Court Record Book, pages are 128-133.

THE WILL OF JOHN LOWRANCE
"IN THE NAME OF GOD AMEN:

"I John Lowrance of the County of Rowan and state of North Carolina farmer, being sick and weak in body but of perfect mind and Memory, Thanks be to God for the same & calling to mind the mortality of My Body and knowing that it is appointed for all men once to die. Do make and ordain this my Last Will and Testament in the manner and form following:

That is to say IMPRIMIS. I recommend my soul into the hands of God who gave it me, and my Body to the Earth from whence it came to be Buried in a decent and Christian manner at the direction of my Executors, In hopes of a joyfull Resurrection through the mercies of my Saviour JESUS CHRIST....

ITEM: I do give and bequeath unto my well beloved wife Anne Lorance one black bald faced horse and one brown horse with a bald face but one eye and my old sorrel horse during her widowhood. Likewise two hundred pounds in money to be raised out of my estate if the money rates at the time when she shall demand it, as it does at this present time Dollar at a ha'penny, but if it should come to its former value a dollar at eight shillings at the above said time of demand then she shall have but thirty pounds likewise the use of my house I now live in, and all my household furniture likewise my whole plantation on the west side of the Creek I now live on, during her widowhood, except Ten Acres of the lower end of my meadow with a strate line from the creek west to the hill which I reserve for the use of my son Jacob. Likewise give unto my Beloved wife four cows and calves of her own choosing two three year old stears, likewise ten sheep of her own choosing, likewise all my Hogs and geese for the support maintenance of these my children, which I had by her during her widowhood and if it should please God to Remove her by death or if she should marry again before my two sons Johsua & Alx'r become of age then all the above moveables to be equally divided between all my children I had of her at the discretion of my Executors. I likewise order that my Wife shall have use of my 'itch plow' and Waggon with the gears belonging to them, likewise my Iron tooth Harrow, likewise the use of Negro Boy called Ben for the time of eight years from the date hereof and no longer and after the expiration of the above said eight years that then my said Negro Boy shall be my beloved son Abrahams property. I also give unto my Son John my money scales. I also give unto my son Abraham my still and eight still Vessels, also one cow and calf and three sheep. I also give unto my son Andrew two sheep. I also give unto my son Joshua both my old and young black mares. I also give unto my daughter Jane my black mare called fley and her yearling colt I give to my daughter Anna. I also give unto my son Jacob my stone horse and my three year old passing mare, colt and one cow and calf. I also give unto my step-daughter Agness two sheep. I also give unto my daughter Catherine two sheep. I also give unto my beloved wife shoud think it best for my son Jacob to live in the House by himself, that then he shall build a House on the East side of the Creek for himself to live in and shall have the use of the land on that side of the Creek on the above said Plantation, and further if it shoud please my beloved wife to Marry again, or if it shoud please God to remove her by death, That then after either of these, I do give unto my son Jacob the whole Plantation I now live on, with a promise that he give or cause to be given unto my two younger sons, Johsua and Alexander each of them when they come of age fifty pounds proc currency of North Carolina, and if my son Jacob shoud not be willing to pay the money that then the above said Plantation shall be equally divided between my two younger sons namely Joshua and Alexander at the discretion of my Executors not withstanding if my son Jacob shoud pay the above moneys to said Joshua and Alexander, that then the said Plantation shall be my son Jacobs not withstanding if it shoud please God to remove my son Jacob by death and he not having a male heir that then the said Plantation I now live on shall be equally divided between my two sons Joshua & Alexander. Nevertheless if my son Jacob should beget a living male heir, that then the above Plantation shall be his property & only his the paying the above said moneys. I also order that what moneys I have at present shall be equally divided between my two sons namely Joshua & Alexander. I likewise order that forty shillings be raised out of my Estate and given unto my daughter Margaret or her first born son. I also order that forty shillings be raised out of my Estate & given unto my daughter Mary or her first born son. Also I order that forty shillings be raised out of my Estate and be given unto my daughter Elizabeth or her first born son and further I order that the rest of my moveable effects such as my Executors shall not think proper to keep or divide amongst the Children, to be sold at public sale and the money arising therefrom to defray these Legacies I give to my daughters or their children.

I also choose and appoint my well beloved Wife Ann Lorance, and my son John Lorance, and my son Abraham Lorance, and my friend John McCorkle to be the Executors of this my Last Will and Testament.

And I do hereby utterly disallow revoke and disannul all and every other former Testaments, Wills, Legacies and Executors by me in any wise before this time named, willed and bequeathed and ratifying and confirming this and only this to be my Last Will and Testament in witness whereof I have hereunto set my hand and affixed my seal this 20th day of April One Thousand seven Hundred and Eighty One (1781).

Signed, Sealed, Published, pronounced and declared by the said John Lowrance as his last Will and Testament in the presence of us."

s/John Lorance Junr:
s/William Irvin
s/John Gray
s/John Gracey

Okay, now – this is the audience participation portion of this book. Before I share with you the items of genealogical value I found in this will, let's have you take a shot at it. Some of the things are very obvious, but others are not. I have provided a table below for you to complete as many things as you can from reading through this will. Take a few moments and read through the will, then complete the table before you turn the page to look at my thoughts. (I'd be interested in hearing from you if you come up with some different things than I do. E-mail me at the address at the beginning of this book, and I may include your thoughts in the next edition!)

I've given you a few easy ones to begin your thinking:

Item	Description
1.	John was alive on April 20, 1781
2.	He did not consider himself in good health
3.	He lived in Rowan County, North Carolina
4.	
5.	
6.	
7.	
8.	
9.	
10.	
11.	
12.	
13.	
14.	
15.	
16.	
17.	
18..	
19.	
20.	

Okay – my turn. Below are the items of genealogical significance I gleaned from the will of this ancestor of mine. Besides learning interesting things about the lives these folks led: horses (10), cows, sheep (almost 20), hogs, geese, 'itch plow' (whatever that was!), etc., what do we learn from this last will and testament of John Lowrance? Here are the obvious:

1. John was alive on April 20, 1781;

2. He did not consider himself in good health;

3. He lived in Rowan County, North Carolina;

4. He owned land, buildings and livestock;

5. His wife was Anne *Lorance* (note the different spelling from his name in the same document);

6. He had at least 13 children living at the time of his will (one of which was a step-daughter):

> — Jacob
> — Joshua
> — Alexander
> — Abraham
> — John
> — Andrew
> — Jane
> — Anna
> — Catherine
> — Margaret
> — Mary
> — Elizabeth
> — Agness (step-daughter)

Applying the next layer of curiosity (and logic!), here are some things that aren't quite so obvious:

7. Anne was probably married and widowed before she married John (hence the step-daughter Agness);

8. John probably had another wife, and had children by that wife. Note his comment that in case Anne remarried, all his moveables that he left to her should "…be equally divided between all my children *I had of her*…"

9. He may have died sometime near the time this will was written;

10. It appears that at least Joshua and Alexander are still living at home, and are not "of age" (i.e., under 21 years old);

11. It seems likely that three of his daughters were then married, as he bequeathed them or their first born son monies (Margaret, Mary and Elizabeth);

12. The opening lines of the will, although somewhat formulaic for the time period, indicate John was a Christian man, so searching local parish or other church records seems logical.

And at the next layer, here are a few things to investigate that aren't so obvious, but worth looking into:

13. John bequeathed his slave for his wife's use for eight years, after which the slave was to go to Abraham. This might indicate that the youngest child would reach age 21 in eight years.

14. It also seems possible that several daughters weren't married: Catherine, Jane and Anna. They were each given livestock, while the three who were most likely married received cash. Since they were treated differently from his other daughters, the reason might be because they were single.

15. It would be worthwhile to investigate William Irvin, John Gray and John Gracey, witnesses to the will. Often witnesses of wills and deeds are family members – (John Lowrance, Jr., one of the witnesses, is of course John Sr.'s son). These men might just be trusted neighbors or a minister, but they might also be sons-in-law, brothers- or fathers-in-law, etc.

Let's see how we did with our curiosity and logic. Based on later research on this family, here's what I found:

The Obvious
1. John was alive on April 20, 1781
This was easy – it was given.

2. He did not consider himself in good health
This was easy – it was given.

3. He lived in Rowan County, North Carolina
This was easy – it was given.

4. He owned land, buildings and livestock
This was easy – it was given. Land Records might indicate when they moved to Rowan County, if he purchased his land from a family member, etc.

5. His wife was Anne Lorance
This was easy – it was given. Look for her under Lorance as well as Lowrance in future research.

6. He had at least 13 children living at the time of his will (one of which was a step-daughter)
Correct. In fact, John had 17 children and one step-daughter! Two sons died before John, and two daughters, aged 6 and 12, were alive at the time of the will, but John didn't bequeath them anything.

Not Quite So Obvious
7. Anne was probably married and widowed before she married John
This is correct. Anne was married and widowed prior to her marriage to John. Agness was her daughter with her first husband.

8. John probably had another wife, and had children by that wife.
Correct. John was married once before, and 10 of his children were born to that wife, and 7 of his children were born to Anne.

9. He may have died sometime near the time this will was written.
Correct. John died April 23, 1781 – three days after he made his will.

10. It appears that at least Joshua and Alexander are still living at home, and are not "of age" (i.e., under 21 years old).
At the time the will was written, Joshua was 14 and Alexander was 3.

11. It seems likely that three of his daughters were then married, as he bequeathed them or their first born son monies (Margaret, Mary and Elizabeth).
Correct. Each of these daughters was indeed married.

12. The opening lines of the will, although somewhat formulaic for the time period, indicate John was a Christian man, so searching local parish or other church records seems logical.
Not determined.

Not Obvious At All But Worth Looking Into

13. John bequeathed his slave for his wife's use for eight years, after which he was to go to Abraham. This might indicate that the youngest child would reach age 21 in eight years.
Nice try, but incorrect. The youngest child in the household was three years old at the time of John's death. (You win some, you lose some!)

14. It also seems possible that several daughters weren't married: Catherine, Jane and Anna. They were each given livestock, while the three who were most likely married received cash. This may be a stretch of logic, but since they were treated differently from his married daughters, the reason might be that they were single.
Correct. At the time the will was drawn, Catherine was 23, Jane was 18 and Anna was 16. All were unmarried at this time. I guessed right!

15. It would be worthwhile to research William Irvin, John Gray and John Gracey, witnesses to the will. Often witnesses of wills and deeds are family members – John Lowrance, Jr., one of the witnesses, is of course John Sr.'s son. These men might just be trusted neighbors or a minister, but they might also be sons-in-law, brothers- or fathers-in-law, etc.
Correct. John Gracey was John Lowrance's son-in-law. John Gray was married to one of John Lowrance's cousins. No connection to William Irvin was determined. Land records might show he was a neighbor.

In this particular will, there are several things beyond genealogical information that caught my eye. Note that John was concerned about the valuation of the pound – 200 pounds were left to his wife if the pound was based on a certain valuation, but only 30 pounds if it was based on another valuation!

Also, note that Anne lost all the moveables (non-real estate) that John bequeathed her if she remarried. This is a very frequent finding in the wills of 18th- and 19th-century men – giving assets to their wives as long as their wives did not remarry, and if they did, they forfeited whatever had been given them.

I have established for you the value of wills, and of looking at the information beyond the surface. But where do you find the wills? What resources are available for you to use this terrific resource in your research?

Since your home computer is generally closer than most county courthouses or state archives locations, I would suggest starting there first. If you're fortunate (extremely fortunate!), you may find your ancestor's will on line. In my researching, that seldom happens, but it is certainly worth the few minutes it takes to type in "Will of Samuel McCollough" in the search box of Google and check out any hits that might provide you what you're looking for.

The **Family History Library** of the LDS Church has microfilmed many, many wills and accompanying probate records from all over the nation. A search in their library catalog may yield the results you are seeking, and within a week the microfilmed document can be available for your review at any local Family History Center.

Original records are generally kept at the county courthouse or the State Archives. Check the website for both to see where best to begin your search for these documents. If your ancestor lived in an area that hasn't been microfilmed, and if you cannot personally travel to the courthouse or state archives location, don't despair. There are a number of options, including hiring a professional genealogist (most will give you price quotes prior to doing the research). A good way to locate a professional genealogist is to contact the **Board of Certification of Genealogists** (*www.bcgcertification. org*) or **The International Commission for the Accreditation of Professional Genealogists** (ICAPGEN) – *www.icapgen.org* – both of which are certifying organizations for professional genealogists. You can search by state, region, or specific topic for which you are searching. For example, you can query for a genealogist in Colorado that specializes in probate searches.

Back to locating the records. Check where your state's probate records are kept by googling _____(name of state) probate records. Some states have many of their records available online, some do not. If that's not successful, go next to the State Archives website and you should be able to find what you are seeking there. (See the Appenidix for a listing of State Archives and Libraries.)

If you are able to go to the location of the records, you'll search an alphabetical name index for your ancestors' name. If you find it, note the case or file number, and provide it to a clerk. He or she will retrieve the case file for you to review. Some archival locations have microfilmed these records, although many have not.

If you are not able to go in person, contact the location where the records are kept (either via e-mail or phone) to determine what their search requirements are. They will let you know if they have a standard form that needs to be used, to whose attention and address the form needs to be sent, and how much the fee will be for the search.

Another excellent source for locating the government agency responsible for preserving (and allowing access to!) probate records is *Red Book: American State, County & Town Sources* (see *Additional Resources* at the end of this chapter). It provides state-by-state research on where various archived records, including probate records, can be located.

Wills and Probate Checklist

____ Locate the state and county where your ancestor died.

____ Determine where probate records are kept in the state and county of your ancestor's death.

____ Determine whether the records are accessible via the Internet, or whether a visit to the repository is required.

____ Consider engaging a local genealogist to do your research in a distant place.

____ Look beyond the obvious in reviewing the will.

____ Check to see if there are any relationships between the testator and witnesses of the will.

Additional Resources

Steven Fisher (editor), *Archival Information (How to Find It, How to Use It)*, (Greenwood Press, 2004).

Sharon DeBartalo Carmack, *The Genealogy Sourcebook*, (McGraw-Hill, 1998)

Loretto Dennis Szucs and Sandra Hargreaves Luebking (editors), *The Source – A Guidebook to American Genealogy*, 3rd Edition, (Ancestry Publishing, 2006). The Source has an extensive and very detailed chapter on Court Records.

Alice Eichholz (editor), *Red Book: American State, County & Town Sources* (Ancestry Publishing, 2004)

7. IMMIGRATION & NATURALIZATION RECORDS

"Give me your tired, your poor, your huddled masses..."
– Emma Lazarus (Statue of Liberty)

Do you feel the correct pronunciation of Celtic should be with a hard C (Keltic) instead of a soft C (Seltic)? Does the thought of sauerkraut for dinner make you hungry all day?

Most of us who call America home will soon hit the ocean as we are doing research on our family lines, some of us sooner than others. It is then that we begin truly earning our dues as genealogists!

So, when that happens, what do you do? Where do you turn?

The first thing to do is determine who you are looking for, and where they were likely to have come from. Perhaps you don't have a clue, but scattered throughout the research you have already done may be an item or two that will prove to be the slender thread you need to find that ocean-going ancestor or yours.

Perhaps it's a census record that shows the birth place of your ancestor as another country, or perhaps it's the birth place of his/her parents. Perhaps it's family tradition that great-great Grandma Marie came from Italy when she was just a babe. Perhaps you notice that the land records you are re-searching contain a lot of ethnic names – buyers, sellers, neighbors. While you formerly assumed that your Castillo ancestors came from either Mexico or perhaps Spain, perhaps all these Irish neighbors provide some credence to the family tradition that they came from Ireland, several hundred years after they were part of the ship-wrecked Spanish Armada.

THE UNITED STATES – THE GREAT MELTING POT

When you consider the ethnic composition of the United States, you can see why we have been referred to as a great melting pot. We've also seen some changes since the country's inception. Following is a comparison of the most frequent countries that have contributed to making America the melting pot that it is. In 2010, the US Census reported that Americans had the following ancestral origins in the following percentages:

Nationality	Percentage
German	15.2%
African American	12.9%
Irish	10.8%
English	7.7%
American	7.2%
Mexican	6.5%
Italian	5.6%
Polish	3.2%
French	3.0%
American Indian	2.8%
Scottish	1.7%
Dutch	1.6%
Norwegian	1.6%
Scotch-Irish	1.5%
Swedish	1.4%
Total Population	**308,745,538**

Source: U.S. Census Bureau, Census 2010 special tabulation

Regardless of the place you find your first clues, it's a big ol' world out there, and you can rest assured that at some point you're going to have to go abroad to continue your research.

Once you know who you are looking for and where they may have come from, a timeframe for their arrival would be helpful. Early in her history, the US began cataloguing and keeping track of immigrants. There is a LOT of data – it is estimated that nearly 50 million immigrants have come to America since her inception. Many of their names have been captured, and you just need to know where to find their names.

In this chapter, we'll discuss some of the places you should look for these foreign ancestors of yours, those who braved months at sea on dangerous vessels to come to America and start a new life.

Passenger Lists

Of course, you have heard of Ellis Island (known as Isola della Lacrime – The Island of Tears — by Italian immigrants) – most genealogists have. But it might surprise you to learn that Ellis Island was only one of many ports of entry for immigrants arriving in the US. While more than 12,000,000 immigrants had Ellis Island as their first port of call in America, that leaves over three times that number to have come to American shores through other ports of entry. In fact, the US government officially took over the tracking of immigrants in 1890; prior to that, the states were responsible for tracking immigrants. As you can imagine, the information and rigor varied state-by-state, and administration-by-administration within those states. Some kept very good records and asked many questions, others kept scanty records with very little information beyond the name of the immigrant and date he or she passed through the port.

Castle Gardens, the predecessor to Ellis Island, was the first point of arrival for 10,000,000 immigrants between 1830 and 1892, the year that Ellis Island opened.

Between 1820 and 1920, immigrants entered the US in the following numbers at the following points:

Baltimore, MD – 1,460,000
Boston, MA — 2,050,000
Charleston, SC – 20,000
Galveston, TX – 110,000
Key West, FL – 130,000
New Bedford, MA – 40,000
New York City, NY – 23,960,000
New Orleans, LA – 710,000
Passamaquoddy, Maine – 80,000
Philadelphia, PA – 1,240,000
Portland / Falmouth, ME – 120,000
Providence, RI – 40,000
San Francisco, CA – 500,000

As you can see, the top ports in order of arrival in the United States were:

New York
Boston
Baltimore
Philadelphia
New Orleans
San Francisco

If you do not know where your immigrant ancestor entered the United States, searching indexes and databases that contain the names of immigrants entering through these ports should be the first step you take. Doing so should cover about half of the immigrants who came to the United States in the first 150 years of our existence.

Other cities also served as hosts to newly arriving immigrants, including Miami, Los Angeles, Savannah, etc. From Alaska to Florida, from Baja California to Maine, from the Canadian and Mexican borders, some experts estimate there were over 300 entry points into the United States. While all were supposed to keep records, some kept better records than others. Some kept complete passenger lists while others lumped their immigrating passengers in with other commodities that were being shipped.

Now – let me surprise you. I consider finding your immigrating ancestors by going directly to passenger lists as an exercise of picking the low-hanging fruit (no, I am not casting aspersions about your ancestors, calling them fruits and/or nuts). Simply stated, if you find your ancestors here without going through other efforts (described later in this chapter), you will be extremely fortunate, and they will be the easier ancestors to find. For every easy ancestor you find (*the low-hanging fruit*), there are probably many, many others that are much better hidden, and will require other sleuthing methods to flush out.

Now, don't get me wrong – it is still exciting and you will have a sense of accomplishment when you discover a family in the passenger lists that you have been trying to find for some time. Consider my joy, for example, when I found this family immigrating to the United States:

Annie Peoples, 32

Charles, 6
Andrew, 5
William, 4

My third-great grandmother was Margaret Peoples, and I have known very little about her and her family. So I decided to see if I could find any Peoples who had immigrated to America. Since Ellis Island has the highest number of immigrant records of any other US port of entry, I went there first. A little searching turned up the names of the family above. After boarding the Assyria in Glasgow, Scotland, they arrived in the United States on September 24, 1924. Family tradition says my third-great grandmother was from Scotland, so this family piqued my interest. Regardless, I was open to her being born elsewhere, especially in Ireland, since the Irish often went to Scotland to live and to work. So it is possible that this family is still related to me. And of course, the Irish and the Scottish exchanged countries of residence quite easily through the years, as they sought employment, marriage, etc.

Note, however, that there is no father listed with this Peoples family. However, the passenger list indicates that Annie was going to see her husband William, who lived in Bryn Mawr, Pennsylvania. Later in this chapter, I will share how I used the Ellis Island passenger list and several other immigration and naturalization sources to locate the husband and glean a great deal of genealogical information for them.

After the federal government took over the responsibility for cataloguing incoming immigrants, effort was made to increase the number of questions and standardize the information gleaned from the immigrants. The questions varied year-to-year. The ship's passenger lists collected an amazing (and sometimes startling!) set of facts about the immigrants, including some wonderful genealogical clues. Many of the questions are similar to those found on the US Census. In 1915, the questions asked (and answered) were:

•Were they a citizen, diplomat, tourist, or a citizen of Canada, China or Mexico?
•What was their age in years and months?
•What was their sex and marital status?
•What was their occupation, and could they read and write?
•What was their nationality and race?
•What was their last permanent address?

- What was the name and complete residence address of a relative or friend in the country from whence they came?
- What was the passenger's final destination (state and town)?
- Did they have a ticket to their final destination?
- Who paid the passage for this individual?
- Did they have at least $50? If not, how much did they have?
- Had they been to the United States before, and if so, where and for how long?
- Were they coming to visit a relative or friend? And if so, who was it and what was their full address?
- Were they a polygamist?
- Were they an Anarchist?
- What was their mental and physical health condition?
- Were they deformed or crippled, and if so, the nature, length of time and cause?
- Did they have any identifying marks?
- What was their height, complexion and color of hair and eyes?
- Where was their place of birth?

You can see why some of this information would make a genealogist's heart flutter! Especially if the information was about that long-lost ancestor you have been trying to find out about.

It is interesting to note that the immigrants completed this information upon entering the ship. Immigration officials at the arriving port would often use the information provided by the immigrants – months before at the beginning of the voyage – to determine whether the immigrant had been truthful upon boarding the ship. Remember your mother always telling you that the truth was always best, since it always remained the same? Well, immigration officials were suspicious of anyone who couldn't provide the same answers that had been provided at embarkation.

And so you ask what I have against using passenger lists to find your ancestors? Nothing, of course. But if you depend solely on passenger lists that are available, either at free sites on the Internet or through subscription services, you may miss many of your ancestors. Not all passenger lists have been indexed. Those that have been indexed have errors – typos, incorrect spellings, illegible handwriting so a name is mis-written or couldn't be deciphered at all by the transcriber, etc. Many immigrants simply weren't included, either on a ship's passenger list or on a manifest of items shipped.

Some – none of them your ancestors, I am certain – simply didn't want anyone to know about them – either at the point of departure or arrival.

The National Archives (NARA) has immigration lists from 1820 through 1982 on microfilm, and many of them are available online through subscription services like Ancestry.com and Fold3.com. You can go to *www.archives.gov/research/immigration/index.html* to learn more about what is available through NARA, but here is a summary:

Immigration records are kept by port of entry into the United States.

Microfilmed copies of passenger lists up to 1955 are available at the National Archives in Washington DC, and some may be available at regional NARA locations. A link from the NARA site will take you to their microfilm catalog so you can see whether certain passenger list microfilms are available at one of the regional facilities.

If you aren't close enough to a regional NARA facility to visit personally, you can order copies of passenger arrival records by using order form NATF 81, or by ordering online.

While the records for most ports have been indexed, records for immigrants who came through Castle Garden (1847 to 1892) or Ellis Island (1892 to 1896) in New York between 1847 and 1896 are incomplete. A partial database is available, listing over 600,000 immigrants who arrived in New York between 1846 and 1851.

Castle Garden has a website (www.castlegarden.org) that lists over 10,000,000 immigrants who came through the port of New York from 1830 to 1892, and Ellis Island has a searchable database of over 22,000,000 immigrants who arrived between 1892 and 1924. The database is accessible by going to *www.ellisisland.org*.

Finally, Ancestry.com has indexed the passenger lists for ships that arrived in New York between 1820 and 1957.

Now, let's get to some of those other records and documents I alluded to earlier.

Naturalization Papers

Immigrants coming to the United States in the 19th and early 20th centuries generally wanted to become American citizens. In order to do so, among other things, potential citizens needed to participate in the naturalization process, which required the completion of naturalization papers. These documents are often chock-full of information that will make a genealogist's heart sing!

Shortly after the United States Constitution was ratified, Congress passed the first Naturalization Act – and established the process for immigrants to become citizens of the United States. As you can imagine, the process evolved somewhat over the years. For example, between 1790 when the first Naturalization Act was passed, and 1906, naturalization documents were filed with territorial, state or federal courts. There seemed to be no rhyme or reason in where immigrants filed their papers. Doubtless some courts were selected because of proximity to where the immigrant was living. Perhaps sometimes courts were selected in other geographic areas because the court and judge had a reputation for being "easy" whereas local magistrates were considered tougher. Regardless of the reasons, this aspect of filing makes the hunt all that much more interesting – a bit of a challenge.

Each state / territory had different forms that asked different questions of aspiring citizens. While all covered the basics, some provide more information than others. Thankfully, in 1906 the federal government stepped in and standardized the process, requiring standard forms and more standardized filing.

When I use the term **naturalization papers**, I am referring to any of several documents that accompanied the naturalization process. Documents include *Declaration of Intention, Naturalization Petitions, Oaths of Allegiance, Certificates of Arrival* and other documents. As mentioned above, some of these documents provided a great deal of information that was of interest to genealogists (and descendants!).

As you search for your immigrant ancestors, it is important to understand the process of naturalization. Immigrants who were interested in becoming citizens of the United States were required to complete a declaration of intention. There was no waiting period and few requirements before they filed this declaration. The declaration of intention is sometimes referred to as **first papers**. Prior to filing a naturalization petition, immigrants had to meet a number of conditions, including filing a declaration of intention (not necessary after 1941), five years residency in the US, be of good moral character and be able to demonstrate a reasonable understanding of English and US civics. Over the years, some of those requirements have been modified (such as residency requirements, length of time between declaration of intention and filing of a naturalization petition, etc.).

After the conditions had been met (residency, etc.), immigrants filed their naturalization petition with the court, then waited for an appointment to be examined.

In *Secrets of Tracing Your Ancestors*, I proposed that genealogy was a bit old fashioned, because information about families was generally found under the male's surname. As you begin combing through naturalization papers, you'll be astounded at how few petitioners were women. You may be tempted to ask yourself whether or not women immigrated, or if they did, why they didn't apply for citizenship. However, an understanding of naturalization requirements helps clarify that mystery. Until 1922, a woman could become a citizen by marrying a citizen, or she could become a citizen when her husband became a citizen. While women were free to apply for their own citizenship, many simply waited until their immigrant husband

NATURALIZATION TERMS

Listed below are a few terms you should be aware of as you begin searching for your ancestor's naturalization papers.

Declaration of Intention – a document signed by the immigrant, declaring their intent to become a United States Citizen. Also called first papers.

Naturalization Petition – a formal petition filed with the courts requesting citizenship. Certain residency and other conditions were required to have been completed prior to filing. Also called second papers or final papers.

Oath of Allegiance – an oath signed by immigrants who wanted to become a US citizen. In addition to pledging allegiance to the United States, it specifically renounced citizenship and titles elsewhere.

Certificate of Arrival – a short document declaring the date, port of entry and ship of arrival for an immigrant.

became a citizen, thus becoming citizens themselves. After 1922, marrying a citizen was not enough – women had to apply for their own citizenship.

As mentioned earlier, the federal government standardized the various naturalization documents beginning in 1906. Though several of the documents provide similar information, there are also important differences that make finding them important. Following are the questions that were asked on each of the documents after that date:

Declaration of Intention
Court and location of filing
Name
Age
Occupation
Personal description (race, complexion, height, weight, color of hair and eyes, distinctive marks)
Place of birth
Date of birth
Current residence
Place from which they emigrated
Ship they arrived on
City of last foreign residence
Married / not married
Spouse's birth place and residence
Renunciation of allegiance and fidelity to another foreign government
Port of arrival in the United States
Date of arrival in the United States
Statements that the immigrant isn't an anarchist, polygamist or believer in polygamy
Statement of the immigrant's intention to become a citizen of the United States
Date the Declaration was filed

The declaration of intention was valid for seven years.

Petition for Naturalization
(Note: this form is sometimes called Petition for Citizenship)

Court and location of filing

Name
Current residence
Occupation
Date of birth
Place of birth
Place from which they emigrated
Date, place and court where they declared their intent to become a citizen
of the United States
Married / not married
Spouse's name, birth date and birth place
Spouse's current residence
Number of children, their names, dates and places of birth and current
residence
Renunciation of allegiance and fidelity to another foreign government
Statement of the immigrant's intention to become a citizen of the United
States
That the immigrant is able to speak English
Date since the immigrant has continuously lived in the United States
A declaration that the immigrant has not filed for citizenship in the United
States before
The certificate number on the immigrant's declaration of intention
The date of the immigrant's certificate of arrival
The names and signatures of two witnesses (US citizens) who attest that
they have known the person has lived continuously in the United States
for at least five years
The two witnesses attest to the good moral character of the immigrant
The occupation and addresses of the two witnesses

Oath of Allegiance
Name
Date filed
Renunciation of allegiance and fidelity to another foreign government
If the immigrant wished to change his name, his former and his new name
was identified
Names and addresses of two witnesses

Certificate of Arrival
Beginning June 26, 1906, immigrants completed a certificate of arrival upon
their arrival in the United States. The form they completed was given to a

clerk at the port of entry. He then checked the ship's passenger list, and if the immigrant was found on the list, a formal certificate of arrival was sent to the naturalization court with the following information:

Port of Entry
Name of the immigrant
Date of arrival
Name of ship

The certificate of arrival was included with the petition for naturalization, unless the immigrant arrived before June 26, 1906.

As you can see, the first three of these documents are laden with genealogical information that is invaluable to a researcher. Even the Certificate of Arrival provides the name of the ship, date and port of entry for the immigrant. Armed with that information, a researcher can then seek the passenger lists for the ship, and perhaps learn much more about the immigrant.

Be sure you go beyond the obvious information contained in the naturalization documents. For example, check out the witnesses. Who are they? How did they know the immigrant? Could they have known him in the old country – were they neighbors? Relatives? As your research on a particular ancestor hits brick walls, you may need to backtrack and find out more about these witnesses who attested to the good moral character of your ancestor.

When immigrants came to America, they often settled near one another. Same language and traditions, same goals and dreams, a common ancestry and former country – all these drew immigrants together. They may have worshipped in the same churches, filed naturalization papers in the same courts, and were perhaps even buried in the same cemeteries.

A friend who was doing research on a German ancestor had hit a stone wall and just had no clue where to go. He had used censuses, naturalization papers and passenger lists to glean all he could about this ancestor of his, and had even traced him to one of the German states, but that's where the trail grew cold. After years of fruitless research, he turned his attention to his ancestor's neighbors. A clue here and a hunch there, and he was able to trace several neighbors to a small village in the German state his ancestor was from. He was eventually able to locate information that not only put his ancestor in that village, but found information that extended his line back several generations further.

So pay attention to those Irish enclaves in Boston, the groups of Italians in New York, Bulgarians in northern New Mexico and Polish in Chicago. When the going gets tough, you may need to enlist the help of some of your ancestors' neighbors!

Census Assistance

As you are searching for the naturalization papers for your ancestors, don't overlook the federal censuses – several will be helpful to you and will enable you to narrow your search.

The 1900 through 1940 censuses all asked whether a person had been naturalized. The 1920 census went a step further by requiring the year of naturalization. That last will be especially helpful, and will assist you in locating your ancestor's naturalization papers.

By census, here are the immigration and naturalization questions asked:

1900
•If an immigrant, the year of immigration to the United States.
•How long the immigrant has been in the United States.
•Is the person naturalized?

1910
•Year of immigration to the United States
•Whether naturalized or alien
•Whether able to speak English, or, if not, give language spoken.

1920
•Year of immigration to the United States
•Naturalized or alien
•If naturalized, year of naturalization

1930
•Year of immigration into the United States
•Naturalization
•Whether able to speak English

1940
•Citizenship of the foreign born
•Residence on April 1, 1935
•Mother tongue

In the *Citizenship* column of the census, where the above questions were asked, these abbreviations were used: AL = Alien, NA = Naturalized, NR = Not Reported, PA = First Papers filed (the immigrant's declaration of intention).

Naturalization & The Civil War
To encourage enlistment during the Civil War, legislation was passed granting citizenship to any foreign-born male who served in the United States army and was honorably discharged. The requirement for a declaration of intention was waived, and the residency requirement was lowered from five years to one year.

So, for example, if you had an ancestor who came to America and fought in the 69th New York infantry, more commonly known as the Irish Brigade, he would have had the opportunity to earn his citizenship in a more expedited manner than most other immigrants.

A Search
Okay – earlier in this chapter I promised you I would tell you how I found the husband to Annie Peoples, how I used various immigration and naturalization resources to learn a great deal of genealogical information, and then how I used various immigration and naturalization resources to learn a great deal of genealogical information about this family. Again, here is the information I found on Annie and her children on the **Ellis Island passenger lists** (*www.ellisisland.org*):

Annie Peoples, 32
Charles, 6
Andrew, 5
William, 4

Here's how I used various sources, starting with the passenger list, to bring this family together:

Annie and her children arrived in the United States on September 24, 1924. From the passenger list, I was able to glean their ages (32, 6, 5 and 4), that they had sailed from Glasgow, Scotland, and that Annie's husband was William, who lived in Bryn Mawr, Pennsylvania. The passenger list also provides me Annie's maiden name and her mother's name, since Annie listed her nearest relative as Mrs. Jane McGarvey of Ramelton, County Donegal, Ireland. I also learned these physical characteristics of Annie and her children: their height, complexion, hair and eye color.

Finally, the passenger list gave Annie's birth place as Ramelton, County Donegal, Ireland, and her children's birth places as Clydebank, Scotland – great genealogical information.

Since Annie and her children came through Ellis Island, I reasoned that William might have also done so. I checked the Ellis Island passenger lists for William, but had no luck there. So – perhaps he entered the United States through some other port. Rather than start trying random ports of entry (which I could do), I decided to see if I could find a clue from other records that might point me to the port of entry William used.

I know that Annie immigrated in 1924, so I decided to see if I could find the family in the **1930 Federal Census**. Using Ancestry.com and with just a little bit of research, I found them in the census, living in Delaware County, Pennsylvania. Here's what I found:

William Peoples, 40, age at first marriage – 26, Year of Immigration – 1923,
    Citizenship status – naturalized
Annie, 36, age at first marriage – 22, Year of Immigration – 1924, Citizen-
    ship status – alien
Charlie, 12
Andrew, 11
William G., 10
Robert J, 4

The names and ages match up pretty well between this census record and the Ellis Island passenger list, although you may note that Annie only aged four years in the six years since she landed at Ellis Island – what a great country! Since their immigration, a fourth child – Robert J. – had had been born to the family. Other interesting information on the census record indicates that William and Annie were both born in Ireland, and the children who immigrated with Annie were all born in Scotland.

The dates of immigration listed in the 1930 census are important for my research. Had I started with this family from the census record only, I would have had a clue what years to be looking for as I searched various passenger lists for their information. William immigrated in 1923 – a year before Annie brought the children.

Based on William's living in Pennsylvania, I decided to look at the passenger lists for Philadelphia. I used Ancestry.com again, and searched their passenger lists for Philadelphia. In moments I discovered the following record for a passenger who had arrived on the ship *Haverford* on April 23, 1923 in Philadelphia, PA:

William Peoples, 35, married, laborer, never been to the US before, from Clydebank, Scotland and married to Annie Peoples of Clydebank, Scotland. He was born in Ramelton, Irleland, and his final destination in the US was Bryn Mawr, Pennsylvania. William declared on the passenger list that he wanted to remain in the United States "Always" – in other words, was immigrating and not just visiting.

An interesting – and genealogically valuable tidbit – was that his ticket was paid for by his cousin, William Montgomery of Bryn Mawr, PA, whom he listed as the relative or person he was going to join. Surely this William Peoples is Annie's husband. (Note: William landed in America, the land of opportunity, with a whole $27 in his pocket!)

Another interesting age-related note: similar to Annie, William only aged five years between his arrival as a 35 year old in 1923 and his age (40) on the 1930 census, seven years later!

Okay – between the passenger lists and 1930 census, I have learned a lot of information about this family. I know:

— their names
— approximate ages
— where they were all born

— where they lived before coming to the US
— where they were living in 1930
— occupations
— the age William and Annie were when they married
— the name of Annie's mother (and most likely Annie's maiden name)
— the name of William's cousin – William Montgomery

While that is a lot of information, I wanted to know more! So next I turned my attention to naturalization records. The 1930 census told us that William Peoples was a naturalized citizen, so there should be some records available to support that, and as pointed out earlier in this chapter, naturalization records are a rich source of genealogical information. If I could find his declaration of intention and petition for naturalization, I would get a ton more information, information that could firm up some of the information I gleaned from the census and passenger lists. I was particularly interested in seeing if I could find birth dates for all the members of this family.

Using Fold3.com, I searched for the naturalization papers for William. I was fortunate to find them almost immediately – both his declaration of intention and his petition for naturalization. Following is information I found in his declaration of intention; I have bolded those bits of information that are new, or that expand on other information I already had:

Declaration of Intention, November 18, 1926, filed in the Court of Common Pleas of Montgomery County, Pennsylvania

Name – William Peoples
Age – 37
Occupation – fireman
Physical description – height, weight, color of hair and eyes
Birth place – Ramelton, County Donegal, Ireland
Birth date – June 1, 1889
Current residence – Ardmore, Pennsylvania
Emigrated to the US from – Liverpool, England
Vessel – Haverford
Wife's name – Annie
Wife was born at – Ramelton, County Donegal, Ireland
Port of arrival of immigrant – Philadephia
Date of arrival – April 23, 1923

His declaration of intention provided great information, especially his birth date. Following is the information I found on his petition for naturalization:

Petition for Naturalization, filed with the District Court of the United States, Eastern District of Pennsylvania, on February 25, 1929:

Name – William Peoples
Age – 39
Occupation – engineer
Physical description – height, weight, color of hair and eyes
Birth place – Ramelton, County Donegal, Ireland
Birth date – June 1, 1889
Current residence – Ardmore, Pennsylvania
Emigrated to the US from – Liverpool, England
Port of arrival of immigrant – Philadephia
Date of departure – April 10, 1923
Date of arrival – April 23, 1923
Vessel – Haverford
Wife's name – Annie
Wife's birth date – July 24, 1891
Wife was born at – Ramelton, County Donegal, Ireland
Number of children – 4
Names, birth dates, birth places and current residence of children:
Charles, April 26, 1917, born Clydebank, Scotland, living in Ardmore, PA
Andrew, October 6, 1918, born Clydebank, Scotland, living in Ardmore, PA
William George, November 6, 1919, born Clydebank, Scotland, living Ardmore, PA
Robert John, June 26, 1925, born in Narberth, PA, living in Ardmore, PA

William's petition for naturalization was witnessed (and his number of years living in the United States was attested to) by William McCrea and Robert James Montgomery. In his declaration of intention, William listed his occupation as fireman, and William McCrea lists his occupation as fireman also – that's probably how they became acquainted. Even more interesting however, is that the other witness was Robert James Montgomery. If you'll recall, William Peoples said his cousin, William Montgomery, was his cousin, and that's who he was going to join. It's certainly worth looking into to see how Robert James Montgomery is related to both Williams (Peoples and

Montgomery!) – another cousin to William Peoples? His uncle, perhaps? Or maybe he is William Montgomery's son. Another thread to pick up and follow for this family.

Now – we have gathered a great deal of information on this family, starting with a random search of the passenger lists for Ellis Island, searching to see if a family member had passed through Ellis Island on their immigration journey.

One bit of information I would like to have gotten would have been a marriage date and place for William and Annie. We know they were both born in Ramelton, and that's where Annie's mom was living when Annie immigrated to the United States, so searching for marriage records in Ramelton and County Donegal would seem to make sense. However – all their children were born in Clydebank, Scotland, so it's possible the wedding took place there – another place to look if nothing turns up in Ireland. The 1930 census also tells us they were married when William was 26 and Annie was 22 – so they were married sometime between 1913 and 1915, based on the information we have on them.

If you're thinking you may want to scour Catholic Church records seeking information on their marriage, you might be wrong. True, William and Annie Peoples hailed from County Donegal, Ireland. But a knowledge of the history of Ireland will tell you that much of County Donegal, including Ramelton, was settled by Presbyterian Scots during the plantation period of Irish history – so don't overlook those records!

So, perhaps I have convinced you that passenger lists and immigration and naturalization records are worth your while to use in your research as a genealogist. But where to you go from here? Where do you find these records? Do you have to go anywhere – to Washington DC to check out microfilms from NARA? Or perhaps to one of NARA's regional centers? Well, those are certainly options, but before you hurry out and purchase an airline ticket, you'll be happy to know that many of these records are online. In fact, every bit of research I presented here on William and Annie Peoples was done from my home office in a few hours!

As you may have noted in my narrative about my research on the Peoples family, I was switching between Ancestry.com for some records and Fold3.

com for others. These two subscription services are my favorites, and I tend to use them more than some of the others that are available. But neither has everything; there is some overlap between the services (some of the censuses, for example), but I have found Ancestry to be stronger on the censuses and Footnote to be stronger on naturalization records. I also used several free services as I searched passenger lists – ellisisland.org was one I mentioned. While I used Ancestry to locate William on the Philadelphia passenger lists, there are other (free) sources where those records are available. The nice thing is that more and more records are coming online at free sites every day.

Many of these records are in book form, and will be available in your local library, or through inter-library loan. Family History Centers are also a valuable resource for all these records, as their collections are extensive.

Alien Registration Records
Not everyone who immigrated to America filed for naturalization. From 1808 to 1828, and again during two periods of our country's history in the 20th century, immigrants who had not been naturalized were required to register, and these documents also provide a plethora of genealogical information. Both of these registrations were as the result of security concerns associated with the outbreaks of World Wars I and II. All resident aliens who had not been naturalized were required to complete an alien registration form. These registrations took place between November 1917 and April 1918, and between August 1, 1940 and March 31, 1944. During both World Wars, any resident or entering alien age 14 or older was required to be fingerprinted and registered. In both registrations, the penalty for not registering was potential deportation.

Following are the questions that were asked of aliens:

World War I
— Full name (including maiden name for females)
— Current residence and length of residence
— Place of birth
— Spouse's name and residence
— Children's names, sex, and years of birth
— Parents' names (including maiden name for mother), birthdates, and birth places
— Names, dates of birth, and current residence of siblings

— Whether any male relatives were serving in the military for/against US
— Whether the alien had registered for selective draft
— Previous military or government service
— Date of immigration, name of vessel and port of arrival
— Whether naturalized in another country
— Whether reported/registered with a consul since 1 June 1914
— Whether applied for naturalization or took out first papers; if yes, when and where
— Whether ever taken an oath of allegiance other than to the United States
— Whether ever arrested or detained on any charge
— Whether held a permit to enter a forbidden area

A full description, photograph and set of fingerprints were also included.

World War II
— Full name
— Name at time of entry to the US, if different than current
— Other names used
— Current address
— Date and place of birth
— Citizenship/Nationality
— Gender
— Marital status
— Race
— Height & Weight
— Hair & Eye Color
— Date, port, vessel and class of admission of last arrival in US
— Date of first arrival in US
— Number of years in the US
— Usual occupation
— Present occupation
— Name, address and business of present employer
— Membership in clubs, organizations or societies
— Dates and nature of military or naval service
— Whether citizenship papers were filed and if so the date, place, and court
— Number of relatives living in the US
— Arrest record, including date, place and disposition
— Whether or not affiliated with a foreign government

As during World War I, a full description, fingerprints and a photograph were included.

As you can see, these records – especially those from 1917-1918 provide invaluable genealogical information.

Finding Immigration & Naturalization Records

Alright – so perhaps I have convinced you that searching for the naturalization papers of your ancestors is worth your while. Your next question will naturally be, "So, where do I find these treasure-laden documents?" The answer varies depending on the records sought and the year your ancestor immigrated to America.

As mentioned earlier in this chapter, prior to 1906, immigration and naturalization was handled by the states, most often at the county level. Therefore, you should begin your research for pre-1906 naturalization records in the county where your ancestor lived. *Sort of.* Many immigrants started their naturalization process (their first papers / letters of intention) in the port where they landed, either because they were so anxious to get the process started, or perhaps they stayed near their port of entry for awhile. Regardless of the reason, if you know where your ancestor entered the country, you may try finding their first papers there.

Back to the counties. Before you plan a cross-country trip to another state and the county where your ancestor lived, a few phone calls and/or internet research may make your search much more pin-pointed – and successful. The repository of immigration and naturalization records varies from state to state. Some states keep those files at the county courthouse. Others have centralized them in the State Archives. Others have handed them over to the state library. Or any combination of the above. When searching for naturalization records in different states, I have had the most luck calling that state's archives (see the Appendix for a state-by-state listing) and asking them where the immigration and naturalization records of the state are kept. Generally the person I have spoken with has an answer for me right off the top of their head. They'll likely know where the records are kept, if the state library has copies of them, if other courts in the state participated in the naturalization process – marine courts, city courts, criminal courts, etc. Some early naturalization records are even included with land records.

Unless you really want to go the county your ancestor lived in, I would strongly suggest you exhaust the Internet trying to locate those records. It is possible they are online, either through a subscription service, or some free website, like a genealogy society for the county in which your ancestor lived. Millions of county naturalization records have been microfilmed and are in the Family History Library of the LDS Church in Salt Lake City, and can be sent to a local Family History Center in your neighborhood.

If you are stymied in your efforts at finding your ancestor in a county's naturalization records, expand your search. Perhaps the county courthouse of an adjoining county was closer to your ancestor than the courthouse in his own county. Perhaps he traveled to a brother or sister's home, or his parents, and filed his naturalization papers there. Be creative if his naturalization papers aren't where you expect them to be!

For post-1906 naturalization records, after the federal government took over the process, those records are kept at the National Archives and Records Administration (*www.archives.gov*) in Washington DC, as well as in their fourteen regional centers (see the Appendix). As with state and county records, the Family History Center also has millions of those records on microfilm.

And of course, as I demonstrated in my search for naturalization records for the Peoples family, many of the immigration and naturalization records are online, either through free services or subscription services such as Ancestry. com and Fold3.com.

Other Sources
In addition to census records, naturalization records and passenger lists, there are many other sources that are available to assist you in finding your ancestors who immigrated to the United States. Many of these records are online, and more are coming online daily. Those that aren't available online are often available on microfilm through the LDS Church, and through inter-library loan across the country. Following are a few that take you beyond the surface in your researching.

Passport Applications
Many who came to America as immigrants left family members in their home country. Human hearts being as they are, many yearned to see their family members after years of absence, and traveled back to their homeland.

Also, as today, business men and vacationers took trips to other countries. Passports were not required until 1941; prior to that they were available and recommended, but not required (except for brief periods during the Civil War and World War I). Even at that, the National Archives has nearly two million passport applications on file for travelers between 1795 and 1925. The applications for these passports sometimes provide genealogical information.

Until the first quarter of the 20th century, the vast majority of passports (95%) were issued to men. This doesn't mean women didn't travel abroad; until the 1920s, women and children traveling with their husbands / fathers were listed on their husband's passport.

Unlike today's passports that are good for ten years, passports in the early years of the United States were valid for two years; therefore, you may find numerous passports for your ancestors.

The information found on passport applications varied through the years, but at a minimum they usually listed at least the full name, birth date and birth place of the individual. Many provided the physical description, which though not particularly of genealogical value, provide an interesting glimpse of an ancestor whom you would otherwise have no way of knowing what he or she looked like. Some provided more information – consider, for example, the application of John Boutrass. His passport application provided the following information:

Application date: September 12, 1900
Name: John Boutrass
Age: 25
Birth date: April 25, 1875
Birth place: Zahle, Syria
Emigrated from: Genoa, Italy
Arrival date: September 1, 1881
Ship he arrived on: Kaiser Wilhelm II
Current residence: Kansas City, Missouri
Date of Naturalization: March 12, 1900
Naturalized at: Criminal Court, Kansas City, Missouri
Physical description: 5-9", high forehead, brown eyes, straight nose, large mouth, oval chin, dark brown hair, dark complexion and long face

Now, I haven't done much research in Syria, but I suspect that their records, if any, would be difficult to research! So this passport application provides LOTS of assistance in learning more about this individual. FYI, Fold3.com has over 700,000 passport applications and related documents available online.

Immigrant Databases
There are many, many immigrant databases online, based typically on country of origin. Many of these can be found quickly by simply Googling them. For example, going to Google and typing in *Italian immigration genealogy*, I received over 160,000 hits, the first one being **Italian Immigration Database** (*www.daddezio.com/genealogy/italian/ships.html*). Going to this website, I found a database that listed the surnames of Italians contained on passenger lists between 1850 and 1930 – and it took me about 35 seconds! I tried this with several nationalities and each yielded a gaggle of websites specific to immigration records of the queried nationality.

According to the 2010 United States census, 47 million Americans (15.2% of us) stated they were of German ancestry – the highest representation of any nationality in America (followed closely by African American at 12.9% and Irish at 10.8%). Since 1 in 7 of us owe our presence here to German immigrants, I think it worthwhile to include information about a great source of genealogical information – the Hamburg Passenger Lists.

For those whose roots extend back to Deutschland, the **Hamburg Passenger Lists** may be the key to finding more information about your ancestors who came to the United States from that part of the world. They provide information about several million Europeans who came to America through Hamburg between 1850 and 1934 (few records were kept during the years of World War I, 1915 – 1919). The nationalities are heavily slanted toward Germans, but individuals from central and eastern Europe also used Hamburg as their point of departure to America and other points. In fact, it is estimated that nearly one-third of the people who emigrated from central and eastern Europe used Hamburg as their jumping-off place.

The passenger lists may be just what you need to locate the town from which your ancestor emigrated. Well-indexed, they provide many genealogical clues to those who emigrated through Hamburg's port including the all-important city or German state.

There are two types of Hamburg passenger lists:

1. **Direct passenger lists** are the lists of those who left Hamburg and sailed directly to their destinations without additional stops at other European ports. The lists for 1850 to 1855 are not complete, but do contain information that may be of assistance (knowing my genealogical luck, my ancestors came between 1850 and 1855 and are not on the portion of the extant lists!). The 1850 to 1855 lists are arranged alphabetically by the first letter of the surname of the person identified as the head of household. After 1855, the lists are arranged chronologically based on when ships left Hamburg port.

2. **Indirect passenger lists** are the lists of those who sailed from Hamburg and stopped at one or more European ports before reaching their final destination. The indirect lists are for the period 1854 to 1910; individuals who left before 1854 or after 1910 are included in the Direct passenger lists.

There are several ways of accessing the Hamburg passenger lists. The LDS Church has an extensive collection in their Family History Library. They have nearly 500 rolls of microfilm containing the passenger lists, and they are available to view by either going to the Family History Library in Salt Lake City, or by renting them for a nominal fee and having them sent to one of their thousands of local Family History Centers around the world. Note, however, that Hamburg State Archives of Germany do not allow the rolls to be sent to a Family History Center in Germany. In Germany, the records must be viewed at a Hamburg State Archives location.

Another way of reviewing information found on the Hamburg passenger lists is through Ancestry.com (*www.ancestry.com/search/db.aspx?dbid=1068*). I searched their 1890 to 1934 database for information on my wife's ancestors, and came up with the following information from the 1896 passenger lists:

Passenger Number	Surname	First Name	State of Origin	Marital Status	Date of Birth	Destination
495083	Blau	Hannie	USA		1873/1874	New York
490134	Blau	Liebe	Osterreich		1858/1859	New York
490136	Blau	Liesel	Osterreich	Ledig	1891/1892	New York
490135	Blau	Moses	Osterreich	Ledig	1884/1885	New York
495081	Blau	Philipp	USA		1869/1870	New York
499949	Blau	Sali	Ungarn	Ledig	1879/1880	New York

Also listed were whether or not family members were in attendance with this passenger, and whether they were a Direct or Indirect passenger. On the results of the Internet search, notice that passengers 490134, 490135 and 490136 are all named Blau. Liebe is about 37 years old, and the other two are ages 4 and 11. I think I would reasonably anticipate that this was a mother and her two children traveling together. (Can't you just see them in your mind's eye: Mother talking to the ship steward as he writes down her name and age, holding the hand of her squirming 4-year-old daughter Liesel who wants to see and experience everything going on around her, with her 11-year-old brother Moses also keeping a watchful eye on Liesel, while also trying to take in all the new sights, sounds, smells, feelings and excitement!)

Note: Since these are official German records, they are written in German (no surprise there!). So, unless *Sie sprechen Deutsch*, you may need some assistance interpreting them. You might try *translate.google.com*; it is a website that provides pretty decent translation services, certainly generally enough to learn some of the main phrases used in these German records. For example, from the chart above, *ledig* means single and *Osterreich* means Austria.

Ethnic Societies

Generally speaking, when immigrants came to America, they tended to cluster in groups, especially for their first few years here. They were among their own, who had the same language, traditions, etc. They were also a wonderful source of assistance to newcomers who were coming to this big land with all new laws, requirements and societal concerns.

Many formed heritage groups through the years – The Irish Americans, The Swedish Connection, The Italians, etc. Often these groups published newspapers, kept records and celebrated weddings and births and noted deaths together. Searching the Internet for information about these societies may yield untold information.

Genealogy Societies

As you have personally experienced, genealogy is an addictive and satisfying hobby. Many others feel this way, and many have joined together to form genealogy societies. These societies are seemingly at every level of our culture: there are family genealogy societies, county genealogy societies, state genealogy societies, regional genealogy societies and ethnic genealogy societies. All are pledged to researching the roots of those within their constituency.

These are often a wonderful source of genealogical information on immigrants. Your Swedish ancestors came to Minnesota in the mid-1800s? Then try the **Swedish Genealogy Society of Minnesota** (*www.sgsmn.org*) to see what immigration records and information they have available. Your Irish ancestors fled the potato famine in Ireland in the mid 1840s and came to Boston? Then be sure and see what the **Boston to Providence Genealogy Society** (*www.iment.com/bos2prov*) has to offer.

Books, Books, Books

There is probably no end to the number of books that have been published and continue to be published about immigrants in America, emigrants from _____ (fill in the blank of your ancestor's country). Many of these have been microfilmed and are available through the Family History Library, and many are available at your local or state library, if not on the shelf, through inter-library loans.

In the 1800s, it was fashionable to write county histories, which often included the biographies of prominent and/or early citizens of the county. I tend to think that my ancestors were largely like me – pretty normal, with occasional flashes of brilliance. Despite this relative normality, I have been successful in finding interesting and genealogically enlightening articles about several ancestors that have advanced my research efforts. Consider the following excerpt about one of my fourth great grandfather's neighbors from *Biographies of Old Schuyler County* (Illinois) Settlers, written in 1878:

WILLIAM DEAN

William Dean was born in county Dennygaul, Ireland, May 3d, 1825, and is a son of John Dean. He received his early education in the district schools of Ireland. At about the age of twenty-two he emigrated to America, landing in New York. From there he went to the western part of Pennsylvania, where he resided two years. He then moved to Schuyler county, Illinois, in the spring of 1850, where he engaged in farming. In March, 1857, he was married to Mrs. Maria Pain, daughter of George and Jane Humphreys; she was born July 10th, 1830. The fruits of their marriage is a family of four children, one of whom is now deceased. Mr. Dean is at present residing on his farm in Littleton township, enjoying good health.

Wow – this short biography helped establish important information about this immigrant, William Dean: his father's name, his marriage and number of children (one of which had died by 1878 when this article was written), his wife and her parents. Dates and places are included. As an experienced researcher you know this secondary source of information might be fraught with errors (for example, knowing a bit about Ireland and the Irish accent, I'd be willing to bet *Dennygaul*, Ireland, is in reality *Donegal*, Ireland!), but the information provided is invaluable and can narrow your areas and timeframes for searches as you look for original documents to support this information. I can use this information to narrow my search for his naturalization papers, knowing that he immigrated to America in about 1847 (at the height of the potato famine!) and came through the port of New York.

Vital Records
While searching for information about your ancestors, don't overlook the value of vital records. Yes, of course – if you knew where your ancestor was born, you could get his or her birth certificate. But perhaps their death certificate will provide some enlightenment – they often carried the birth place of the individual, and often listed the parents' names. Consider the death certificate of immigrant Matilda Cunningham, who died June 13, 1930 in Hardin, Ray County, Missouri. Here's the information I gleaned from her death certificate:

She was born in Woodstock, Ontario, Canada
Her birth date was December 6, 1853
Her father's name was George Powell
Her father was born in Ireland
Her mother's name was Matilda McCardle
Her mother was born in Ireland
She was married to Oliver S. Cunningham
She was buried in the City Cemetery in Richmond, Missouri

There was a place on the death certificate for the clerk to indicate if she was foreign born (she was), how long she had been in the United States. While the clerk for Matilda's death didn't see fit to complete this section, had he done so, it would have narrowed our search for the immigration records for her and her parents, and possibly her husband.

There is a lot of information here to lead me other places to find original records. Using the information I have gleaned from her death certificate, I can search for her naturalization papers, or passenger lists of the ship that carried her parents from Ireland to Canada.

HISTORY LESSONS!

I am not a historian, but here are a few other historical events that might have affected your ancestors and spurred their immigration to America:

1607: Jamestown founded

1600 – 1650s The Plantation Period in Ireland – Ulster is "planted" with Scots loyal to the British crown; many Irish flee to the wilds of America (one of my Irish ancestors included!)

1620: Pilgrims land at Plymouth Rock

1630: Puritans begin heading for America

1638 – 1655: Sweden sends colonizers to America, founding New Sweden in Delaware

1648 – 1650 – Germans flee from religious persecution

1681: William Penn and the Quakers found Pennsylvania

1707: Scots flee England as a result of the merging of England and Scotland

1745: The English sentenced Scottish Jacobite rebels and sympathizers to America

1789: Many French nobility fled France for America during the French Revolution

1798: The rebellion called the 1798 Uprising in Ireland fails, and many rebels flee to America

1846-1848: Irish potato famine brings approximately one million Irish immigrants to America

1849: Britain repeals Navigation Laws, for a variety of reasons (economic, agricultural, etc), Norwegian immigrants flock to Canada and on to America

1867 – 1869: Successive crop failures in Sweden spur another round of mass immigrations to America; many headed to Iowa and Illinois

1876 – 1900: Italian men immigrate to America in huge numbers as a result of declining economic conditions in Italy

1890 – 1915: Polish immigration due to poor economic, religious and political conditions in southern Poland

1910: Revolution in Mexico sent many immigrants north of the border

1933 to 1940: Jewish refugees fleeing from Nazi Germany come to America

1945-1950: Poles flee the Communist reign established by Russia after World War II

Doubtless I have left out some of the historical issues you are aware of that spurred emigration from your ancestors' native land (e-mail me and tell me, so I can include it in future editions!), but at least this will give you an idea of where to begin or continue your research.

History

An important clue to searching for your ancestors goes back to your junior high school days – *History*. Knowing the history of your ancestors' countries of origin may help you pinpoint them and their dates of immigration to America. I have mentioned several times in this book the Irish potato famine, a result of a blight that hit successive potato harvests in the mid 1840s. Since the potato was the mainstay of the Irish diet, the consequences were brutal. It left over 10% of the population dead, and another 10% to 15% emigrated from Ireland. Estimates place the number of Irish immigrants to America during this time at about one million! If you feel like your chances of finding your Irish ancestor are one in a million – perhaps you should check the immigration records during this period!

Don't Forget the Rest of the Family!

When researching your immigrant ancestors and looking for clues that will establish dates and places, and perhaps links to the next generation and beyond, don't be so focused on your direct-line ancestors that you forget about their siblings. Let's use Matilda Cunningham, for a moment. As we discussed above, we learned from her death certificate that while she was born in Canada, her parents were both born in Ireland. But we don't know where exactly. Searching the death certificates of Matilda's siblings may yield that information. Perhaps the clerk who completes the death certificate for one of her siblings won't ignore the question that asks when the deceased came to the United States, thus giving clue to when Matilda may have come. It may also list more than Ireland as the birth place for her parents.

Immigration & Naturalization Checklist

____ Passenger lists are a good place to find immigrating ancestors.

____ Naturalization papers were the responsibility of the territories, states and counties prior to 1906, when the federal government took over the immigration process.

____ Don't forget that the 1900 through 1940 censuses have immigration-specific questions.

____ Naturalization papers can provide tremendous genealogical information.

____ Don't overlook other sources where immigrants may be found: genealogy societies, county histories and books

____ Look beyond your direct-line ancestors for potential clues and information.

Additional Resources

Steven Fisher (editor), *Archival Information (How to Find It, How to Use It)*,
(Greenwood Press, 2004).

Sharon DeBartalo Carmack, *The Genealogy Sourcebook*, (McGraw-Hill, 1998).

Roger Daniels, *Coming to America: A History of Immigration and Ethnicity
in America*, (New York: Harper Collins, 1990).

Christina K. Schaefer, *Guide to Naturalization Records of the United States*,
Genealogical Publishing Company, 1997.

Henry Steele Commager, *Immigration and American History*, Pantheon
Books, New York.

Loretto Dennis Szucs and Sandra Hargreaves Luebking (editors), *The Source
– A Guidebook to American Genealogy*, third edition, edited by Ancestry
Publishing, 2006. The Source has an extensive and very detailed chapter
on Immigration and Naturalization.

Lubomyr R. and Anna T. Wynar, *Encylopedic Directory of Ethnic Newspapers
and Periodicals in the United States*.

For more in-depth treatment of these issues, pick up a copy of my *Mastering
Immigration & Naturalization Records*, 2nd Edition, Cold Spring Press, 2013.

8. LAND RECORDS

"No man but feels more of a man in the world if he have a bit of ground that he can call his own." — Charles Dudley Warner

Perhaps as you came upon this chapter, you thought I had lost my mind. You might have asked, "What possible good can land records be to a genealogist?"

Well, I am glad you asked! It is true that most land records don't provide the significant genealogical information that other records may provide, but they none-the-less serve an important genealogical purpose. First, a land record can establish where a particular individual was at a certain time in his life. While not as common, land records may also provide relationship information, if for example, several members of a family bought or sold a tract of land together, or if members of a family served as witnesses to a deed. Using this information, intrepid genealogists may be able to turn up other family members in nearby locations in either land records or more genealogically focused records such as birth and death records, military records, etc. And finally, land records may be some of the few records that are in existence, especially from colonial times – a good reason to glean every bit of information you can from them.

Land Record Definitions
As you research land records, some of the terms are bound to be archaic or unclear to you. Following are some definitions that should help:

Bounty Land Warrant – a warrant granting land to individuals to reward them for enlisting and/or previous military service.

Buyer Index – An index of deeds that is alphabetical based on the buyer's name.

Deed – the document used to transfer land ownership from one person or entity to another.

Grant – also known as a first-title deed or patent. A grant is the transfer of land from either the federal government (for public-domain states) or state / colony (state-land state) to an individual or entity.

Grantee – buyer in a land transaction.

Grantee indexes — the name given to an index to deed books containing records of land transactions, alphabetized by the name of the buyer (grantee). Also called an indirect or reverse index.

Grantor – seller in a land transaction.

Grantor index – an index to deed books containing records of land transactions, alphabetized by the name of the seller (grantor).

First-title grant – the original granting or transferring of land from the state or federal government.

Headright – land granted for immigration or for bringing immigrants to an area. Practiced during colonial times.

Indiscriminate survey – a survey that was not part of a larger survey grid or area.

Patent – the federal government granted land to individuals through a patent (sometimes called a grant).

Plat – the legal description of a parcel of land, generally determined after a survey.

Public Domain States – those states where lands were granted by the federal government to individuals. They consist of the thirty states not considered State-land states (see definition) (mostly western states).

Running index – name given to indexes of deed books where names of buyers and/or sellers are grouped together alphabetically by first letter of surname, but not alphabetically within the letter.

Seller Index — an index of deeds that is alphabetical based on the seller's name.

State-land State — those states or colonies where lands were granted by the states to individuals. They consist of the thirteen original colonies, along with Hawaii, Kentucky, Maine, Tennessee, Texas, Vermont, West Virginia.

Warranty Deed – a deed that is warranted (guaranteed); the title in a land transaction.

Which Records to Look For

I'll address a number of types of records and share the elements of the records that are of most interest to genealogists.

First, let's briefly discuss the process in which your ancestors may have participated to obtain land.

At the outset of the country, lands were often granted (given or sold) to individuals for a variety of reasons: as enticement to settle or to bring others to settle in a particular area, and as rewards for enlistment and/or service in the military. When an individual wished to obtain land, he filed an *application* or *petition* to the entity holding title to the land. In colonial times, this petition may have been to the King of England, the governor of one of the colonies, or to another individual or entity who had been given responsibility to administer the distribution of lands. The application would have contained the individual's name, and depending on locality, may also have included his age, country of citizenship, evidence of military service (another clue that might lead to other information about the individual – see the *Military Records* chapter), and other interesting genealogical tidbits. His application and supporting documents would have been kept in a case file, put together by the person administering the transaction.

Once the application was approved, the individual would have been issued a warrant. This allowed the individual to request a survey of the area he had been granted. Most pre-Revolutionary era surveys were done using the metes-and-bounds system. It was eventually replaced by the township and section system most of us are familiar with, but metes-and-bounds surveying and property descriptions continued to be used well into the 19th century.

This metes-and-bounds system used the physical attributes of the land to describe the property. Consider the following property description of one of my ancestors in North Carolina in 1806:

Beginning at the black oak near John Cowan's corner running east 25 chains to a stake then north 13 west 9 chains to a post oak 12 degrees west 11 chains and 95 links to a hickory tree
Thence north 75 degrees, east, 12 chains to a black oak
Thence east 20 chains to a post oak
Thence north 3 chains 50 links to a post oak
Thence north 80 degrees east seven chains to post oak
Thence north 31 degrees east 14 chains and 50 links to a hickory
Thence north 59 degrees east 25 chains to a post oak
Thence north 33 chains and 50 links to a black oak
Thence north 78 degrees west 50 chains to a post oak
Thence south 24 degrees west 54 chains and 50 links to a post oak
Thence south 4 degrees east 41 chains to a post oak
Thence 22 chains and 50 links to the beginning and including 560 acres more or less and all the woods, ways, waters and watercourses, and all and every appurtenances thereunto belonging,

Thankfully, many of our second-generation founding fathers realized that basing land boundaries on topography and flora would eventually result in problems of identifying lands accurately – trees die or get cut down, streams are rerouted due to erosion or man-made interference, rocks are moved, etc. As mentioned earlier, this method of surveying was replaced with the township and section method (sometimes called the rectangular survey system). Most of the United States use the rectangular survey system, but some do not. Louisiana, for example, uses an old French surveying method in addition to the township and section method, Hawaii uses a separate system developed during the Kingdom of Hawaii days and several other states (Texas and New Mexico) use a mixture of methods relying on old Spanish and Mexican land grants and the township and section method.

In the township and section method, townships, ranges and sections are used. A township consists of 36 sections, each of which is 640 acres, or one square mile. Each section can then be divided into smaller parcels. A typical land description in the town and section method might be "SE 1/4 of section 23, T4N R3E," which interpreted, is "The southeast quarter of section 23, township 4 north, range 3 east."

Back to the process. In addition to the steps mentioned above (application, warrant, survey, grant), an individual could also have been issued land as a result of a lottery or as a purchase. After land was obtained, regardless of the method, the individual's name was entered into a tract book, and then on a plat map.

Once payment was received for the land (as well as other requirements – residency, installment payments, etc.), a patent was given to the individual. As you can imagine, the day an individual received a patent for his land was a red-letter day, and patent documents often were among his prized possessions, passed down for generations.

In summary, the land grant process generally followed the following pattern:

Petition/application: warrant: survey: grant: patent (first title grant)

This would be a good place to say a word or two about military bounty land warrants. Prior to the Revolutionary War, the colonial governments offered military bounty land warrants to men to entice them into military service or to reward them for their service. After the Revolutionary War, the United States government and various states used military bounty land warrants to attract and/or reward men for military service. These military bounty land warrants began in 1788 and were used until 1855. Until later in the process, the land warrant could only be used in specially designated districts called military districts, primarily Ohio, but also in a few other states, including Arkansas, Georgia, Illinois, Kentucky, Missouri, New York, Pennsylvania, South Carolina, Tennessee, and Virginia. This was a way for the federal government to reward those who served under her flag, and at the same time foster western expansion.

A military bounty land warrant did not in and of itself grant land. It was the means whereby the former service man could enter the process described above to receive land. The warrant was surrendered to receive a survey on a predetermined area of land (some warrants were exceptionally generous, granting hundreds, if not thousands, of acres of land). Once a survey was completed, a grant was given and the veteran owned the land. Or not. Although the exact number isn't known, researchers of military bounty land warrants have concluded that a very small percentage of veterans actually used their land warrants – perhaps fewer than 10%. Not wanting to move to Ohio or other military districts, many veterans simply assigned (for remuneration, of course!) the land warrant to someone who was interested in the land, either for themselves, or for speculation. The warrant was simply signed, much like endorsing a check, and assigned to someone else. There are no records that indicate who redeemed and who did not redeem their land warrants for themselves, versus selling them to others.

In addition to assigning or executing their military bounty land warrants, many veterans simply didn't execute their warrants, and in most cases, those unredeemed warrants have been lost to history.

Some of the original colonies used bounty land warrants to attract and reward soldiers for service during and after the Revolutionary War. Often, these warrants provided for land elsewhere in the colony. Like the federal military bounty land warrants, some were redeemed, some were sold, and still others simply went unredeemed.

During the War of 1812, none of the states used military bounty land warrants; those were issued only by the federal government at that time. Several of the so-called Indian Wars in western states spawned a revival of military bounty land warrants, primarily in Illinois and Missouri. Several of my ancestors, including Leonidas Horney and his father Samuel, received and executed military bounty land warrants in Illinois for service in either the War of 1812 or the Black Hawk War. For his service during the War of 1812, Samuel received military bounty land warrants and he also received them for his service during the Black Hawk War. His son Leonidas may have received and redeemed military bounty land warrants for his service during the Mexican War.

As well known as military bounty land warrants are, only about 7% of the land distributed by the federal government was through that process.
A little over a quarter of the lands distributed by the federal government were through homesteads. The Oklahoma Land Rush in 1889 is one of the more well-known homesteading events, perhaps given its dramatic race to locate land (and the scoff-law Sooners, who snuck in ahead of the appointed

time!) Those who claimed lands through homesteading, generally had to reside on the land for five years and make improvements on the land.

A quick (and short!) note about military bounty land warrants for the Civil War – there were none!

As you can see, whether lands were given as part of a military bounty land warrant, or granted by a state or federal government, a variety of documents were produced in the first land transactions. Transaction documents included:

— case files
— grants / patents
— plat maps
— surveys
— patents
— warrants

Most government entities kept these documents in books – case files, plat books, tract books, patent books and warrant books. These land records are located in the State Archives of each individual state as well as in the National Archives. Excellent sources for finding more about these documents are the research outlines provided by the LDS Church at www.familysearch.org. From the FamilySearch *Home* page, go to *Get Help*. Select *Research Wiki*, then in the box below Or find research articles, type _____ (*name of state*) *land and property records*. You'll be provided a list of articles that have been written about land and property records in the state you asked about, and these research helps are invaluable for assisting you in finding where a state's land records are kept.

These research helps will give you the history of land distribution for the state you have selected, and where to find the federal and state records pertaining to land grants purchases.

State-Land & Federal-Land States
In searching for land records, it is important to know how lands were originally granted – whether by the state or the federal government. Depending on the answer, your search for first-title deeds will take you in different directions.

The original 13 colonies and a handful of other states (Hawaii, Kentucky, Maine, Tennessee, Texas, Vermont and West Virginia) are known as state-land states – those states whose first land claims were granted by the states.

The remaining 30 states are known as federal-land states (also known as public-domain states), and in those states, the federal government was the first to grant land titles.

The federal government distributed over a billion acres of public domain lands through various processes, including military bounty land warrants, homestead grants, donation or cash sales and private land claims (these latter were for individuals who could prove title to lands received from France, Mexico or Spain, prior to ownership by the US). All of these transactions were the responsibility of the **General Land Office (GLO)** or the **Bureau of Land Management (BLM)**, the successor organization to the GLO. Records of those transactions are included in the National Archives.

Unfortunately, most of the GLO/BLM records have not been microfilmed. Those that have been microfilmed are available through the Family History Library of the LDS church. Otherwise, you may be able to get copies of the various records (case files, applications, etc.) by contacting the National Archives at:

Textual Reference Branch
National Archives and Records Administration
7th and Pennsylvania Avenue, NW
Washington, DC 20408

When you write to the National Archives, include all the information you know about the transaction: full name of the purchaser, state, land office legal description of the land, and if you have it, the certificate type and number of the patent.

Note that the GLO/BLM has the records for first-title transactions only. Once land was transferred from the federal government to individuals, subsequent sales, foreclosures, quit claims, bequeaths, etc. were handled and recorded at the county level of each state.

For state-land states (the thirteen original colonies and seven other states), to get copies of a land grant, you'll need the name of the grantee (buyer) of

TAKING THE MEASURE OF YOUR ANCESTORS

Sure, you're familiar with feet, yards and miles. But how up-to-speed are you on your ancestors' measurement terms? When your ancestor wrote about rods and perches, he wasn't talking about going fishing for the weekend! Read on:

Acre – 43,560 square feet. 14,520 square yards. 10 square chains. 160 rods.

Application – also called a petition or memorial, this document was usually the first step taken by a person seeking a grant of land, whether to purchase or to have it given to him.

Chain – a chain is 66 feet long, and consists of 100 links. An acre is 10 square chains.

Furlong – a furlong is 660 feet, or 10 chains. There are 8 furlongs in a mile.

Link – a link is 7.92 inches long. There are 100 links in a chain.

Mile – 5,280 feet. 1760 yards. 80 chains. 640 acres.

Patent – also called a first-title deed, a patent is the first deed granted for land.

Perch – a perch is 16.5 feet, 5.5 yards long. There are 25 links in a perch. There are 4 perches in a chain, and 40 perches in a furlong.

Plat – a plat is the specific lot within a tract of land.

Pole – a pole is 16.5 feet, 5.5 yards long. There are 25 links in a pole. There are 4 poles in a chain, and 320 poles in a mile.

Rod – a rod is 16.5 feet, 5.5 yards long. There are 25 links in a rod. There are 4 rod in a chain, and 160 rods in an acre.

Vara – a vara is 33.33 inches.

Warrant – a document or certificate that entitled an individual or entity to receive a portion of land.

the land. Some records are also indexed by the name of the grantor (seller). Those indexes are called grantor indexes, and buyer indexes are called grantor indexes. If the county where the records are located has only grantee indexes, your search will be more difficult – since you'll need to search all the transactions in the area, and around the time of the land transaction. Unless, of course, you kow the name of the man who sold the property to your sixth great grandfather!

State land records are generally found in the county where the grant was given, and many states also include them in their state archives.

Okay – so you've found some information – a deed, an entry in a tract book showing that one of your ancestors purchased some land, etc. Now what do you do with that information? Here are some thoughts:

1. Record the information. Make good notes so that you, or someone reviewing your research, can find the information again. Enter the name of the document, database or website where you found the information, the name of the source and everything necessary to be able to locate the information again.
2. Either print the information, photocopy it, copy it word-for-word, or abstract the information. Abstracting is valuable and saves time, but be sure you include all the salient information: the source, the document, the critical information, etc.
3. Review the information with an open mind – don't be so focused on finding what you are looking for that you miss clues or information that might lead you to other family members.
4. Develop a research plan for and surrounding the documents.

Regarding Number 4 above, a research plan should begin with the document or information at hand, and fan out from there, including all other logical research sources. To illustrate, I have provided the abstract of a deed below, and a possible research plan beginning with the deed:

Source: Delaware County, Ohio Deed Book #5, pages 526-528. Abstract found at *kinexxions.blogspot.com/2009_05_01_archive.html*

Deed between Jonas Joslin and his wife Ruth to James Joslin and Jonas Joslin Junior

This indenture made and concluded this 10th day of January in the year of our Lord **one thousand eight hundred and sixty two** by and between **Jonas Joslin and Ruth his wife of Delaware County in the state of Ohio** of the first part, and James Joslin and Jonas Joslin Junior witnesseth that the said Jonas Joslin and Ruth his wife for and in consideration of eight hundred dollars fifty cents to them in hand paid or secured to be paid the receipt whereof is hereby acknowledged, given, granted, bargained, sold, released, conveyed and confirmed and by these presents give, grant, bargain, sell, release, convey and confirm unto the said James and Jonas Joslin Junior and unto their heirs and assigns forever a lot of land viz., lot number 16 in the west tier of lots in the fourth section of the third township in the nineteenth range of the United States Military lands and within the county of Delaware and supposed to contain **one hundred acres more or less,** to have and to hold the above described premises with all the privileges and appurtenances threreunto belonging or in any wise appertaining unto him the said Jonas Joslin Junior and James Joslin and unto their heirs and assigns forever and the said Jonas Joslin and Ruth his wife for their heirs and executors and administrators covenant and promise to and with the said James Jonas and Jonas Joslin Junior their heirs and assigns that they are lawfully seized of the premises aforesaid that they have good right and full authority to sell and convey the same in manner aforesaid and that the said Premises are free and clear from all encumbrances. And further that they the said Jonas Joslin and Ruth his wife their heirs executors and administrators will well warrant and truly defend the premises aforesaid unto the said James and Jonas Joslin Junior and unto their heirs and assigns forever against the lawful claims of any persons or person whomever **except a reservation of the use of the above described Premises during our lives.** In testimony whereof the party to the first part here hereunto set our hands and seals the day and year above written.

Jonas Joslin (seal)
Ruth Joslin (seal)

Signed and sealed and delivered in presence of:

Nathan Carpenter
Sophia Weaver

I highlighted a number of items I felt had genealogical value in this deed. Below are some of the more *obvious* tidbits of data we can glean from the above deed:

1. Jonas Joslin was alive on January 10, 1862

2. Ruth Joslin was alive on January 10, 1862

3. Jonas and Ruth were married ("Jonas Joslin and his wife Ruth")

4. Jonas and Ruth owned land in Delaware County, Ohio

5. The land was conveyed to James Joslin and Jonas Joslin Junior

6. We might assume that James and Jonas Joslin Junior were related to each other (brothers, perhaps?) and maybe to Jonas and Ruth also (Jonas Junior would imply a relationship between the two Jonases).

Applying the next layer of curiosity (and logic!), here are some things that aren't quite so obvious:

7. James and Jonas Junior had probably reached adulthood (at least age 21), since they were purchasing land.

We might assume that Jonas Junior is older than James, even though James's name is mentioned first in the deed. Most families name the eldest son Junior, rather than younger sons. Be careful with this assumption, however. I have examples in my own ancestral family tree where that wasn't the case.

And at the next layer, here are a few things to investigate that aren't so obvious:

Understanding the historical timeframe will help me understand if $800.50 for "100 acres more or less" represents a bona fide sale, or if it was really more along the lines of a gift, with a token payment being received therefore. Other deeds in the same area around the same timeframe may shed light on this aspect of the transaction. A gift would further indicate that James and Jonas Junior were related to Jonas and Ruth.

Did you catch that the deed called for Jonas and Ruth to continue to live in the home on the property (the Premises) during their lives? This almost assuredly establishes some familial relationship between these four individuals.

Are the witnesses related in any way to the buyers and/or sellers? Ruth's brother and sister? Son-in-law? Daughter-in-law?

Since James and Jonas Junior are agreeing to let Jonas and Ruth live in the house for the rest of their lives, it is probable that Jonas and Ruth are elderly.

From this point, I develop a research plan to see if I can springboard off this information to find more genealogical information. Below are some of the places I may go in my search about this family:

Research Plan

1. First, I will check the 1860 and perhaps 1850 federal censuses for Delaware County, Ohio to see if I can locate this family. A census record will help me determine for certain whether James and Jonas Junior are brothers and the sons of Jonas and Ruth. It will establish their ages for me also. A census will also give me the birth states of the individuals involved in the transaction.

2. I'll check land records prior to 1862 to see when Jonas and Ruth first purchased the land they sold. It may indicate when they first arrived in the area.

3. I'll check military records to see if Jonas Sr., Jonas Jr., or James were Union soldiers, and if so, whether they applied for a pension. Their pension application may provide me additional information about his family.

4. While the surnames of the witnesses to the deed — Carpenter and Weaver — don't ring any immediate bells, perhaps they are Ruth's brother and sister, or perhaps a son-in-law and a married daughter. It is certainly worth looking into. Scanning 1860 and 1850 censuses for those surnames may yield further information on those individuals and their families.

5. I'll check grantors and grantees deed indexes to see if I can find any other lands that may have been purchased or sold by any of these four individuals.

6. If I am reviewing in person the tract books from which this deed was extracted, I will also check the vital records books to see if I can find marriage or birth information for any of these individuals.

7. I'll check the Family History Library to see if they may have microfilmed vital statistics or religious records from Delaware County, Ohio.

Land Records Checklist

___ The LDS website Familysearch.org has excellent Research Guides to assist your land records search.

___ Gain an understanding of Land Record terms.

___ Determine the state and county where your ancestor may have purchased or sold land.

___ Determine a time frame within which your ancestor may have purchased or sold land.

___ Learn where to look for records for any given state.

___ Go beyond the obvious information found in land records – look for genealogical clues.

___ Use information found in land records as a springboard to other, more genealogically focused records.

Additional Resources

Steven Fisher (editor), *Archival Information (How to Find It, How to Use It),* (Greenwood Press, 2004).

Sharon DeBartalo Carmack, *The Genealogy Sourcebook*, (McGraw-Hill, 1998)

E. Wade Hone, *Land & Property Research in the United States*, (Ancestry. com, 2008)

Patricia Law Hatcher, *Locating Your Roots: Discover Your Ancestors Using Land Records,* (Cincinnati: Betterway Books, 2003).

Loretto Dennis Szucs and Sandra Hargreaves Luebking, (editors), *The Source – A Guidebook to American Genealogy*, 3rd Edition, Ancestry Publishing, 2006. The Source has an extensive and very detailed chapter on land records.

Some of my ancestors!

9. GETTING THE MOST OUT OF VISITING CEMETERIES

"I didn't attend the funeral, but I sent a nice letter saying that I approved of it." – Mark Twain

Sometimes, despite your best efforts, you just seem unable to unearth any records that will give you information about an ancestor or his family. You've exhausted all the records you can think of with no luck. It may be time to get out some maps, fuel up the car, dust off your shoes and make a road trip to a cemetery.

We all have one thing in common with our ancestors – we are all going to die! Often headstones in cemeteries will provide us with a few clues about those ancestors. Birth dates, death dates, age at death, relationships to others buried nearby, etc. are all typical of information found on tombstones. Since state laws governing the requirement to keep birth, death and marriage records didn't come into existence until recently (some as recent as the beginning decades of the 20th century), sometimes cemeteries and cemetery records may be the only places you'll find genealogical information on the individuals and families you're seeking.

Visiting cemeteries may be one way to break through the log jam you're experiencing for a particular ancestor or two. I have had the opportunity to prowl through more than a few cemeteries during my genealogical sojourns. I have had some tremendous luck, but I have often left frustrated because I did nothing more than eliminate the cemetery from further consideration as a place to find information about my ancestors! And there have been times when I found some little bits of data, only to discover after I had returned hundreds of miles to my home, that there had been other relatives buried in that cemetery whose information I hadn't recorded. Because of those experiences, I have provided a few suggestions about how to make the most of your cemeterial field trip.

Bring Plenty of Names

Before you head out on a scouting trip to a cemetery, I suggest that you bring with you the names of other families that are related to you beyond your direct-line ancestor. Before going, make sure you are familiar with the names of extended family members: sons-, parents-, brothers- and sisters-in-law may well be resting in the same cemetery as your ancestor, within just a few feet or yards of your ancestor. This seems especially to be the case in rural cemeteries. Be sure and look at the tombstones that are located adjacent to or nearby the graves of your ancestors. Family members are often buried near each other, and in small town or county cemeteries, often large sections of the cemetery are devoted to individuals related to one another.

It is also important to have a good working knowledge (written or in your head) of the time period you are looking for. If your ancestor died in the 1850s and the section of the cemetery you are in only has tombstones from the turn of the century (19th or 20th!) that's a clue that you may not be in the right part of the cemetery.

Photo Recording

Once you have located the tombstones of your ancestors, make some record of what you have found. Digital cameras are inexpensive and invaluable for recording the information on the tombstones. Film cameras generally do a good job too, although you won't know until you have developed the film whether the picture you took is useable. (And by then, you may be hundreds of miles away!) With decent digital cameras available for around $50, I think they are well worth the investment! Whether you are using a digital or film camera, I suggest bringing a flash if your camera isn't equipped with one. Tombstones whose inscriptions are in the shade (either facing away from the sun or under a tree) may not yield a good photograph without a flash.

Also, it seems that I am always at cemeteries in low-light conditions – early mornings or at dusk. I also suggest taking a tablet or pad of paper (or some electronic device like a Blackberry, I suppose!) and record the information in writing. Files are corrupted or lost, computer hard drives crash, photos are accidentally erased from memory cards, film pictures don't come out quite right. This dual recording helps protect and preserve the information you may have traveled many miles to capture.

PRESERVED HISTORY

Thelma Green Reagan memorialized the efforts of those who seek to preserve and share information found in cemeteries in a poem:

The Recording of a Cemetery
Today we walked where others walked
On a lonely, windswept hill;
Today we talked where others cried
For Loved Ones whose lives are stilled.

Today our hearts were touched
By graves of tiny babies;
Snatched from the arms of loving kin,
In the heartbreak of the ages.

Today we saw where the grandparents lay
In the last sleep of their time;
Lying under the trees and clouds -
Their beds kissed by the sun and wind.
Today we wondered about an unmarked spot;

Who lies beneath this hallowed ground?
Was it a babe, child, young or old?
No indication could be found.
Today we saw where Mom and Dad lay.

We had been here once before
On a day we'd all like to forget,
But will remember forever more.
Today we recorded for kith and kin

The graves of ancestors past;
To be preserved for generations hence,
A record we hope will last.
Cherish it, my friend; preserve it, my friend,

For stones sometimes crumble to dust
And generations of folks yet to come
Will be grateful for your trust.

Note: The author could not be located to gain permission to use her poem. However, she granted permission to use it on the website *tioga.nygenweb.net/faces.htm*, and the owner of that site granted permission to use it here.

Family Cemeteries: Check with Local Genealogical Societies
Often, especially in rural and agricultural communities, families merely designated a plot of land in a corner of one of their fields to serve as a family cemetery. Sometimes these cemeteries are not catalogued and are difficult to find. Prior to your visit to the area where your ancestor lived, touching bases with the local genealogical society to see if they know of any family cemeteries in the vicinity is a good idea. A favorite activity of genealogy societies around the world is locating and recording information from local and family cemeteries.

Speaking of family cemeteries and recording and preserving them, I recently stumbled across a listing on the internet (at www.findagrave.com) for a cemetery where a number of my ancestors were buried. A fellow genealogist went to a great deal of effort to record information found in the Thompson Family Cemetery in Schuyler County, Illinois, the final resting place of several generations and lines of my ancestors. I have been to this small-ish family cemetery, and appreciate the difficulty in transcribing all this information, much less transcribing it and making it available on the Internet.

This fellow genealogist provided information on over 120 individuals in this small family cemetery out in the middle of the country. He also provided a number of comments and important genealogical information based on his personal knowledge and research. Some of the information I already knew through my own research, but I was able to glean additional information on other ancestors through his efforts.

As an experienced genealogist, you'll know that you should be cautious about using information from headstones, especially for such things as birthdates. Memories dim (or fibs are perpetuated!) about the birth dates of individuals. You can usually consider the death date pretty accurate, owing to the closeness of the event to the individual's need for the headstone.

Internet Listings for Cemeteries
Before you fuel up the car and head out in search of cemeteries, you might spend a few minutes with Mr. Mac or Mr. PC and see if you can find anything about your ancestors' cemetery on the Internet – it may save you time and a trip! I initially stumbled upon the online information about Leonidas Horney and his family when I was poking and prodding on the Internet. I had found information about the cemetery quite accidentally.

But a concentrated search of cemeteries in the areas where your family were from may yield great rewards for you also.

There are a number of genealogy websites that I have found useful. Some of the better ones include:

www.ancestorsatrest.com/cemetery_records/ — Ancestors at Rest has a large database containing many free death records: coffin plates, funeral cards, death cards, wills, memorial cards, cemeteries, vital stats, obituaries, church records, family bibles, cenotaphs and tombstone inscriptions. This is a subscription service.

www.usgennet.org/usa/topic/cemetery/ — This site, sponsored by the **American History and Genealogy Project (AHGP)**, provides transcriptions and photos for cemeteries throughout the United States.

www.findagrave.com — This website grew out of the passion of one individual (Jim Tipton) who was fascinated by graves, and began categorizing the graves of famous people. His work is now aided and abetted by over 500,000 volunteer contributors. Several of the links lead you to sites that are subscription-based, but many others do not. They boast 109 million graves and more than 70,000 website visits daily. I checked several obscure relatives from the turn of the last century and found the transcription of their headstones here. I also searched for my 3rd great grandfather, a Civil War veteran, and found a photo of his tombstone. Included with the photo was a long biographical paragraph about him from a county publication.

www.interment.net — This is a free online library of burial records from thousands of cemeteries across the world, for historical and genealogy research. They also have their own blog.

www3.sympatico.ca/bkinnon/cemeteries.htm — This search engine serves as a gateway to a number of free cemetery transcription websites.

www.usgennet.org/usa/topic/cemetery/ — **US Gen Net** is a nonprofit historical-genealogical web hosting service on the Internet.

www.usgwtombstones.org — The purpose of this project is to organize volunteers who will work together to create a lasting tribute to ancestors.

Volunteers will transcribe tombstone inscriptions and have that work archived for the future and made easily accessible to all.

If you have a cemetery near where you live, you might consider checking as many Internet sites as you can find to see if the cemetery has its information transcribed there. Most (if not all) of these Internet sites welcome the addition of information about new cemeteries.

A fellow genealogist was following the thread of a trail for several of his ancestors who were born in the 1830s. He had found and followed them through the 1850, 1860 and 1870 censuses, where they appeared to have lived and died childless. As he followed the thread of their lives, it took him to a small family cemetery in Illinois. He located their tombstones, and to his vast surprise, he discovered not only their names, but the names of eleven children! Their tombstone epitaphs included the names and dates of birth and death of all of their children, each of which had died either in infancy or early childhood – all between censuses. It is likely that had he not made this discovery, this couple would have continued to be childless through their continuing lives in his records. But because he made the effort to seek out their graves, he was given a bonus of uniting this family.

Church & Sextons' Records
Many cemeteries you will visit may be small – from a few dozen graves to a hundred or so. But if your ancestor was buried in the cemetery of a large church or in a municipal cemetery, finding the tombstones of your ancestor by just wandering around would be a colossal waste of time. Fortunately, for larger, more formal cemeteries than family grave plots in the corner of an ancestor's field, records will most likely have been kept.

Church burial records will generally list the names of all those who were buried in the church's cemetery, along with a location, at least general (northwest quadrant, back, east side, etc.). These records will share anything from the name of the deceased and burial date to a great deal more genealogical information: name, birth date, birth place, son or daughter or wife or husband of, death and burial dates, etc. But don't expect to walk up to the church and inspect their burial register – registers of the age you are seeking may well be kept at a central location, another building or even at the minister's home. A call ahead of time to ascertain the existence and location of the church's burial records is advisable.

LIVING IN THE SHADOWS

Even though this chapter focuses on cemeteries, let me share a few items from the 1830 census to point out one of the values of cemetery stalking. Consider the following census record for one of my ancestors:

1830 Census — Tuscarora township, Mifflin County, Pennsylvania

Head of Family: Joseph Cunningham
2 males under 5 years, 0 females 5 to 10 years
2 males 5 to 10 years, 1 female 5 to 10 years
2 males 10 to 15 years, 0 females 10 to 15 years
0 males 15 to 20 years, 1 female 15 to 20 years
1 male 30 to 40 years, 1 female 30 to 40 years

The first six United States Censuses did not identify women and children in the census, other than via tally marks. A woman who lived in the records shadow of her father's household and then married and moved to the records shadow of her husband's household may have truly been unidentified any place else but on her tombstone! Censuses didn't include her name until the 1850 US census. Tax rolls didn't list her name. Her husband's name is on the land records of the land they lived on.

Children fared no better – oftentimes the only place we will find their name and birth date – even a knowledge of their existence if they were born and died between censuses – is on their tombstone.

Tombstones give a name to the women and children of the early years of our country's history, shining a bright light on those formerly used to genealogical shadows.

Sexton's records are kept for large municipal cemeteries. Like church burial records, the information could be sparse or very extensive. I have seen some that provided various sets of the following information:

Name of the deceased
Who they were related to, and what that relationship was
Birth date
Birth place
Death date

Cause of death
Occupation
Surviving relatives
Military affiliations
Last residence
The physical location of the grave – block, row and plot

To see the sexton's records, prior to going to the cemetery, call the cemetery and ask to speak with the sexton, or the person who keeps the sexton's records. Explain your mission and ask if he would be willing to let you see the cemetery's burial records to try and identify the spot where your ancestors are buried.

With the proliferation of information on the Internet, more and more of these records I have been writing about are finding their way onto the web. I have found them to be a sparse but growing resource. It's certainly worth your effort to try and find the information on the Internet ahead of time.

Funeral Home Records
For years I made the mistake of blowing right past this information – not giving them much notice at all. However, I have since learned the error of my ways, and have discovered that they will often provide a great deal of information, sometimes more than I am able to glean from other sources. Consider, for example, these funeral home records I found through USGenWeb on several families in rural Missouri that I have been researching:

Coday, Flora Della: Hartville; died in Mansfield Hospital at 3:15 a.m. on Feb. 20, 1972; homemaker; born Dec. 9, 1886 in Wright County; d/o Joseph Matlock and Angeline Whittaker; 1 daughter Violet Moody of Hartville MO; 3 sons Farris Coday of Willard MO, Joe Coday of Hartville MO and Russell Coday of Exeter CA; 1 brother Walter Matlock of Gardenia CA; 7 grandchildren; 7 great-grandchildren. Burial Steele Memorial Cemetery.

Or how about this one:

Coday, Marvin Calvin: Mansfield; died in Baptist Hospital at 7:00 a.m. on July 11, 1967; farmer; born Oct. 1, 1891 in Wright County; s/o Thomas Coday and Lullao Johnson; h/o Mabel Vina; 3 daughters Hazel Jones and Jeannie Rippee of Hartville MO and Effie Lea Walling of Marshall MO; 5 sons Harold Coday of Springfield MO, Murrell Coday of Mountain Grove MO, Reed Coday of Columbia MO, M. C. Coday Jr. of Hartville MO and Daniel Coday of Mansfield MO; 1 sister Lillie Skinner of Teague TX; 20 grandchildren; 5 great-grandchildren. Burial Dennis Cemetery.

These funeral home records provided tons of information previously unavailable to me from other sources. Consider the information that was contained in these short records: husbands, wives, brothers, sisters, children's names and places of residence, daughters' married names, and the cemetery in which they were buried. Most funeral home records I have reviewed also include their birth and death dates. Of course I can't count on all the information being perfectly accurate, but it provides me more clues and threads to follow, not only for them but for others of their loved ones – my ancestors!

I was able to take this information and match up families from other information I had on them, matching sons and daughters to their parents, when before they were just names without families.

So – if you run across funeral home records, don't turn your nose up at them! Sometimes you'll find them online, while others may come from contacting the funeral homes in the areas you are researching, either by phone or e-mail.

Cemetery Cautions
I have a couple of cautions to share as you prepare to search through cemeteries:

1. Don't try to straighten sagging tombstones – you may do more harm than good!
2. Don't rub chalk or some other substance on tombstone to try and "bring out" the inscription. It may damage the tombstone.
3. A few years ago it was fashionable to take "rubbings" of tombstones – placing a paper or thin cloth over the face of the tombstone and rubbing a crayon or chalk to take an imprint of the inscription. This can harm tombstones, the pressure you apply could cause the stone to fall or break off, etc. (How terrible would that be!?)
4. In older cemeteries that are not well kept, tall grass may harbor snakes, ticks and other undesirable fiends. Wear good shoes and long pants.

5. Some suggest it is not advisable to go alone, especially to remote cemeteries.
6. Be sure and record the information exactly as it appears on the stone – don't correct spelling, dates, etc., that you "know" to be incorrect.

Cemetery Summary

In summary, here are my suggestions for making your trip to an ancestor's cemetery successful and enjoyable:

1. Know the information you are looking for.
2. Know (and bring with you) all the information you have about the ancestor and his or her relatives – approximate dates of death, maiden names of the women, etc.
3. Bring a quality camera (preferably digital) with a flash.
4. Bring a pen, paper, and your smartphone or tablet of choice.
5. Check with local genealogical societies to locate family cemeteries, and see if the society has recorded any of the local cemeteries.
6. Contact the Church or sexton to see if burial records are available and if you can see them. If not, at least get burial location information from them for your ancestors.
7. Wear comfortable shoes and clothing. You may be kneeling, brushing grass or dirt away from headstones.
8. Bring along a healthy sense of adventure!

Remember — if you have hit a brick wall in your research and simply cannot find information on those elusive ancestors or yours, consider stalking a few cemeteries to try and extend your knowledge about these ancestors and their families.

Getting the Most Out of Visiting Cemeteries Checklist

____ Identify the state(s) your ancestor may have died.

____ Determine which cemetery your ancestor was buried in.

____ Know the names of family members with different surnames (daughters' married names, in-laws, etc.)

____ Take a digital camera to use for taking pictures of tombstones. Don't forget the flash!

____ Take a pen and paper to write down information from tombstones.

____ On a visit to the cemetery, watch closely for other family members who may be buried there.

____ Use the power of the Internet to glean all the knowledge possible before jumping in the car for a cemetery field trip.

Additional Resources

Steven Fisher (editor), *Archival Information (How to Find It, How to Use It),* (Greenwood Press, 2004).

Sharon DeBartalo Carmack, *The Genealogy Sourcebook*, (McGraw-Hill, 1998)

Arlene Eakle, *How to Search a Cemetery,* (Genealogical Inst., 1974) (Note – this book is out of print, but may be available in your local library, or perhaps through inter-library loan.)

10. MILITARY RECORDS

"Nothing in life is so exhilarating as to be shot at without result."
– Winston Churchill

Leonidas Horney
Born September 4, 1817
Born in Guilford County, North Carolina
Married Jane Crawford
Married September 2, 1841
Married in Littleton, Schuyler County, Illinois
In May 1863, the following children younger than 16 years of age were still living in the home:

• William Jeffrey Horney, born 14 March 1849
• Mary Jane Horney, born 30 January 1851
• Emilia Ann Horney, born 16 July 1857
• Adelia Horney, born 27 August 1860

Residence: Littleton, Schuyler County, Illinois
Physical description: 5'8 1/2" tall, dark hair, dark brown eyes and a fair complexion
Occupation: farmer
Enrolled as a Captain in the 10th Missouri Volunteers on 5 August 1861 in St. Louis, Mo
Promoted to Major in the 10th Missouri Volunteers regiment 19 April 1862
Promoted to Lieutenant Colonel in the 10th Missouri Volunteers regiment 3 October 1862
Wounded 3 August 1862 at Corinth, Mississippi (flesh wound to right leg – not serious)
Killed in action 16 May 1863, Champion Hill, Mississippi

Jane Horney was 39 years old on 28 August 1863
Jane Horney received a pension of $30 per month as a result of her husband's death in battle.

Jane Horney died on 20 February 1907.

Now you might think that the above information was gleaned from many different civil documents – birth and marriage certificates, death certificates, census records, etc. If you thought that, you would have been wrong. All the information listed above came from just a few military documents as a result of Leonidas's service during the Civil War.

It is surprising how much genealogical – and just plain interesting — information is available from military records.

Speaking of interesting (not to mention genealogically rich), **Union Civil War** induction papers provide the following information:

• Age
• Birth date and birth place
• Serious illnesses the candidate may have had prior to enlisting
• Injuries the candidate may have had prior to enlisting
• Height
• Weight
• Color of eyes
• Color of hair
• Color of complexion
• Size of head
• Size of hands
• Size of chest
• Size of abdomen
• Condition of genitals (oh my!)
• Length of neck

Must have been quite a physical these young men were subjected to! Among other things, a nation-wide compilation of these records tells us that the average Union Civil War soldier was 5'8" and weighed 143 pounds.

The information found in military records can be a significant source of genealogical information for genealogists. Information I have gleaned from pension records, for example, has enabled me to piece families together, and records of military service have made my ancestors seem like real people to me. And I suspect, with just a little effort on your part, you may have many of the same experiences. Read on and you'll get a few clues on how best to find your ancestors among the military records of our nation.

American Wars

In her storied history, Americans have fought in a number of wars. If you are not sure whether one of your ancestors fought, see if they were of military age (roughly 16 to 35) during any of these wars:

- King Philip's War (1675-1676)
- King William's War (1689-1697)
- Queen Anne's War (1702-1713)
- French and Indian Wars (1754 to 1763)
- Revolutionary War (1775 to 1783)
- War of 1812 (1812 to 1815)
- Blackhawk War (1832)
- Mexican-American War (1846 to 1848)
- Civil War (1861 to 1865)
- Spanish-American War (1898)
- Philippine War (1899 to 1902)
- World War I (1917 to 1918)
- World War II (1941 to 1945)
- Korean Conflict (1950 to 1953)
- Vietnam War (1965 to 1973)
- Gulf War / Desert Storm (1991 to 1992)
- Gulf War / Iraq War (2003 to 2011)

If they were of military age during any of those wars, it may well be worth your time to check out military records for genealogical information. Each of the wars / "conflicts" the United States was involved in generated varying amounts of records that may provide helpful to you in your hunt for information about your ancestors.

Where to Begin

First of all, decide what you want to know for whom. Perhaps your interest is in whether or not an ancestor served in the military, and if so, what battles he was engaged in. Or perhaps you really don't care about that, but would like to glean any genealogical information about that particular ancestor that might be included in military records.

When beginning your search, use common sense. If you are trying to find information from military records about an ancestor that was born in 1855, you probably won't find him listed in enlistment or service records during the Civil War! (However, you may find him mentioned in a pension application by his father or his widowed mother — more on that later.)

Let's use my third great grandfather as an example. Leonidas Horney was born in 1817. That would have made him the ripe old age of 44 at the time the Civil War broke out in 1861. Was he too old to participate in the Civil War? Perhaps. But it also put him at about the age of senior military officers. So, I might as well check Civil War military records to see if he may have served.

However, before I rush off to look for Leonidas in the Civil War, I shouldn't overlook other wars that were waged during his lifetime. I know from my eighth or ninth grade history classes that the Blackhawk War was fought during the early 1830s in Illinois and present-day Wisconsin — Michigan territory at the time. (Mr. Berry at Holmes Junior High in Colorado Springs would be so proud of me for remembering that!). I also know that Leonidas was living in Illinois at that time, and would have been about 15 years old – probably too young, but worth a look. Another possibility is that he may have served during the Mexican War. So I should check those records also.

I googled *Leonidas Horney Blackhawk War* and got a number of hits. None of them showed him as being in the army during the Blackhawk War, but one of the hits listed him as a private in Company E of the Illinois Foot Volunteers during the Mexican War, assigned to Captain Mear's company.

As a bonus, however, my search for *Leonidas Horney Blackhawk War* yielded some information about his father, Samuel Horney, who served in the Blackhawk War when he was 44 years old. A link also took me to a photo of the old gentleman, along with a link to a compiled biography about him. Make a mental (and physical!) note of this information and move on!

In Leonidas' case, I had a bit of a clue, in that I have a picture of him in a Union Civil War uniform. I also knew that family tradition held that he had enlisted in Missouri – not in Illinois. So as a shot in the dark, I got on the Internet and entered *Missouri Civil War Records*. I received 234,000 hits to my request and selected the first one: *Index to the Civil War in Missouri.*

Once I got to the website, one of the options was *Index to Officers in Missouri Military Units*. I selected that, and within seconds had the following information:

Leonidas Horney, original commission: Captain, 10th Missouri Infantry

Subsequent promotions:
Major 10th Missouri Infantry
Lieutenant Colonel 10th Missouri Infantry.

This was important information. While it might not look like genealogical information, it provides me an important element in researching military records – his military unit. US military records were kept by military unit.

Armed with your ancestor's name and military unit, it's time to move a step forward to learning more about this gallant forbear of yours. There are a number of routes you can take, but all lead to the National Archives.

The National Archives
At some point in your search for the military records of your ancestors, you will cross paths with the National Archives of the United States of America. The website for NARA (National Archives and Records Administration) is www.archives.gov. The repository of US military records, the National Archives may yield you a wonderful wealth of genealogical information, if you only know (or learn) how to use them. The National Archives has the following military records available for research:

• Volunteer military service
• US Army military records
• US Navy records
• US Marine Corps
• US Coast Guard and its predecessors (Revenue Cutter, Life Saving Services, and Bureau of Lighthouses)
• Civil War Service and pension records

The feds are slowly moving to the digitized world through partnerships with for-profit organizations, and a very small percentage of their records are becoming available online. The key word here is *slowly*…unfortunately, many, many records held by the federal government (especially those for individuals who served since World War I) are available only by snail mail: fill out a request, mail it, wait up to two months for a response, etc. (In lightning fast response to new technology, you can now send a query about the status of your request via e-mail after your request has been in for ten days!) The cost for a successful search is $25. When you complete the form requesting the information, you'll be given the option of paying by credit card, or they will invoice you for the successful search. There is no charge if their search is unsuccessful.

However, many of the records can be viewed in person. (At $25 a search, it doesn't take much to justify the cost of a trip, especially if you have multiple lines and ancestors to research!) Military records for the 20th century are kept at:

National Personnel Records Center
Military Personnel Records (NPRC-MPR)
9700 Page Avenue
St. Louis, MO 63132-5100

They contain the military personnel, health and medical records of discharged and deceased military veterans from all branches of the armed forces (more on this later).

Records of military personnel prior to 1912 (World War I) are located in Washington DC at:

National Archives
700 Pennsylvania Avenue
Washington, DC 20408-0001

Following are the records held at this National Archives location:

• Volunteer military service (1775 to 1902)
•US Army military records (1789 to 1917) (Officers prior to June 30, 1917, enlisted men prior to October 31, 1912)
• US Navy records (1798 to 1902)
• US Marine Corps (1789 to 1904)
• US Coast Guard and its predecessors (1791 to 1919)
• Civil War Service and pension records (Union as well as Confederate)

Researching at the National Archives

When you visit a National Archives facility to do research, it's not exactly like strolling into your local library to do a research project. There are special rules you'll need to follow; here are a few:

- Upon arrival your first time, be prepared to watch a short presentation (15 minutes or so) on researching at the National Archives.

- To view original documents, you must register to obtain a Research Identification Card. Bring a photo ID and be able to describe your research project. It must be a project that can be reasonably pursued at NARA.

- No more than four original document searches may be made at any one time.

- Lockers are provided for personal belongings, including purses, briefcases, etc. Light jackets or sweaters may be worn in the research rooms, but if you remove them, you may be asked to put them in your locker. Lockers cost a quarter, but the quarter is returned when you retrieve your items.

- You will not be allowed to bring notebooks, personal notes, etc. into the research rooms. You may bring a laptop computer in, and possibly a digital camera (but you must get permission for the latter first). Note: Some research rooms have few electrical outlets.

- Cotton gloves are available for use, although not required.

- Self-service and staff photocopying is allowed, depending on the section and the items to be copied. Self-serve copies are $.25 each.

- You may not use ink pens in your note taking. Either bring a pencil, or one will be provided for you. Do not bother bringing your own paper, notebooks, journals, etc. NARA will provide paper and note cards for you.

- Special instructions are provided in how to search through original documents: keep them in order, only view one document at a time, return them to the exact place you found them, view the documents while they lay flat on the table, etc.

- As of this writing (but check before you go!), hours of public operation are Monday, Tuesday and Saturday, 9:00am to 5:00pm, Wednesday through Friday, 9:00am to 9:00pm.

- Pull times (where staff will go and pull your requests from the archives) are 10:00am, 11:00am, 1:30pm and 2:30pm, with an extra pull time of 3:30pm Wednesday through Friday. No records are pulled from the stacks on Saturdays or evenings.

These rules and regulations may sound a little over the top, but they are necessary to preserve these precious documents so they will continue to be available to researchers for generations to come. Rather than be annoyed (or amused), appreciate the effort – after all, these requirements have ensured that these original documents have been preserved so that you can view them!

Whether you view records online of visit one of the National Archives locations, you'll want to have an idea of what kinds of records are available. Here are some of the types of military records available:

Bounty Land Warrants
The Continental Congress discovered a way to pay its veterans or their widowed and orphaned dependents by giving them cash or (preferably) public lands. Laws passed between 1776 and 1855 authorized granting warrants for land to those who had served in the Revolutionary War, the War of 1812, the Indian Wars and the Mexican War.

The documents in a Bounty Land Warrant file are similar to those contained in pension files. They are particularly rich in genealogical data if it is the widow or children of the veteran who applied for the Bounty Land Warrant.

Enlistment Records
Enlistment records of soldiers can be very interesting. At a minimum, they will tell you the name, rank, date and place that the individual enlisted. They may also tell you such interesting tidbits as their occupation, age, physical description (height, weight, hair and eye color, complexion, size of hands and feet, etc.) and marital status.

Record of Events
Generally, not much of genealogical value is listed in the Records of Events.

They are generally sort of journal entries that trace the movement of troops. Often, they are little more than places and dates that the various companies and regiments were stationed or marching to.

These would be of interest if you wanted to trace an ancestor's movements through the war. In the case of the Civil War, it would be interesting to see if any of your ancestors engaged in battles against one another. A number of my ancestors lived in and around border states during the Civil War, and both the Confederate and Union armies had members of my family fighting for them.

Compiled Military Service Records (CMSR)

Compiled Military Service Records (CMSRs) serve as the records for Union Army soldiers. Each soldier will have one for each regiment in which he served. An index of CMSRs is available on the NARA website as well as on the CWSS website.

Pension Records

Pensions were applied for by military men, their widows and / or their minor children. (Note – Confederate soldiers' pension applications were made to the state from which they served, not the federal government. Those records are held at the state level.) Because of the need to ensure that the applicant was indeed related to the former soldier, a great deal of information was often requested to substantiate the relationship.

A widow, for example, would have had to provide the date and place of their marriage (and often the name of the person who performed the marriage). She would often be required to provide either the marriage certificate, or a certified record signed by the minister who performed the ceremony. If the widow had children under the age of 16, she also needed to provide proof of their birth in the form of a birth certificate, or a government-certified document that provided the child's name, birth date and birth place – all genealogical nuggets.

Available Records by War

Let's take look at some of the records available at NARA for several wars and conflicts. Generally speaking, the earlier the war, the less information will be available. For example, if you are hoping to find health records for an ancestor who fought in the Revolutionary War, you are out of luck. But you might be successful in finding a pension application for the same individual. As your search moves into the twentieth century, available information again gets sparse due to federal laws protecting individual privacy. Below, war-by-war, are the records available for your perusal.

Pre-Revolutionary Wars

The records available prior to the Revolutionary War will not provide much in the way of genealogical interest. Generally speaking, these records are limited to soldiers' names and the colonial units with whom they served. In the 300+ years since Americans have been fighting wars, many of the records have been lost through carelessness, fire, etc.

As scanty as these records may be, there is still value to finding an ancestor's name listed in them. First, it may give you a clue where they lived at the time of their enlistment. While it is possible that they went to another state to enlist, it is not probable, transportation being what it was in those days. However, you might want to check surrounding states, as, depending on where a fellow lived and where enlistments were taken, it may have been closer for him to ride twenty miles to enlist in neighboring state, than ride one hundred miles to enlist in his own state.

If, for example, you find Ambrose Hawkins listed in a Rhode Island colonial unit during King George's War (1744 to 1748), that may provide a thread for further research, since he had seemingly disappeared from his home state of Massachusetts. And you might note that enlisted in the same unit is a Timothy Hawkins. Brother? Father? Son? Uncle? Cousin? Perhaps he is none of the above, but it is certainly worth noting in your research papers for further research at another time.

Revolutionary War

To give it a try, head to the NARA website at *www.archives.gov/research/military*. Once there, scroll down a bit and on the right-hand side you'll see a listing of American wars. Select *American Revolution*, then click on the hyperlink (on the left side of the page) labeled *Online Catalog*, and you'll arrive at a search screen where you can input what you are looking for; I then entered *Revolutionary War*, and received 2,440 hits, 582 of which were online.

Numerous of the links you select will warn you that most of the records from the Revolutionary War period were destroyed by fire in 1800 or 1814, the latter due to the hostilities surrounding the War of 1812. According to the NARA website, the current collection housed in the National Archives was:

> …begun in 1873 by means of purchase, gifts, or transfers from other agencies. The compilation of military service records was begun in 1894, under the direction of the War Department's Record and Pension Office. Information about individual soldiers was meticulously copied onto cards as a means of consolidating information about individuals, as well as preserving the original source documents, including muster rolls, pay rolls, returns, and other records.

Of the 582 hits that came up with my request, I selected the link listed as Compiled Service Records of Soldiers Who Served in the American Army During the Revolutionary War, compiled 1894- ca. 1912, documenting the period 1775-1784. I was taken to a screen that described what I was going to be able to see. Among other things, it told me:

- The creators of the document (War Department and War Department Records and Pensions);
- Dates the records covered (1775 to 1784);
- Arrangement (jackets/envelopes designated Continental Troops, or alphabetically by state, then by organization then alphabetically by soldier's name, chronologically by year);
- Access restriction (none, for these records);
- Microfilm number (M881);
- The Finding Aid type (Index);
- Online resource URL (*www.Fold3.com/documents/8731977/revolutionary-war-service-records*)
- Online resource note: Records in this series have been digitized and made available online by our partner, Footnote.com, for a fee. The digitized records on Footnote.com are available free of charge in all NARA Research Rooms.

The last bullet point says records have been digitized and made available through Footnote.com. It is important to note that Footnote.com changed its name to Fold3.com. Now, I happen to have a subscription to Fold3.com (good deal), so I whisked to their website to see what I could find. As a stab in the dark, I typed in *Revolutionary War Quillen*, and received sixty hits. I selected *Robert Quillen*, and found the following:

Robert Quillen
1st Virginia Regiment, Private

There wasn't any information on the card beyond his name, rank and regiment, but at the end of the card, there was a comment that said his records were filed under the name Robert Quillin – apparently the difficulties of getting my surname correct extend back to at least that time! I checked there, and there were a number of records under Robert Quillin; one of them, a Pay Roll record, looked like this:

```
_____ /_____ 1 ____/ Va. ____.

Appears with the rank of _____ on a

Pay Roll
of Capt. William Lewis' Co., Capt. Charles Pelham's
Co. and Capt. Joseph Scott's Co., of the 1st Virginia
Regiment, commanded by Colonel Richard Parker,

Revolutionary War
for the month of ....................., 17___
Commencement of time............, 17___
Commencement of pay.............., 17___
To what time paid...................., 17___
Pay per month........................, 17___
Time of service......................., 17___
Whole time of service..............., 17___
Subsistence..........................., 17___
Amount................................, 17___
Pay due to sick, absent..............., 17___

Casualties:
_____

Remarks:
_____
```

In addition to his payroll record (which indicated he was paid $6.67 per month for his service!), there were a number of other records, including his compiled service record, and numerous muster sheets (roll calls). I also found that he received a land warrant for his service, issued February 1808 (nothing like timely payment for his service – three decades after the fact!)

Encouraged by my success with the Compiled Service Records (CMSR), I thought I'd try something that might provide a little more genealogical data – like a pension application. Back to the 582 Fold3 hits, I discovered a link to *Case Files of Pension and Bounty-Land Warrant Applications Based on Revolutionary War Service, ca. 1775-ca. 1900*. As with the CMSR, the digitized records for this collection are held by Fold3.com. Going back to Fold3.com, under the search string *Revolutionary War Pensions*, I entered the name *Quillen*, and received 17 hits. Our friend Robert from above didn't appear to be there, but I found the pension for John Quillin. Below are excerpts from his pension application – I have **highlighted** the genealogical data that exists:

State of North Carolina
Stokes County

On this **24th day of August, 1833**, personally appeared unto me…John Quillin, aged seventy-six years, who being first sworn according to law at his own place of residence in the afore-mentioned county, doth on his Oath make the following declaration in order to obtain the benefit of the Act of Congress passed 7th June 1832. First he states that from the infirmities of old age together with the fact that at certain times the loss of his memory makes it impossible for him to remember the precise dates of his service as a soldier of the Revolution, but as well as he can recollect, he entered the service of the United States under the following named officers who served as hereinafter stated. That he first entered the service as a drafted private in Surry County, North Carolina in Captain Henry Smith's company of militia infantry…. (following this were officers' names and descriptions of campaigns John was on)….Near the Savannah River, the applicant states that he hired a certain William Fields as a substitute to serve the balance of his tour in order that he might **return home to his wife who was in a delicate situation** at the time…

Of the seven interrogatories prescribed by the War Department, he answers them as follows (to wit):

1st – that **he was born in Cumberland County, North Carolina**

2nd – that he has no record of his age, only traditionary that **he was born in March 1757**

3rd – that he lived in **Surry County North Carolina when called into the service**....

4th – answer as above

5th – that from his being subject to fitts and consequent loss of his recollection, he cannot name all the officers any more than he has named already or Regiments

6th – that he does not remember of receiving a written discharge, and if he did, he has lost it

7th – he has no one present, but has a number of individuals that will testify as to his character as to veracity and belief of his services as a soldier of the Revolution, there being no clergyman for a considerable distance from him renders it very inconvenient for one's certificate.

The pension application was signed by the attorney and Justice of the Peace (same man) who took his testimony and statement. There were ten pages in the pension application, including the cover of the envelope all the papers were in, as well as seven other pages, including statements from several neighbors and a man who averred that he served with John during parts of his service. But let's check out the genealogical information available from this pension application:

1. **State of North Carolina, Stokes County** – identifies where John was on a certain date;
2. **24 August, 1833** – the certain date John was at Stokes County, NC;
3. **...at his own place of residence**... — The statement was taken at his residence on the above date in the above-stated county and state;
4. **aged seventy-six** — he was seventy-six (76) years old on 24 August 1833;
5. **return home to his wife** — He was married;
6. **his wife who was in a delicate situation** – this was often a euphemism for pregnancy (but could also have meant she was very ill);
7. **born in Cumberland County, North Carolina** – John's birth place;
8. **he was born in March 1757** – John's birth month and date, according to *traditionary*....

As you can see, this 250-year-old document has a cache of wonderful genealogical tidbits for us for this gentleman, a patriotic if not failing-memoried soldier of the Revolution!

Author's note: I selected John Quillin's pension more or less out of a hat to demonstrate this research source and technique. Just prior to sending the first edition of this book to my publisher, I discovered than my fifth great grandfather was John Quillin, born March 1757 in Cumberland County, North Carolina – this very man! As I said, sometimes your ancestors are just dying to be found, and will help you any way they can!

Back to the NARA website, following are a few of the 100s of Revolutionary War records that are available:

Revolutionary War Rolls, 1775–1783 (Muster rolls and payroll records)

Compiled Service Records, 1775–1784 (consist of a jacket-envelope for each soldier, labeled with his name, his rank, and the unit or organization in which he served. The jacket-envelope contains card abstracts of entries relating to the soldier as copied from original muster rolls; payrolls; rank rolls; inspection, provision, and clothing returns; receipts for pay and bounty; accounts for subsistence, pay, rations, clothing, and ordnance; abstracts of muster and pay rolls; and correspondence.)

Indexes to Compiled Service Records, 1775–1783 (This series consists of eight card indexes showing name of soldier, sailor, or civilian; his organization, rank, or profession; and cross-references to other spellings of his name.)

Case Files of Pension and Bounty-Land Warrant Applications Based on Revolutionary War Service, ca. 1775-ca. 1900. (Applications and other records pertaining to claims for pensions and bounty land warrants. The files contain information pertaining to a soldier's rank, unit, and period of service, his age or date of birth, his residence, and sometimes his birth place. Application files submitted by a soldier's widow may include her name, age, residence, date and place of marriage, and date and place of death of her husband. Some files contain copies of marriage or other family records.)

Lists of Revolutionary War Officers, 1775-1783. (Lists of regimental and company officers for each of the states and one for the Continental Line, giving each officer's name, rank and organization; a list of officers named in the "Journals of Congress….")

Bounty Land Application Warrant Application Files, 1812–1855 (This series consists of approximately 360,000 bounty-land application files submitted by veterans or their heirs based on service between 1790 and 1855. The majority of the claims are based on service in the War of 1812, Indian wars, and the Mexican War.)

Registers of Muster Rolls, 1775–1782, (Muster rolls but also contain information concerning some payrolls that were in the Record and Pension Office. They contain such information as the dates and places of troop musters, the names of the companies, and the names of their commanding officers.)

Benedict Arnold's Oath of Allegiance (okay – so unless you are related to Benedict Arnold, there isn't much genealogical value here, but I just thought it was interesting!)

And over 750 more! As you go to the links for each of these records, if you click on them, you will be able to learn more details about what is included in the collection, and whether or not it is online. Unfortunately, few of these records are online, but more are being added all the time. As of this writing, only seven of the 759 collections were online.

You may have noticed that I frequently state that more and more records are coming online every day, and such is truly the case. Earlier in this chapter, I detailed a search that eventually unearthed the pension application of my fifth great grandfather, John Quillin. Since the first edition of the *Troubleshooter's Guide* was published a few years ago, John Quillin's pension is now online. I was able to find it quickly by simply Googling *John Quillin, Revolutionary War pension application* (you can see it at: *http://revwarapps. org/s9461.pdf*). So if you are having trouble navigating the NARA website (or other websites) in search of pension or other records, be sure and try Googling for the information you are seeking.

War of 1812
Just to brush you up on your history. The war of 1812 was fought on US soil and in US coastal waters from 1812 to 1815, between the United States and its former parent and nemesis, Great Britain. It was the War of 1812

that gave us the National Anthem (you thought it was the Revolutionary War, didn't you?!).

There are over 180 collections of records spawned by the War of 1812 that provide important information. Unfortunately, at the time of this writing, most of the records are not available online or even through inter-library loan. It seems that slowly (ever so slowly), the government is moving that direction with many of their war records, but at least at this point, it will take a personal visit to see them. At the time of this writing, in fact, only one of the collections – War of 1812 Prize Case files – is available online through Fold3.com. So if you'll want to see any of the records on the War of 1812, you'll need to plan a trip to the National Archives in Washington DC to search these records. Alternately, you can complete the appropriate forms and mail them in, waiting (and waiting) for your request to be researched, copied and mailed to you.

However, Ancestry.com has compiled the information for nearly 600,000 men who served during the War of 1812, and those records are online. While you won't be able to see an image of the original document, they have summarized (compiled) the information from each service record. At a minimum, you'll be able to see if an ancestor was enlisted during the War of 1812, his state, company / regiment and rank.

The NARA website contains an excellent article entitled Genealogical Records of the War of 1812, written by Stuart L. Butler (currently located at *www. archives.gov/publications/prologue/1991/winter/war-of-1812.html*). If you are looking for ancestors from this time period, it would be worth your time to read what he has written. Searching the NARA website yields, among others, the following collections that might be worth reviewing:

War of 1812 Prize Case files, 1812-1816 (Consists of libels for the condemnation of enemy property seized as a prize during the War of 1812, answers, motions, interrogatories, depositions, claims of owners and other interested parties.) This is the only War of 1812 collection available online to date.

Pension and Bounty Land Warrant Application Files, 1812-1900. (Consists of approximately 180,000 pension and bounty land warrant application files relating to claims based on service between 1812 and 1815. The files generally contain documentation submitted in support of a claim, such as the original application form, affidavits, and statements from witnesses. The records document the veteran's name, age, place of residence, and service data including dates, places of enlistment and discharge, organization, and rank.

Carded Records Showing Military Service of Soldiers Who Fought in Volunteer Organizations During the War of 1812, 1812-1815. (Consists of jackets giving name of soldier, his organization and rank, and cards on which information from original records, such as muster rolls, pay rolls, and various other original records has been copied.)

Index to War of 1812 Pension Application Files, 1812-1816 (Consists of microfilmed images of the faces of envelopes that contain the War of 1812 pension application files. On the face of each envelope are the name of the veteran, the pension claim or file numbers, and other identifying information.)

Muster of Volunteers organized during War of 1812, 1812-1815. (Contains muster rolls for volunteer organizations which had service in the War of 1812. The series also includes orders for pay, pay rolls, pay accounts, certificates of discharge, and papers concerning powers of attorney and bonds furnished.)

And over 175 other collections! If you google *War of 1812 war records*, you'll be surprised at how many sites come up devoted to this war, especially many outside of the NARA holdings. Here are a few:

- *www.cyberdriveillinois.com/departments/archives/databases/quincyhome.html* — a listing of Illinois residents who were veterans of the War of 1812;
- *www.sos.mo.gov/archives/soldiers/* — database containing information about Missouri residents who were veterans of the War of 1812;
- *lva1.hosted.exlibrisgroup.com* – this odd-looking web address belongs to the Library of Virginia. In the Search box, type *War of 1812* to learn about the databases available about this war;
- *www.ohiohistory.org/resource/database/rosters.html* — the Ohio Historical Society index to the roster of Ohio War of 1812 veterans.

And so on – many states kept documentation on the War of 1812, and many of their records are available online.

Mexican-American War

The Mexican War was fought between 1846 and 1848. It was a training ground for many of the soldiers and officers who would later fight side-by-side or nose-to-nose (as foes) in the American Civil War.

Enlistment, muster records and pension applications are available for veterans of the Mexican-American War, as are bounty land warrant applications. Unlike the Revolutionary War records, the bounty land warrant applications are included with the pension applications for the Mexican-American War. These records are available through NARA – by requesting the records via mail and waiting for a response.

Ancestry.com had a couple of sets of Mexican-American War records, but nothing as extensive as for other collections. For example, one of their collections was titled *Record of the services of Illinois soldiers in the Black Hawk War, 1831-32, and in the Mexican War, 1846-8*. Searching it didn't yield much information beyond names on muster rolls – not as exciting as some other information, but at least might show if an ancestor was alive at the time of that war.

Civil War

For my money, the Civil War is the most exciting of the American wars for which to do genealogical research. First of all, I love the Civil War and am drawn to it – perhaps because I had so many ancestors involved in it, a number of whom shed their life's blood to help preserve the Union. (It has been estimated that one in seven adult men in America saw action in the Civil War.) Secondly, it was during the Civil War era that the government went into over-drive in keeping records of those who served her. They kept records on a long list of things: service, roll calls, pay, prisoners, casualty, death and burial, pension applications, etc., etc. As a bonus, many of those records provide important genealogical information.

More than 2.8 million American men (and a few hundred women) served during the Civil War – about 7% of the population. And when you figure that roughly 50% the of population were men, that means that approximately 14% of the males in the United States served during the Civil War – about 1 in 7. So if your ancestor was between the ages of 18 and 45 during the Civil War years, there's a good chance you'll find information about him in military records of one of the respective armies.

Civil War Soldiers and Sailors System (CWSS)
The Civil War Soldiers and Sailors System (CWSS) is a great starting place for discovering whether an ancestor served during the Civil War, and if so, what branch of the service, and even whether he served with the Union or the Confederacy. To start your search, go to *www.civilwar.nps.gov/cwss*, then select *Soldiers* or *Sailors*, then enter the name of your ancestor. If he served during the war, following is the type of information you can expect to find:

Leonidas Horney
Regiment name: 10th Missouri
Side: Union
Soldier's Rank – In: Captain
Soldier's Rank – Out: Lt. Colonel
Alternate name:
Notes:
Film Number: M390, roll 23

Most of the information is understandable. The film number is the NARA microfilm number where this information was found.

Back on the CWSS title page, you can click on the Regiment link to find a history of your ancestor's regiment – its formation date and place, major battles and assignments it received, total lost officers and soldiers, etc.

The CWSS title page also provides links to Congressional Medal of Honor Winners, prisoner records for Union prisoners held at Andersonville and Confederate prisoners held at Fort McHenry, and the location of graves for soldiers buried at National Parks (like Gettysburg). There is also a link to information about over 10,500 battles and skirmishes fought during the Civil War. Of those encounters, 384 were considered principal battles.

While all of these tidbits of information are interesting, they provide an important piece of information: your ancestor's army (Union or Confederate), the state he served with, and his regiment number. Since federal records are kept by state and regiment, this is important information to have. Using this information, you can order copies of your ancestor's service records from NARA.

Many of the soldiers who were involved in the Civil War fought with state

---

CONGRESSIONAL MEDAL OF HONOR WINNER

Ever wonder what it takes to be a Congressional Medal of Honor winner? During the Civil War, such medals were often given for capturing the enemy's flag, or for carrying and defending one's own regimental flag. (Kind of gives new meaning to the Boy Scout game of Capture the Flag!) Here is one that's a little different than that, from the CWSS website:

Name: Murphy, Charles J.
Rank: 1st lieutenant
Citation State: Virginia
Unit: 38th New York Infantry
Citation Place: Bull Run
Citation Date: 21 July 1861
Date Issued: 5 April 1898
Citation: Took a rifle and voluntarily fought with his regiment in the ranks; when the regiment was forced back, voluntarily remained on the field caring for the wounded, and was there taken prisoner. Rank: First Lieutenant, and Quartermaster

So this 1st Lieutenant, who was normally a Quartermaster (behind the lines, not usually in harm's way), took up arms and fought with his regiment, then stayed on the field, caring for the wounded, and was eventually taken prisoner.

---

militias. Military records for those units are held at the state level. If that's the case, you are in luck, as many of the state records have been digitized and are available online. If the state militia became part of the regular army, their records will also be held at the National Archives.

Following are records that should be searched for your ancestors:

Union Army Records

There are far more records available for soldiers who served in the Union army than there are for those who served in the Confederate army. For those ancestors who served in the Union Army, there are four groups of records that are of particular interest:

• Draft records
• Compiled Military Service Records (CMSR)

- Pension applications
- Compiled Records showing service of military units in volunteer Union Organizations

Draft Records

In March 1863, the federal government instituted a draft for all men ages 20 to 45. The draft ran through the end of the war in 1865. The information listed in the draft records included:

- Name
- Place of residence
- Place of birth (sometimes)
- Age as of July 1, 1863
- Occupation
- Marital status
- State, territory or country of birth (naturalized citizens were eligible for the draft, as were those who had stated their intention of naturalizing)
- Military organization (if he was already in a volunteer unit)
- Physical description (sometimes)

Men in this age range were exempt from service if:

- They were in the military of the United States at the time of the draft
- They served in the US military during the present war, and were honorably discharged
- They were physically or mentally disabled
- They paid someone to take their place ($300 to $1,000)
- They were the only son of a widow
- They were the sole support for infirm parents
- They were a widower with dependents

The government did not keep records of those who were exempted; rather lists of those who were exempted may be found in local newspapers of the time. They are often grouped by their exemption class.

As interesting and information-filled as they are, none of the draft records have been microfilmed. They are kept by state and congressional district within each state. Congressional districts from the Civil War era can be found in *The Historical Atlas of United States Congressional Districts 1789-*

1983 (Kenneth C. Martis, New York: The Free Press). Most larger libraries – especially those with genealogy sections – will have this book available. Also, some diligent searching on the internet should be able to locate congressional districts from 1860 in each state. At the time of this writing, your only option for seeing draft records is to either visit the national Archives in Washington DC or mail a request for a copy of the draft record using NATF form 86 for your request. You may also order online by going to *eservices.archives.gov/orderonline.*

As with so many other military records we have been discussing, many Civil War draft records are finding their way online. If searching by *Congressional District* doesn't yield results, simply google *Civil War Draft Records* for the area you think your ancestors lived. If that doesn't work, you can check out subscription websites like Ancestry.com and Fold3.com, or free websites like FamilySearch.org.

CIVIL WAR DRAFT DODGERS?

Accounts from Civil War-era newspapers often provided lists of men who were exempted from the draft. Sometimes, they also provided interesting anecdotes about those who sought exemption. Following are a few from the New York Times of Sunday, August 23, 1863:

> A young man recently went to Lewiston, ME, to be examined, but he stuttered so badly no one could understand him. He was exempted. He was never known before to stutter in his life.

But the following young man wasn't as fortunate:

> A conscript who has lost six upper front teeth was examined last Tuesday by a surgeon in Boston and accepted. He'll do for the cavalry.

And how about this poor young fellow, the son of a patriotic mother (I love their editorial comment at the end!):

> One lady in Providence, whose drafted son strove to be exempted on the claim of being the sole support of an aged mother, declared that she could, as heretofore, support herself without any of his aid, and she hoped that he would be made to go. Nice old lady, that.

Compiled Military Service Records

Every volunteer soldier has had compiled for him a Compiled Military Service Record (CMSR) for each regiment he served in. It contains basic information about his service while in that regiment. Information contained within the record might include enlistment information, leave (vacation) requests, muster (roll call) records, and injury or illness reports. If your ancestor was killed in action, this will most likely be found in the CMSR, or information about his discharge if he survived. An index of CMSRs is available on the NARA website as well as on the CWSS website. CMSRs are also among the military records available at Ancestry.com, Fold3.com and FamilySearch.org.

When I requested the service record for Colonel Leonidas Horney, my third great grandfather, I received documents that included the following:

- The date and place of his enlistment;
- His date of birth;
- His height, hair and eye color and color of complexion;
- The rank he enlisted as;
- The name of his regiment and company;
- The commanders he reported to;
- Several muster sheets showing his presence on specific dates (muster sheets are like roll calls);
- A copy of a letter from his commanding officer granting him a two-month leave;
- Several documents detailing his promotion from Captain to Major to Lieutenant Colonel;
- Two casualty sheets, one detailing a slight leg injury sustained at the Battle of Corinth and the other reporting his death in the Battle of Champion Hill, Mississippi on May 16, 1863.

Pension Records

As mentioned at the outset of this chapter, pension records often provide us with a great deal of information. When I searched for the Civil War pension record for Colonel Horney, I found a plethora of information about him and his family. As shown at the outset of this chapter, after Leonidas's death, his widow completed a series of affidavits that contained the following information:

- Her full maiden name;
- Her age and birth date;
- Her birth place;
- The date and place she married her husband;
- The name of the person who performed their marriage ceremony;
- The names, birth dates and ages of all their children 16 years of age and younger;
- The names and birth dates of those children who had died.

That was truly a great genealogical find!

Copies of pension records for Union army soldiers can be gotten by sending NATF Form 85 (not Form 86; Form 85 is used for pensions). You may also order online by going to *eservices.archives.gov/orderonline*. Many pension records are also available at Ancestry.com and Fold3.com.

Compiled Records of Volunteer Union Organizations
Volunteer units often worked in concert with and under the command of the regular army. Their compiled records are also kept at the National

---

COMPILED SERVICE RECORD DOCUMENT

Throughout this military records section, reference has been made to Compiled Service Records. Following is a depiction of what one of these documents looks like:

_____Reg't Inf. Vols
_____ Age ____
Rank _____ Co. _____
Captain _____

Enlisted _____
Where _____
Mustered in _____
Where _____
Remarks _____

Mustered out _____
Where _____

Archives. As an added bonus, records about these volunteer units are often kept at the state level, and many of those are available online.

Confederate Army Records

There are fewer records available for the Confederate Army, as many did not survive the war:

• Compiled Military Service Records
• Compiled Records showing service of military units in volunteer Confederate Organizations

Note: The federal government did not grant pensions to Confederate soldiers (imagine that!); but all states that had Confederate soldiers later granted pensions.

Compiled Military Service Records (CMSR)

As with the Union army, every Confederate soldier has had compiled for him a Compiled Military Service Record (CMSR) for each regiment he served in. It contains basic information about his service while in that regiment. Information contained within the record might include enlistment information, leave requests, muster records, and injury or illness reports. If your ancestor was killed in action, this will most likely be found in the CMSR, or information about his discharge if he survived. An index of CMSRs is available on the NARA website as well as on the CWSS website.

A special note about Confederate army records. Both Compiled Military Service Records (CMSR) and Records of Events were kept for Confederate units. They are often not as complete as Union records of the same type, as many Confederate records did not survive the war. Pensions were granted to Confederate veterans and their widows and minor children by the states of Alabama, Arkansas, Florida, Georgia, Kentucky, Louisiana, Mississippi, Missouri, North Carolina, Oklahoma, South Carolina, Tennessee, Texas, and Virginia. Note that the states granted these pensions, not the federal government; those records are contained in the State Archives of the state where the veteran resided after the war, not in the National Archives.

Copies of Confederate army (but not pension) records can be found at Ancestry.com, Fold3.com and FamilySearch.org. They are also held in the

National Archives and can be ordered by sending NATF Form 86. You may also order online by going to *eservices.archives.gov/orderonline.*

Pension Records

Pension records can be a valuable source of genealogical information. Each state decided at different times when and if they would provide pensions to Confederate veterans, and who was eligible for those pensions. Below is the location of the offices for each of the states that granted Confederate pensions, and a little about their collections:

Alabama Department of Archives and History
624 Washington Avenue
Montgomery, AL 36130-0100
Telephone: 334/242-4363
Website: *www.archives.state.al.us/index.html*

In 1867 Alabama began granting pensions to Confederate veterans who had lost arms or legs. In 1886 the State began granting pensions to veterans' widows. In 1891 the law was amended to grant pensions to indigent veterans or their widows.

Arkansas History Commission
1 Capitol Mall
Little Rock, AR 72201
Telephone: 501/682-6900
Website: *www.state.ar.us/ahc/index.htm*

In 1891 Arkansas began granting pensions to indigent Confederate veterans. In 1915 the State began granting pensions to their widows and mothers.

Florida State Archives
R. A. Gray Building
500 South Bronough Street
Tallahassee, FL 32399-0250
Telephone: 850/487-2073
Website: *dlis.dos.state.fl.us/archives/genealogy.cfm*

In 1885 Florida began granting pensions to Confederate veterans. In 1889 the State began granting pensions to their widows. A published index, which provides each veteran's pension number, is available in many libraries.

Georgia Department of Archives and History
5800 Jonesboro Road
Morrow, GA 30260
Telephone: 678/364-3700
Website: *www.sos.state.ga.us/archives/*

In 1870 Georgia began granting pensions to soldiers with artificial limbs. In 1879 the State began granting pensions to other disabled Confederate veterans or their widows who then resided in Georgia. By 1894 eligible disabilities had been expanded to include old age and poverty.

Kentucky Department of Libraries and Archives
Research Room
300 Coffee Tree Road
Frankfort, KY 40601
Telephone: 502/564-8704
Website: *www.kdla.ky.gov*

In 1912, Kentucky began granting pensions to Confederate veterans or their widows. The records are on microfilm.

Louisiana State Archives
3851 Essen Lane
Baton Rouge, LA 70809-2137
Telephone: 504/922-1208
Website: *www.sos.la.gov/HistoricalResources/ResearchHistoricalRecords/Pages/default.aspx*

In 1898 Louisiana began granting pensions to indigent Confederate veterans or their widows.

Mississippi Department of Archives and History
PO Box 571
Jackson, MS 39205
Telephone: 601/359-6876
Website: *www.mdah.state.ms.us/*

In 1888 Mississippi began granting pensions to indigent Confederate veterans or their widows.

Missouri State Archives
600 W. Main
PO Box 1747
Jefferson City, MO 65102
Telephone: 573/751-3280
Website: *www.sos.mo.gov/archives/*

In 1911 Missouri began granting pensions to indigent Confederate veterans only; none were granted to widows. Missouri also had a home for disabled Confederate veterans. The pension and veterans' home applications are interfiled and arranged alphabetically. Typically, the pension file is small, perhaps four to eight pages, containing a standard application form and may include letters of recommendation from family members or others.

North Carolina State Archives
Physical address:
109 East Jones Street
Raleigh, NC 27601-2807
Telephone: 919/733-7305
Website: *www.ncdcr.gov/archives/Home.aspx*

Mailing Address:
4614 Mail Service Center
Raleigh, NC 27699-4614

In 1867 North Carolina began granting pensions to Confederate veterans who were blinded or lost an arm or leg during their service. In 1885 the State began granting pensions to all other disabled indigent Confederate veterans or widows.

Oklahoma Department of Libraries, Archives and Records Management Division
200 Northeast 18th Street
Oklahoma City, OK 73105
Telephone: 800/522-8116 (nationwide) ext. 209
Website: *www.odl.state.ok.us*

In 1915 Oklahoma began granting pensions to Confederate veterans or their widows.

South Carolina Department of Archives and History
8301 Parkland Road
Columbia, SC 29223
Telephone: 803/896-6100
Website: *scdah.sc.gov/Pages/default.aspx*

A state law enacted December 24, 1887, permitted financially needy Confederate veterans and widows to apply for a pension; however, few applications survive from the 1888-1918 era. Beginning in 1889, the SC Comptroller began publishing lists of such veterans receiving pensions in his Annual Report. From 1919 to 1925, South Carolina granted pensions to Confederate veterans and widows regardless of financial need. These files are arranged alphabetically. Pension application files are typically one sheet of paper with writing on both sides. Also available are Confederate Home applications and inmate records for veterans (1909-1957), and applications of wives, widows, sisters, and daughters (1925-1955).

Tennessee State Library and Archives
Public Service Division
403 Seventh Avenue North
Nashville, TN 37243-0312
Telephone: 615/741-2764
Website: *www.tennessee.gov/tsla/*

In 1891 Tennessee began granting pensions to indigent Confederate veterans. In 1905 the State began granting pensions to their widows. The records are on microfilm.

Texas State Library and Archives Commission
PO Box 12927
Austin, TX 78711
Telephone: 512/463-5480
Website: *www.tsl.state.tx.us/arc/genfirst.html* (Genealogy)
Website: *www.tsl.state.tx.us/arc/index.html* (Archives and Manuscripts)

In 1881 Texas set aside 1,280 acres for disabled Confederate veterans. In 1889 the State began granting pensions to indigent Confederate veterans and their widows. Muster rolls of State militia in Confederate service are also available.

Library of Virginia
Archives Division
800 East Broad Street
Richmond, VA 23219
Telephone: 804/692-3888
Website: *www.lva.lib.va.us/*

In 1888 Virginia began granting pensions to Confederate veterans or their widows. The records are on microfilm.

In addition to these records, the Family History Library of the Church of Jesus Christ of Latter-day Saints has a large collection of microfilmed Confederate records. They can be seen in Salt Lake City, or ordered for viewing at any local family history center. You can start learning about their collection by going to www.familysearch.org.

After all is said and done, there is tremendous interest in Civil War records, and there are currently many records online and more coming all the time. Local county genealogy societies, state veterans groups, etc., continue to add to the voluminous amount of Civil War records out there. Have an ancestor who served in the Civil War from Missouri? Then Google Missouri Civil War records and see what you find (as of this writing, I got over 4.3 million hits). Now, most won't have what you're looking for, but some may. The first hit I got was from the Missouri State Archives, and it had muster sheets for my third great grandfather listing all the important military information (service branch, regiment, company, etc.), but also included information about where he lived, where he was born, his height and hair color, and where he was killed.

World War I

One of the richest genealogical finds from World War I are the draft registration cards for 24,000,000 men living in the United States. Male citizens and aliens living in the United States between certain ages were required to register for the draft. In May 1917, the Selective Service Act was passed that instituted the draft in the United States. There were actually three draft registration periods:

1. June 5, 1917 – for all men between the ages of 21 and 31;
2. June 5, 1918 – for all men becoming 21 after June 5, 1918, (a supplemental registration, considered part of the June 5, 1918 registration was held August 24, 1918) and
3. September 12, 1918, for men aged 18 through 45.

The 24,000,000 men represented a little over one quarter of the US population at the time, and about 98% of the adult males in that age range. As mentioned above, there were three different draft registration periods covering three different classes of men. Of course, it would have been too easy to use the same registration card for each period, but generally, the information requested the following information for these men:

• Full name
• Home address
• Age in years
• Birth date
• Race
• Native born, naturalized or alien
• If an alien, what country are they a citizen of
• Occupation
• Employer's name
• Employer's place of business
• Nearest relative
• Nearest relative's address
• Brief physical description (height, weight, build, hair and eye color)
• Signature of the registrant

From a genealogical perspective, what's not to love about such a record?!

Even more impressive is that during the period when many of these men were born (1872 to 1900), many of the states and territories did not require birth records to be kept. So in the draft registration cards, you have the men themselves providing their birth dates, addresses, etc (instead of someone else in the household answering questions for the census enumerator, or a spouse or child completing the questions on a death certificate, etc.).

Through the years we have pondered about and researched what my great grandfather's birthday and birth place were. Depending on which census we looked at, his birthday was reported as January 1880, January 1881 and October 1881. His birth place had been reported as Virginia and Tennessee. Of course, we didn't know if he was providing that information or if someone else in the household had been providing the information, and was remembering incorrectly. But his World War I draft registration card tells us what he believed:

• Name – Ed Quillen
• Home address – RR 1, Ralston, Pawnee County, Oklahoma
• Age in years — 37
• Birth date – January 15, 1881
• Race — White
• Native born
• Occupation — Farmer
• Employer's name
• Employer's place of business
• Nearest relative – Wife, Dollie Quillen
• Nearest relative's address – RR 1, Ralston, Pawnee Co., Oklahoma
• Brief physical description: 5'11", medium build, black hair, blue eyes

Since each draft registration period used a slightly different draft registration card, I have provided a facsimile of each of the cards used during this time. You may either print each card and use it as a template for writing down the information you find for your ancestors, or you can simply use it to decipher the questions that were asked – the type on some of the microfilmed documents is difficult to read. The following pages contain those templates.

(Note – If you would like to receive them electronically, e-mail me at wdanielquillen@gmail.com and I'll send them your way You may also download them for free from my website at *www.essentialgenealogy.com/forms_records.*)

Draft Registration Card used during the June 5, 1917 Registration – Page 1
For all men between the ages of 21 and 31

	REGISTRATION CARD

1	Name in full _____	Age in Years
	(Given name) (Family name)	

2	Home
	Address (No) (Street) (City) (State)

3	Date of Birth _____
	(Month) (Day) (Year)

4	Are you (1) a natural-born citizen, (2) a naturalized citizen, (3) an alien, (4) or have you declared your intention (specify which)?

5	Where were you born? _____
	(Town) (State) (Nation)

6	If not a citizen, of what nation are you a citizen or subject?

7	What is your present trade, occupation, or office?

8	By whom employed?
	Where employed?

9	Have you a father, mother, wife, child under 12, or a sister or brother under 12, solely dependent on you for support (specify which)?

10	Married or single (which)?

11	What military service have you had? Rank _____ Branch _____ Years _____ Nation or state _____

12	Do you claim exemption From draft (specify grounds)? _____

I affirm that I have verified above answers and that they are true

_____
(Signature or mark)

If person is of African descent,
cut off this corner

Draft Registration Card used during the June 5, 1917 Registration – Page 2

	REGISTRAR'S REPORT
1	Tall, medium, or short (specify which)? _____ Slender, medium, or stout (which)? _____
2	Color of eyes _____ Color of hair _____ Bald
3	Has person lost arm, leg, hand, foot, eye, or both eyes or is he otherwise disabled (specify)? _____

I certify that my answers are true, that the person registered has read his own answers, that I have witnessed his signature, and that all of his answers of which I have knowledge are true, except as follows:

_____

_____

_____

(Signature of Registrar)

Precinct _____

City or County _____ _____

State _____ (Date of Registration)

Draft Registration Card used during the June 5, 1918 Registration – Page 1
For all men becoming 21 after June 5, 1918

Serial No. _____		Registration No. _____

1	Name in full _____ (Given name) (Family name)	Age in Years
2	Home Address _____ (No) (Street or RFD) (City or Town) (State)	
3	Date of Birth _____ (Month) (Day) (Year)	
4	Where were you born? _____ (City or Town) (State) (Nation)	
5	1. Native of the United States 2. Naturalized Citizen 3. Alien 4. Declared Intention 5. Noncitizen or citizen Indian (Strike our items or words not applicable)	
6	If not a citizen, of what nation are you a citizen or subject? _____	
7	Father's Birth place _____ (City or Town) (State) (Nation)	
8	Name of employer _____ Place of employment _____ (No) (Street or RFD) (City or Town) (State)	
9	Name of nearest relative _____ Address of nearest relative _____ (No) (Street or RFD) (City or Town) (State)	
10	Race – White, Negro, Indian (Strike our items or words not applicable)	

I affirm that I have verified above answers and that they are true

P.M.G.O   _____
Form 1   (Signature or mark)

If person is of
African descent,
cut off this corner   REGISTRATION CARD

Draft Registration Card used during the June 5, 1918 Registration – Page 2

	REGISTRAR'S REPORT	
1	Tall Medium Short $\quad\quad\quad\quad$ (Strike out words not applicable)	Slender Medium Stout
2	Color of eyes _____ $\quad$ Color of hair _____	
3	Has person lost arm, leg, hand, foot, eye, or is he palpably physically disqualified (specify)? _____ _____	

I certify that my answers are true, that the person registered has read his own answers, that I have witnessed his signature, and that all of his answers of which I have knowledge are true, except as follows:

_____

_____

_____

_____

                                                   (Signature of

Registrar)

_____

      Date of Registration)

(The stamp of the local board having jurisdiction of the area in which
the registrant has his appointment shall be placed in this box)

172

Draft Registration Card used during the September 12, 1918 Page 1
For men aged 18 through 45 as of June 5, 1918

REGISTRATION CARD

SERIAL NUMBER				ORDER NUMBER	
1					

First name	Middle name	Family Name

2 PERMANENT HOME ADDRESS

(No)	(Street or RFD Number)	(City or town)	(County)	(State)

3. Age by Years	4 Date of Birth		
	(Month)	(Day)	(Year)

RACE

				Indian	
White	Negro	Oriental	Citizen		Non-Citizen
5	6	7	8		9

U.S. CITIZEN			ALIEN	
Native Born	Naturalized	Citizen by Father's Naturalization Before Registrant's Majority	Declarant	Non-Declarant
10	11	12	13	14

15
If not a citizen of the U.S., of what nation are you a citizen or subject? _____

PRESENT OCCUPATION	EMPLOYER'S NAME
16	17

18 Place of Employment or Business

(No)	(Street or RFD Number)	(City or town)	(County)	(State)

NEAREST RELATIVE	NAME	19	
	ADDRESS	20	
		(No) (Street or RFD Number) (City or town) (County) (State)	

I AFFIRM THAT I HAVE VERIFIED ABOVE ANSWERS AND THAT THEY ARE TRUE.

P.M.G.O   _____
Form No. 1   Signature or Mark of Registrant

MILITARY RECORDS

**Draft Registration Card used during the September 12, 1918
Registration – Page 2**

REGISTRAR'S REPORT

DESCRIPTION OF REGISTRANT

HEIGHT			BUILD			COLOR OF EYES	COLOR OF HAIR
Tall	Medium	Short	Slender	Medium	Stout		
21	22	23	24	25	26	27	28

29 Has person lost arm, leg, hand, eye, or is he obviously physically disqualified?   (SPECIFY)

30 I certify that my answers are true, that the person registered has read or has had read to him his own answers, that I have witnessed his signature or mark and that all of his answers of which I have knowledge are true, except as follows:

_____
Signature of Registrar

Date of Registration _____

(The stamp of the local board having jurisdiction of the area in which the registrant has his permanent home shall be placed in this box)

As you can see from one of the questions on the draft registration cards, the government registered everyone – citizens and non-citizens alike. So if you had an immigrant male ancestor who was living in the United States during one of these draft registration periods, and he was between ages 18 and 45, there is a 98% chance that he completed a draft registration card.

Now, you may be asking yourself: "Where do I find these wonderful records?!" There are several correct answers to this question, as these records are kept in several places:

1. The National Archives
2. Ancestry.com, FamilySearch.org and several other fee and free websites
3. Other pay-for-service genealogy services
4. Family History Library of the LDS Church
5. Other free locations

Taking them one at a time:

National Archives: All 24,000,000 of the draft registration cards have been microfilmed and are available by request from the National Archvies, either by using NATF form 86 or ordering online at eservices.archives.gov/orderonline. The records are located at Microfilm list M1509, and the rolls are numbered according to state and county. You can go to *www.archives.gov/research/military/ww1/draft-registration* to see which roll a particular state and county is on. If none of the other options below have your ancestor's draft registration card available, try either the National Archives or the LDS Church.

Ancestry.com and FamilySearch.org: Both Ancestry.com and FamilySearch.org provide access to all 24,000,000+ WW I draft registration cards online.

Other pay-for-service genealogy services: There are a number of other pay-for-service websites that provide access to World War I draft registration cards, including www.archives.com and www.findmypast.com, to name a couple.

Family History Library of the LDS Church: The Family History Library of the LDS Church has microfilmed all 24,000,000 draft cards. So you can go to Salt Lake City, Utah to see them, or order them through your local

Family History Center and view them locally. However, to do that, you'll need to know what state and county your ancestor lived in and registered for the draft.

Other free locations: As of this writing, there are several states, counties genealogy societies, and individuals who have taken it upon themselves to put draft cards for their area online. Just google *World War I draft registration cards* for the most up-to-date listing of available sources.

World War II
In the World War II era, we run into government privacy laws that protect personal information newer than 75 years. However, there are still some records available to you – some open to the public, and others open only to veterans or their next of kin (or those whom they allow to gain access).

For those who are veterans or their next of kin, service records, including World War II draft registration cards, are available. For access to veteran's records, the government defines next of kin as the veteran's widow or widower (who has not remarried), son or daughter, father or mother, brother or sister of the deceased veteran. If you are related to the veteran, but not considered next of kin (such as a grandchild, niece, nephew, cousin, etc.), then you are considered part of the *general public* (aka the unwashed masses…).

To get copies of records for a veteran for whom you are next of kin, or if you have authorization from either the veteran or next of kin (or if you are the veteran!), contact:

NARA – National Personnel Records Center
Military Personnel Records
9700 Page Avenue
St. Louis, MO 63132-5100
Tel: 314-801-0800, Fax 314-801-0800

Alternately, you can go online and request records at their evetrecs web link — *www.archives.gov/veterans/military-service-records*. While part of this process is online to expedite the process, a part of the process that must be completed is that you must print, sign and date the request, then either fax or mail (sort of defeats the purpose of the online option!) the request to the National Personnel Records Center.

PRIVACY LAWS – 75 YEARS

Federal privacy laws prohibit the release to the general public of veterans' records until 75 years have passed since their creation. With few exceptions, veterans and their next of kin can get access to the veteran's records. Anyone else besides veterans and their next of kin are considered the general public, and they must wait until the records have aged 75 years before access will be granted.

If you do find yourself in the general public domain and you are looking for information for a veteran who is a relative (albeit not next of kin), you still have a chance. According to the NARA website, either the veteran or his next of kin can provide you authorization to access and get copies of his record. Here's a sample letter provided on the NARA website:

I authorize the National Personnel Records Center, or other custodian of my military service record, to release to (your name or that of your company and/or organization) the following information and/or copies of documents from my military service record.

The letter must identify the specific records requested, and must of course be signed by the veteran or his next of kin. Authorization letters are good for one year from the date of signature. If the veteran has died, either a death certificate or obituary of the veteran must accompany the authorization.

If you are not the veteran whose records are being sought, and not the next of kin, you must complete Standard Form 180 (SF 180). The form is on the NARA website at *www.archives.gov/research/order/standard-form-180.pdf*. For records that are not at least 75 years old, you must have a signed authorization from either the veteran or his next of kin.

About 600 archives personnel deal with about 4,000 requests each day for veterans' records – that's a lot of records to sort through, copy and mail out! Time marches on — no pun intended there (well, maybe a little), even though we are writing about military records – and as it does so, more and more military records become available. Such is the case for one of the groups of draft registration records from World War II. A great source of genealogical information from the World War II era is the draft registration cards of approximately 10 million men who registered for the draft. There were seven drafts associated with World War II. As of this writing, three of them are still within the government's 75-year privacy laws protection, but one group isn't. Known variously as the **fourth registration** or the old man's registration, a draft registration was conducted on April 24, 1942 and registered men whose birthdays were between 28 April 1877 and 16 February 1897. These men were between 45 and 64 years old, and were not currently serving in the military.

Information available on the draft registration cards includes the following:

Name
Age
Birth date
Birth place
Current residence
Employer information
Name and address of someone who would always know the whereabouts
    of the registrant
Physical description of registrant (race, height, weight, eye and hair colors,
    complexion)

Additional information such as mailing address (if different from residence address), serial number, order number, and board registration information may also be available.

As with the World War I draft registration cards, this is immensely interesting and valuable genealogical information. However, the database is incomplete. In a (relatively) modern day tragedy, records from the following states were destroyed before they could be microfilmed – they are gone forever:

Alabama
Florida
Georgia
Kentucky
Mississippi
North Carolina
South Carolina
Tennessee

For the rest of the draft registration cards – still a massive number – you can find them at Ancestry.com, Fold3.com, FamilySearch.org and other subscription and free websites.

The organization of the records is straightforward – first by state, then alphabetically by surname. Below and on the next page are templates for the World War II draft registration cards. As with World War I cards, you can copy these pages, e-mail me to get copies (*wdanielquillen@gmail.com*) or download them for free from *www.essentialgenealogy.com/forms__records*.

World War II Draft Registration Card – Fourth registration – Page 1

REGISTRATION CARD – (Men born between April 28, 1877 and or before February 16, 1897)		
Serial Number U_____	1. Name (Print) _____ (First)　　(Middle)　　(Last)	Order Number _____
2. Place of Residence (Print) _____ (Number and street)　(Town, township, village or city)　(State) (THE PLACE OF RESIDENCE GIVEN ON THE LINE ABOVE WILL DETERMINE LOCAL BOARD JURISDICTION; LINE 2 OF REGISTRATION CERTIFICATE WILL BE IDENTICAL) 3. Mailing Address _____ (Mailing address if other than place indicated on Line 2. If same, insert word *same*)		
4. Telephone _____ (Exchange)　(Number)	5. Age in Years Date of Birth _____ (Mo)　(Day)　(Yr.)	6. Place of Birth _____ (Town or Country) _____ (State or Country)
7. Name and address of person who will always know your address		
8. Employer's name and address.		
9. Place of Employment or Business. _____ (Number and street or RFD number)　(Town)　(County)　(State)		
I AFFIRM THAT I HAVE VERIFIED ABOVE ANSWERS AND THAT THEY ARE TRUE. D. S. S. Form 1 _____ (Revised 4-1-42)　(over) (Registrant signature)		

World War II Draft Registration Card – Fourth registration – Page 2

REGISTRAR'S REPORT

DESCRIPTION OF REGISTRANT						
RACE		**HEIGHT** (Approx)	**WEIGHT** (Approx)	**COMPLEXION**		
White		**EYES**		**HAIR**	Sallow	
Negro		Blue		Blonde	Light	
Oriental		Gray		Red	Ruddy	
Indian		Hazel		Brown	Dark	
Filipino		Brown		Black	Freckled	
		Black		Gray	Light brown	
				Bald	Dark brown	
					Black	

Other obvious physical characteristics that will aid in identification _____

_____

I certify that my answers are true; that the person registered has read or has had read to him his own answers; that I have witnessed his signature or mark and that all of his answers of which I have knowledge are true, except as

follows:_____

_____

_____

Signature of Registrar)

Registrar for Local Board _____

(City or County)   (State)

Date of Registration _____

(The stamp of the Local Board having jurisdiction of
the registrant shall be placed in the above space)

Another excellent source of information for the men and women of World War II are the enlistment – not draft — records for those who enlisted between 1938 and 1946. Titled World War II Army Enlistment Records, it lists over nine million men and women who enlisted in the Army, National Guard, Army Air Corps and Navy and is found at *aad.archives.gov/aad/series-list.jsp?cat=WR26*. Check out the wonderful genealogical information available on these records:

Name
Residence (state and county)
Date of enlistment
Rank
Branch
Term of enlistment
Nativity (state or country of birth)
Year of birth
Race and citizenship
Education
Civilian occupation
Marital status
Box and film reel number

Other Resources

As you begin to plow the fertile ground of military records in search of your ancestors, understand that that there are far more records available than I can possibly list in this book. Veterans' census records, indexes to old soldiers' homes, indexes for soldiers' cemeteries, and Veterans' societies are just a few of the other resources that are available. The Church of Jesus Christ of Latter-day Saints has published a sixty-page research outline for military records that gives an excellent overview of the records that are available to researchers: **US Military Records – Research Outline, Intellectual Reserve, Inc**. It is available through the LDS Church Distribution Center in Salt Lake City, Utah (Tel. 800/537-5950) for a small fee. Or you can view it online: go to www.familysearch.org, select *Get Help* (near the top right-hand side), then click on *Research Wiki* and then in the *Search* box, type *US Military Records – Research Outline*, then search for it alphabetically. It is an excellent document.

In the meantime, here's a sampling of websites and locations where you'll find military records:

- *www.civilwar.nps.gov/cwss* — the Civil War Soldiers and Sailors System (CSWW) is a great starting place for discovering whether an ancestor served during the Civil War;
- *www.archives.gov* – the home page for NARA – the National Archives and Records Administration website, where you can learn about the nation's military records holdings;
- *www.familysearch.org* – many of the records held by the National Archives have been made available to the LDS Church, and this is your gateway to their collections;
- *www.Fold3.com* – one of the online subscription services available for genealogy research;
- *www.ancestry.com* – another of the online subscription services available for genealogy research;
- *www.militaryindexes.com* – a nice summary of US military records available online by war / conflict.

Military Records Checklist
____ Identify an ancestor you think may have served in the military.

____ Determine (if possible) the branch of service in which your ancestor served.

____ Determine what military records are available to research online.

____ Understand the process for obtaining records (Internet, mail request, personal visit).

____ Select a record to search.

____ Request or print Form 85 or 86, complete and mail to the National Archives for your ancestor. Or request records online at eservices.archives.gov/orderonline.

____ Consider subscribing to one of the subscription genealogy services that has military records collections.

___ States often have more online records available for their veterans than the National Archives do. Don't forget to search there.

___ Remember that more and more records are coming online daily. Check frequently.

Additional Resources

Beers, Henry Putney, *The Confederacy: A Guide to the Archives of the Confederate States of America*, Smithsonian Institution Press, (August 1986)

General Index to Pension Files 1861–1934, National Archives and Records Administration Microfilm Publication T288.

Hewett, Janet B., editor, *The Roster of Union Soldiers, 1861-1865*, 33 volumes. Wilmington, North Carolina, Broadfoot Publishing, 1997.

Intellectual Reserve, Inc., *US Military Records – Research Outline* (a publication of the Church of Jesus Christ of Latter-day Saints)

Johnson, Richard S., *How to Locate Anyone Who is or Has Been in the Military*, 7th edition, Fort Sam Houston, Texas: Military Information Enterprises, 1996.

Military Service Records in the National Archives of the United States, National Archives and Records Administration (pamphlet produced by NARA).

US Military Records – Research Outline, Intellectual Reserve, Inc. (Available at www.familysearch.org.)

Kenneth C. Martis, *The Historical Atlas of United States Congressional Districts 1789-1983* (New York: The Free Press, New York City, New York).

US War Department, *The War of Rebellion: A Compilation of the Official Records of the Union and Confederate Armies*, reprint: Gettysburg, Pennsylvania, The National Historical Society.

Loretto Dennis Szucs and Sandra Hargreaves Luebking (editors), *The Source – A Guidebook to American Genealogy*, third edition, edited by Ancestry Publishing, 2006.

11. CHURCH RECORDS

"The church is always trying to get other people to reform; it might not be a bad idea to reform itself a little, by way of example."
— A Tramp Abroad (Mark Twain)

Compared to churches, states and countries are by and large late entrants into the records-keeping business. Compared to churches – particularly the Catholic Church — they are pikers. Often, church records – records of births, baptisms, christenings, marriages and deaths – predate government records by decades, even centuries.

Whether your ancestors were Catholic or Baptist, Lutheran or Methodist, Mormon or Methodist Episcopalian, church records are a great source of genealogical data for those researchers who are savvy enough to know how to search for them. And since they may be some of the only records available for a particular time period, they can often help you break through some of those genealogical walls you have been encountering in your research. As an added bonus, church records like birth, death and marriage often carried additional information, such as the names of parents, grandparents, aunts, uncles, Godparents, etc.

Throughout history, sometimes the line between church and state was blurred. In some countries, there was a state religion, to which everyone belonged by default, and where careful records were kept, since these served as tax rolls as well as church rolls. I doubt the founding fathers of those countries understood what a boon those records might eventually be to genealogists the world over – they used them quite differently. Lutheran Germany, Anglican England, Catholic Italy and other countries were strict adherents to various religious persuasions. Even America in its earliest days wasn't immune – New York was founded by the Dutch, Pennsylvania by the Society of Friends (Quakers), Virginia, Georgia and South Carolina were predominantly Anglican (Episcopalian), and the Puritans in the New England States. Carrying those teachings of their former countries forward on the American continent, pastors and priests were expected to keep copious notes on their parishioners. In many cases, those records have found their way onto the Internet, into State Archives and Libraries, genealogy societies, etc.

Often, as stated above, these church leaders were keeping records of births, deaths and marriages long before state governments got into the act. Some southern states didn't require recording of births, deaths and marriages until well into the 20th century, New York and Virginia didn't require it until the mid-19th century, etc. And yet, thanks to countless pastors, priests and reverends, (and/or their clerks!) we have records of genealogical value extending back to the earliest days of our country's infancy.

Consider the value of the information below from Zion Evangelical Lutheran Church, Lykens, Dauphin County, Pennsylvania:

Name	Death Date	Age
Austin L. Keagle	5 August, 1877	1
Christanna Sporl	9 August, 1877	84
David Minich	12 October, 1877	19 years, 1 months, 29 days
Sarah Ann Thomas	14 November, 1877	6 years, 8 months, 12 days
Abraham L. Koppenhver	20 December, 1877	13 years, 4 months, 1 day
Mrs. Clara Keast	6 February, 1878	23 years, 8 months, 20 days

(The above information is located at *ancestorsatrest.com/church_records/ zion_lutheran_church_records.shtml*)

While that information is great, especially when the minister / clerk began providing the years, months and days of the age of the deceased, sometimes the information went much further. Consider some of the additional information provided by the Catholic parish priest in Inch, Ireland for deaths that occurred in his parish between 1788 and 1872:

Surname	First name	Date	Remarks
Gibson	William	24 December, 1788	of Ballygalley
Graham	William	24 December, 1788	of Annacloy, father of Ann

Rea	William	21 June 1792	(wife or William Rea) of the Rann of The Rann, Grandfather of Edward; Edward Rea married Ann Thompson and was father of John, James and Edward Rea
Maxwell	Edward	25 January, 1793	son of John Waring Maxwell and wife of Dorothy of Finnebrogue
Kirkwood	Thomas	15 January, 1794	Quaker and Scottish stock – now extinct

As you can see, sometimes church death records go beyond just telling us a little about the deceased. Several other entries from this Catholic Church in Inch contained remarks that the individual had been one of the early settlers in the parish, or that there were once many of the same surname in the parish but they were all gone with the death of this individual, etc.

Baptism Records

I remember a conversation I once had with a fellow genealogist who was thrilled that he had found some church baptismal records for some of his ancestors, but he was frustrated that some of them didn't seem to match up with other records he had for those same ancestors. He was assuming that his ancestors were baptized as infants. But that is a dangerous and often inaccurate assumption to make. Some churches baptize their infants. Others baptize when the individual reaches the **age of accountability** (able to distinguish right from wrong) – and that age varied between age 7 and early teens. Still other churches didn't recognize baptisms of other churches, so their adult converts were baptized. Some congregations even decided that as a sign of recommitment, the entire congregation was rebaptized, regardless of their age. So be cautious when making age-based assumptions when you find baptismal records.

As you begin researching church records, understand that while Church records can provide wonderful information, sometimes they are difficult to track down and may require a little ingenuity and additional effort on your

---

GREAT GOBS OF INFORMATION, WITH A CAUTION!

Now – a caution for you – I am not going to mislead you. While Church records provide a tantalizing prize, they can be as elusive as some of your ancestors!

I consider myself a pretty savvy researcher, and I have to admit finding Church records sometimes tries my best efforts, not to mention my patience. I have come to expect to be able to find great gobs of genealogical information out on the web, or at least be able to identify it and then follow the thread to where I can find it.

I found that a little extra persistence was required to find some of these Church records. Some are available online. Others are available via microfilm from various organizations. Others are available by a visit to a local parish, synod or Church office.

There are many records online, but it seems as though they are sort of hit-and-miss. They are often not organized the way I think they should be!

Be persistent and exercise your best detective skills, and you could reap great rewards as you search for Church records!

---

part. They may be held at a local parish / church, at a minister's home, or at a county, state or even national level.

Let's Begin

Okay, so you believe me when I say church records can be a great source of genealogical data but they can sometimes be difficult to find. Where do you start?

I'd suggest beginning by trying to determine your ancestors' denomination. This may be difficult, or it may be a slam dunk. Perhaps your family has been (place denomination name here: _____) for hundreds of years. If that's the case, then you have a good starting point. If your ancestors were predominantly Catholic, when you are starting your search through church records, you can largely ignore the Baptist, Lutheran, Methodist, etc., records that are online.

But if you don't know, that makes your search a little more difficult. Perhaps there are other telltale clues that will help you. For example, I recently discovered that the family Bible that belonged to my great grandmother was a Catholic Bible. Who knew? (Not me – that's for sure!) While that's not a sure thing, it's a clue to follow up on. Did your ancestors tend to be buried in a certain denomination's cemeteries? Several of my lines go back to Pennsylvania, and death records I have for those families indicate they were buried in the local M. E. (Methodist Episcopalian) cemetery. Was the family Bible you have in your possession printed by the Baptist Missionary Society? Another clue.

Once you have determined your ancestor's (probable) church affiliation, you of course need to determine where they were from. You'll be able to narrow your search a great deal if you know a location.

Of course, you need to know an approximate time frame in which to search for records.

So – armed with those critical components – church affiliation, location and approximate timeframe – you're ready to proceed. I would first try online resources, since I really like to do genealogical research from my home office. Your great grandmother was a Catholic from Houston, and was born in the late 1800s / early 1900s? Then pull up Google and type *Catholic Birth Records Houston, Texas*. When I did that, I got many hits, one of which was *www.catholicarchivesoftx.org*. It is for the Catholic Archives of Texas, and includes over 20,000 feet of microfilm on such topics as sacramental (birth, marriage, death) records, school records, Catholic newspapers, etc.

If nothing comes up, or none of the records is what you're looking for, your next step may be to see if you can contact the church itself. When I made the above search, I discovered a link that told me that St. Vincent's was the only Catholic Church in Houston in 1896, and that is was part of the Galveston archdiocese. You can see if St. Vincent's still exists. I checked, and the original building does not, but another St. Vincent's was built to take its place. Contacting the priest at the current St. Vincent's and asking for information about the records you are seeking is a good step. The priest should be able to tell you if the records exist, and where they might be found. If he doesn't know, your next stop would be the Archdiocese of Galveston. Some churches keep their records locally. Others consolidate them at the state or national level. As you contact local ministers in search of records,

CHURCH TERMINOLOGY

Before you launch your search for church records, it might be good to start out with an understanding of church terminology. Following are some terms you may run into in your research. Knowing what they are may be helpful as you search out records.

Affinity – a relationship determined by the Catholic Church that may preclude marriage between two individuals (i.e. — two people who are too closely related).

Association – Baptist churches typically are part of an association.

Bann – formal announcements of upcoming marriages (Catholic).

Conference – Methodist congregations are part of a conference.

Diocese – local Catholic congregations are parishes, several of which are part of a diocese.

Disparity of worship – an impediment to marriage for a Catholic. This would be the case if the proposed spouse was not Catholic. It is possible to get a dispensation (see below) – if a dispensation for disparity of worship is in place for your ancestor, then his / her spouse was not Catholic. (Note: also called Disparity of Cult.)

Dispensation – a church act authorizing a Catholic priest to perform a marriage that might otherwise not be allowed.

Sacrament – as it applies to genealogical research, sacraments of the Catholic Church that are of interest are baptism, confirmation and marriage. Look online for Catholic Sacramental Records.

Synods – Local Lutheran and Presbyterian congregations join into synods.

they should be able to direct you to sources within their Church where you will be most likely to find the church records for which you are looking.

Some of my best success has come from going to Google and searching for records by typing things such as:

Catholic sacrament records for _____ (location)

Baptist marriage records for _____
Moravian birth (death, marriage) records for _____
Lutheran records for _____

I have also had great success when I append Ancestry.com or Fold3.com to the above information strings:

Ancestry.com Catholic records
Fold3.com Moravian records,
Etc.

If you have a subscription to either of these fee-based services (or access to them though your local library or Family History Center), you may find they allow you greater information than you'll otherwise find on free websites.

Another website that has provided me with success in finding church records is *ancestorsatrest.com/church_records/*.

While the search for church records can be a bit frustrating, it can also be rewarding. Give it a try – the rewards are worth the extra effort.

Church Records Checklist
____ Identify the ancestor you are researching.

____ Identify your ancestors' religious affiliation, residence and timeframe.

____ If you're not sure of your ancestors' religious affiliation, are there clues, such as Bibles, cemeteries they were buried in, pastors who married them, etc?

____ First check online resources for Church records.

____ If you run into brick walls in searching for online Church records, contact the local church in the area where your ancestor lived and attended church. Determine where the Church keeps its records. You may need to contact the next highest division of the Church.

____ Turn to subscription services if you constantly run into roadblocks on free websites.

____ Be persistent.

Additional Resources

Loretto Dennis Szucs and Sandra Hargreaves Luebking (editors), *The Source – A Guidebook to American Genealogy*, third edition, (Ancestry Publishing, 2006).

For more in-depth treatment of these issues, pick up a copy of my *Mastering Family, Library & Church Records*, 2nd Edition, Cold Spring Press, 2014.

12. BIBLE RECORDS

"Bible reading is an education in itself." — Lord Tennyson

As you search for your elusive ancestors, especially those who were born prior to the twentieth century, birth, death and marriage information gets more and more difficult to find. If you are fortunate and exercise your detective skills particularly well, you may find some of those records.

If you have an ancestor that is being particularly elusive, perhaps it is time to turn your attention to bible records. Perhaps inspired by all those begats that pepper the early books of the Bible, many of our ancestors kept records of important family events such as births, deaths and marriages in the center section of the family bible. In some cases, these references may be the only recorded incidences of those particular events.

If you are like me, you are fortunate in that the family bible for your ancestors has fallen into your hands. My dear great grandmother kept a meticulous record of family vital events – and recorded that same information for her extended family. The center section of her family bible contains information about hers and her husband's ancestors back to the 1700s. Literally hundreds of names, dates and locations are recorded in her elegant handwriting.

Among her records, I found a clue as to how my grandmother gathered these records. Included among her personal effects was a half-sheet of paper, yellowed with age, in a flowing masculine script, but different from my great grandmother's lovely handwriting. It listed the genealogical information about one line of the family. Checking my great grandmother's entry in the family bible, I noted that her entries for this family were identical to that which was on the half sheet of paper. So my assumption is that she asked family members to provide genealogical information about their families, and at least this person provided his family's information on this half-sheet of paper.

This brings us to two important points:

1. Don't assume that the information in the center section of the family bible was written at the time of the event. It could have been many years later, and
2. Always consider that the information may not be correct, because it was added years after the event.

So how will you know? Well, there are several things you can do. First, does the information agree with other information you may have – censuses, vital records, etc? Second, check the publication date of the bible. If the publication date is later than many of the dates in the bible, then you'll know for certain that the dates were added after the events occurred.

In addition to the center section of the family bible, don't forget to check the pages of the Bible itself. Sometimes individuals would annotate information in the margins, next to a Biblical name. Say, for instance, someone named their daughter Abigail after that great Biblical heroine:

> Now the name of the man was Nabal; and the name of his wife Abigail: and she was a woman of good understanding, and of a beautiful countenance…
> (1 Samuel 25:3)

Written in the margin next to this scripture might be:

Abigail McCollough, born 3/15/1877

In addition, slipped between the pages of the bible might be obituaries clipped from newspapers, programs from funerals, etc. As I wrote that, I pulled down our old family bible to see what treasures my grandmother and her mother may have slipped between the pages for safekeeping. I found letters from young and older grandchildren, postcards from favorite trips, a Western Union wire from a soldier during WW II, photographs of my grandfather early in his career, newspaper clippings featuring births and deaths, a funeral program for my great grandfather, the center section with genealogical information I have mentioned before, my great grandmother's marriage certificate, and numerous other genealogical entries. There was even a picture I had drawn at about age 5 of my grandmother and her dog!

I also noted that the bible was a Catholic Bible, so perhaps that was a clue to my great grandparents' religious affiliation.

Through my years of genealogical research, I have come to understand how truly fortunate I am to have this record in my hands. But I have also learned that while not many genealogists share that luck, there are places where genealogists can go to find that information.

Preserving and recording Bible records has been one of the quests of many organizations, particularly local and state genealogical societies. One of the more prolific groups in this regard is the Daughters of the American Revolution (DAR). Founded in 1890, this great organization is dedicated to preserving the history of those who fought to earn America's freedom. They have been busily gathering and preserving bible records almost since their inception. The DAR has a chapter in every state, and many of the state DAR chapters that I checked online had a blurb on their website home page about that particular chapter's work in collecting bible records, especially those states on the eastern seaboard and the south. And these aren't just the Bible records for ancestors of the DAR, but for whatever records come into their hands. I didn't add up the totals, by their collection is immense.

Most chapters referenced multiple books of biblical records, generally multiple volumes. The New York chapter, for example, has a 266-volume set of bible records! The North Carolina chapter has twenty volumes, and there is a southern collection featuring numerous volumes. Many of them are included in the Family History Library microfilm and microfiche collections. Here is a sampling of a few below:

- Daughters of the American Revolution (North Carolina). *Genealogical Collection*. Salt Lake City, Utah: Genealogical Society of Utah, 1971. (On 54 Family History Library films beginning with 860336). This collection includes family histories and transcripts of bible, cemetery, church, will, marriage, death, and obituary records. There is a surname index to this collection.
- Kirkham, E. Kay. *An Index to Some of the Family Records of the Southern States: 35,000 Microfilm References from the NSDAR Files and Elsewhere*. Logan, Utah: Everton Publishers, 1979. (Family History Library book Ref 973 D22kk vol.1; fiche 6089183.)
- Lester, Memory Aldridge. *Bible Records from the Southern States*. 7 vols. in 6. Chapel Hill, North Carolina: M.A. Lester, 1956–1962. (Family History Library book 975 D28L; film 978067.) These volumes often

provide birth, marriage, and death dates, as well as marriage places. The entries are arranged alphabetically by bible owner.

• Martin, Ruth. *North Carolina Bible Records.* 8 vols. (Family History Library book 975.6 D2mr; fiche 6049149–56.) Series one (vols.1–7) has bible, church, and cemetery records. Series two (vol.1) has Bible, birth, and marriage records, and genealogies.

• Kirkham, E. Kay. *An Index to Some of the Bibles and Family Records of the United States: 45,500 References as Taken from the Microfilm at the Genealogical Society of Utah.* Two Volumes. Logan, Utah: Everton Publishers, 1984. (Family History Library book 973 D22kk; fiche 6089184 [set of 4 fiche.) Volume 2 includes Illinois.

To quickly scan DAR chapters that have collected and catalogued Biblical records, simply google *Daughters of the American Revolution, Bible Records.*

Many other genealogy societies have also gotten into the bible records preservation act. I tend to do a lot of research in Illinois, and was delighted to find that the Illinois State Genealogical Society has been busy gathering and recording information from family bibles since 1988. They do not limit their collection to Illinois residents – they simply recognize the value of the information, regardless of the state of residency. To date, they have produced two volumes of transcribed bible records. The books are called *Illinois State Genealogical Society, Family Bible Records, Volumes 1 and 2.* They are both available on microfilm through the Family History Library, (film #s 1954965 and 1954966).

Through the years, a number of websites have sprung up to assist individuals in locating biblical records. Some I have used in my research include:

Ancestor Hunt Bible Records – *www.ancestorhunt.com/family_bible_records. htm.* This website lists nearly 200 surnames for which they have Bible records (The Lindsay Family Bible, the Quillen Family Bible, etc.). Of course, not only Lindsay and Quillen surnames are found in those bibles, so a surname index provides information about other surnames contained in the organization's bible holdings. As of this writing, the index contained over 2,400 surnames and represented over 22,700 individuals – and it grows constantly!

Ancestry.com – *www.ancestry.com* has a nice collection of family bible records, regional and state bible records (Southern Bible Records, New York

Bible Records, Virginia Bible records, etc.) and various and sundry other transcriptions of bible records. To access most of these records, you must have a subscription to Ancestry.com (or visit your local library and Family History Center and use their subscriptions).

Bible Records Online – *www.biblerecords.com*. This great website has nearly 1,200 family bibles in their collection, representing thousands of surnames. A surname index allows you to quickly see if your family's bible records are represented, and if so, the years the records cover. Pictures of the Bible pages and transcriptions of what is written there are on the website.

FamilySearch.org – the LDS Church has also been a prolific collector of bible records. To see what their biblical holdings consist of, go to www. familysearch.org, click on Search, then Catalog then select Search by Subject in the box on the left, and type in Bible Records.

Fold3 – *www.Fold3.com*. Like Ancestry.com, Fold3 has thousands of family bible records, some by surname, some by state and region. To access most of these records, you must have a subscription to Fold3.com, or visit your local library and Family History Center and use their subscriptions.

The Virginia State Library — *www.lva.virginia.gov/public/guides/bible. htm*. I am fortunate to have several of my lines go back to Virginia. They are a state that is really tuned into genealogy and vital records. That carries through to their interest in bible records. The Virginia State Library has over 6,000 family bible records.

If you are one of those fortunate enough to have come into possession of your family's bible, by all means, please be active in sharing that information with organizations that keep those records. Contact your local genealogy society – city, county or state, your state library, several of the organizations above (Bible Records Online, Ancestor Hunt Bible Records, etc.), Daughters of the American Revolution, etc. Share your good fortune with others who may be hunting exactly the information you have in the bottom file cabinet drawer in your office. When you contact the organization(s), they will provide you with instructions on how to share the information.

The Virginia State Library (*www.lva.virginia.gov/public/guides/bible.htm*) has an awesome biblical records collection; following is the information they provide to those who are willing to make their family bible information available:

How to Have Your Family Bible Records Placed in the Virginia State Library Archives and Manuscripts Collection

Family bible records represent an extremely valuable source of information for the researcher. As a result, The Library of Virginia actively seeks copies of privately held bible records related to Virginia residents.

If you can bring your original bible to the Archives, we will make arrangements to copy the family information for the collection at no charge.

If you cannot visit the Archives, please make good quality photocopies of the title page of the Bible showing the date of publication, and any pages which record dates of birth, death, marriage or other important family information. Send the copies you make along with information about the Virginia counties of residence of the families shown in the record to:

The Library of Virginia
Description Services Branch
800 East Broad Street
Richmond, Virginia 23219-8000

Potential donors may contact:
Lyndon H. Hart, III
Library of Virginia
800 East Broad Street
Richmond, Virginia 23219-8000
(804-692-3743)

Several years ago I came into the possession of a family history which included compiled biographies for members of one of my family lines – the Throckmortons. The book was published in 1930. As I perused its pages, I noted there were numerous references to the genealogical information that had been included in the book from the Throckmorton family bible. There was even a picture of the bible, open to one of the pages that contained genealogical information. The earliest genealogical date in the bible was 1693. I began trying to search for the owner of the bible. While references to the bible's center genealogical sections were made throughout the book, I was interested in seeing if I could get a copy of those sacred pages. I've not yet had success, but will continue trying. Perhaps future editions of this book will include my successful hunt!

Bible Records Checklist

____ Identify the ancestor you are researching.

____ Check to see if anyone in the family has the family bible.

____ Check various sources where either your family bible, or family bibles that contain information about your family, may exist (FamilySearch, genealogical societies, etc.)

____ Share your good fortune! Contact organizations that preserve and catalog family bible information.

____ Be persistent.

13. OLD NEWSPAPERS

"Accuracy to a newspaper is what virtue is to a lady; but a newspaper can always print a retraction." – Adlai E. Stevenson

One of the early and very visible oracles of Americana is the newspaper. Newspapers made their appearance very early on the stage of American history, and have been an important source of information and news for centuries. Fortunately, many of these newspapers have been preserved and are available in various formats to genealogical researchers.

Sometimes, your best genealogical efforts just aren't enough to find all the family members you're looking for, to establish connections you just know are there, etc. When you hit one brick wall after another in trying to establish those connections, or extend back another generation or two, you might want to consider turning to newspapers to see if they can be of assistance.

Newspapers can provide a wealth of information, whether vital records types of information (birth announcements, death and funeral notifications, marriages, etc.), but they may also provide other sorts of information that will help further your genealogical research. The following sections provide a little about the information that may be gleaned from perusing a newspaper from your ancestor's home town.

Birth Announcements

Life events such as births, deaths and marriages were big deals and were especially of interest to small town citizens and were usually carried in the local newspaper. Such announcements generally provide information about the parents, at least, and often grandparents.

Obituaries

At the other end of the spectrum of life from birth announcements are obituaries. Obituaries can also be sources of genealogical information that might otherwise be elusive. Consider the obituary for my second great grandfather, Jonathan Baldwin Quillen:

J. B. Quillen died January 21, 1920, aged 74 years, 8 months, and 3 days.

He had been in poor health for two years and bore his suffering with patience and said the Lord was with him in his last hours and that he was willing and ready to go. Everything was done for him that willing hands could do. We will miss our dear grandfather, but our loss is Heaven's gain.

He leaves an aged widow and seven children to mourn his loss.

The remains were laid to rest in the Curtis Cemetery eight miles south of Hartville last Thursday.

Dearest father, thou hast left us here,
Thy loss we deeply feel

But 'tis God that hath bereft us
He can all our sorrows heal.

Peacefully we know you're resting,
In that home so bright and fair,

And we know when life is ended,
We will meet our father there.

Marie Hensley

****

Several days later, the following appeared in the same paper:

Card of Thanks

We wish to thank our kind friends and neighbors for their kindness and help shown us during the sickness and death of our dear husband and father.

Mrs. J. B. Quillen
Lizzie Hensley and family
Emmet Quillen and family
Bud Quillen and family

Ed Quillen and family
Henry Quillen and family
Creed Quillen and family
Evan Quillen and family

A couple of genealogical gems are available through his obituary:

• His birth date. Calculating it from the exact number of years, months and days would place his birth date on May 18, 1846.
• We know where he was living when he died
• We know where he was buried in Curtis Cemetery, 8 miles south of Hartville
• His wife was alive in January 1920, when he died
• He had seven living children (he may have had more, but seven were alive at the date of his death)
• The married name of one of his daughters
• Also – almost overlooked – the poet who penned the poem that was included with the obituary was Marie Hensley – possibly a daughter of Lizzie Hensley, writing a poem for her grandpa!

This obituary was interesting to me on several levels. First, it points out the risk of using an obituary or death certificate to get the birth date of individuals. As pointed out above, using the obituary to calculate his birth date (he was "...aged 74 years, 8 months, and 3 days..." when he died) yields a date of May 18, 1845. However, other records I have list his birth date as May 25, 1845. So – the hunt continues for the right birth date!

I learned from this obituary the married name of his daughter, Lizzie.

The obituary indicated he left seven children and a widow. However, I know that he had nine children, so two must have died before his death. The card of thanks several days later listed the seven living children, so by process of elimination I knew which two hadn't survived his passing.

Many of the obituaries I have reviewed through the years, especially those covering rural areas, will say something like: "JB Quillen died last Friday...." While I may have the date of the newspaper, that doesn't help me determine what *date* he died on. If that is the case for one of your ancestors, the Appendix has a calculator that will help you determine the specific date of your ancestor's death. You can use it to determine what date a person died on if the obituary simply identifies a day of the week. Let me give you an example. This is the opening sentence of the obituary for my 2nd great aunt, Lizzie Leticia Quillen Henslee:

> Lizzie Henslee, 86, daughter of J.B. and Sarah Minera Quillen, was born April 3, 1887 near Nashville, TN and died Wednesday.

Her obituary appeared in the newspaper on June 20, 1963. As you can see, it is important for me to learn what date Wednesday was relative to the date the obituary was published, so that I can pinpoint exactly the date of her death. If you go to the Appendix, you'll look in the index and determine that for 1963, you should use Table C. Table C then tells you that June 20 was a Thursday, so the Wednesday before that was June 19, 1963. If you don't have my book at hand and you need to determine a date, there are a number of day-of-the-month calculators on the Internet. One I have used is: *www.searchforancestors.com/utility/dayofweek.html*. Check it out and then bookmark it.

Several years ago I was doing research on a great uncle to whom I had been very close, William Lynn McCollough. I knew the small town in which he was a prominent businessman, and reasoned that any newspaper that covered that town would surely have run an obituary, if not a story about him. His town was very small and did not publish its own newspaper; however, the major city about fifteen miles away did, so I found microfilmed copies of that newspaper in the state library and began scanning copies from around the date of his death. Not only did I find his obituary and a nice story about him, but I also discovered that in its first edition of each year, the newspaper published a list of those who had died during the previous year. After I learned that list was there, I could search many years very rapidly, looking for other family members. I was successful in finding the obituaries and death dates of several other family members, and was able to go to their obituaries and glean more information on them and their families.

There are a number of online sources for obituaries: **Legacy.com** (*www.legacy.com/NS/explore/*) is one I have used extensively for deaths that have occurred in the previous 85 years or so.

Wedding Announcements
These are always fun and informative little news blurbs to run across. First

of all – wedding announcements (generally) meant happy times for your ancestors. Secondly, I cannot recall an engagement or wedding announcement from a newspaper that *didn't* include the maiden name of the bride and the names of the bride's and groom's parents! The late 19th and early 20th centuries are the timeframes when these announcements became fairly standard in American newspapers, regardless of the social stature of the couple.

Society pages

Don't overlook the society pages! In small towns, births and deaths, weddings and visits from distant family members were important news, and society pages often yield information that will lead to further discoveries. I had a friend who discovered one of her ancestors had a sister that my friend hadn't known about, because of an entry in the Society page of the local newspaper that went something like:

> Ada and Phil Anderson celebrated their 15th wedding anniversary last Saturday at the city park. Among invited guests, her sister's daughter, Miss Anna Smithson from Toledo, was in attendance.

My friend had no idea that her ancestor Ada had a sister (much less a niece!) until she ran across this rather obscure society page article. Not only did she learn the sister's married name (Smithson, probably – although you have to consider that it could have been the niece's married name), but she also learned she may have been living in Toledo.

To find copies of old newspapers, understand that online access to newspapers is somewhat scanty, although several subscription and free services have sprung up in recent years that are adding to their collections all the time. But compared to other records (censuses, for example), the vast majority of newspapers that have been published in the US are not online. Companies that offer online access to newspapers include www.newspaperarchive.com, www.genealogybank.com, ancestry.com, Fold3.com and others.

In addition to fee-based services, I have been successful in locating old newspapers at the following locations:

- Chronicling America at *chroniclingamerica.loc.gov*; once you locate the title of the newspaper for which you are looking, click on the title, and then you can click on "Libraries that Have It" near the top of the record for holdings.

- WorldCat at *www.worldcat.org/advancedsearch*, lists all types of library holdings.

Getting Started

To begin your search of old newspapers for information that might be of use to you about your ancestors, you must first determine when and where your ancestor may have lived at the time of the event for which you are searching. If your ancestor's town was too small to have a newspaper, expand your horizons, checking to see if the county or perhaps a nearby town may have published a newspaper during your ancestor's time in the area. It may be in a nearby larger town, but don't overlook nearby smaller towns also – even though a small town wasn't large enough to publish a newspaper for their town, if they could take in several surrounding towns and the county, they may have published from a small town.

Next, you need to determine whether or not a newspaper covered the location of the event during the correct timeframe. If you determine that newspapers were in fact being published at that time and in that place, you need to determine whether or not the newspaper is online, and if not, what your other options are – has the newspaper been microfilmed, and if so, how can you get access to those microfilms? If the newspaper hasn't been microfilmed, are archival copies available, either for you to review or for someone you hire / talk into going to review them?

One quick way to determine whether or not the newspaper in your ancestor's local home town was microfilmed is to contact the city or county library in the area where your ancestor lived. If they don't know, then try the state library. Between those three locations, you are sure to find out not only if the newspapers were microfilmed, they will be able to tell you if they are available through inter-library loan.

Another avenue is to contact the local (town or city, county) genealogical society. They will most likely know whether the local newspapers have been microfilmed, and whether they are available via inter-library loan.

Both the local library and the local genealogical society can also tell you whether the local newspaper(s) have been abstracted, at least the critical parts such as births, deaths, weddings, etc. Many local genealogy societies do these abstractions as part of the work they do with their society.

If the local branches of the library don't have microfilms or abstracts of the area newspapers, you should have more luck at the state library level. Most state libraries have made an effort to gather the local newspapers and have them on microfilm. Sometimes they don't extend back as far as you'd like (the Colorado State Library, for example, only has the local newspapers back to 1906). State libraries that have microfilmed copies of newspapers almost always participate in inter-library loans, at least with other state libraries.

Newspaper directories such as those found at the end of this chapter in *Additional Resources* are also helpful in locating obscure newspapers. There's no need to rush out and purchase these books – most libraries will have copies for you to peruse.

If you fail in your local quest for information on newspapers, you'll need to expand your search. As you do so, you will sooner or later run into the **United States Newspaper Program (USNP)**. In the early 1980s, this program received funding from the National Endowment for the Humanities to locate, preserve and microfilm newspapers from the earliest beginnings of our country to today. Money was provided to one organization in each of the 50 states, Puerto Rico and the Virgin Islands (it was usually the largest repository of archived copies of newspapers in each state that was funded). Some did more with their funds than others.

Microfilm copies of newspapers are generally available to researchers anywhere in the country through inter-library loan. The USNP website includes links to each state, where you'll find information about which newspapers (names and dates) have been microfilmed, and where you can find out more information about accessing those microfilmed copies. A joint effort in tandem with the Library of Congress, the goal was to create a national digital database of historically significant newspapers.

The **Chronicling America project** boasts over sixty million pages for over 200,000 newspaper titles of historically significant newspapers from within the United States.

On the Library of Congress website, you can download information about microfilmed newspapers that are currently held in their collection. The website is *www.loc.gov/rr/news/news_research_tools/newspapersinmf.html*, and from there you will be able to see which newspapers are available on microfilm. (Note: Don't be misled by the titles. The titles might indicate that records are only between 1948 and 1983, but the holdings go back much further than that, some even pre-dating the Revolutionary War!)

The Library of Congress & Inter-library Loan
If you're unable to get to Washington DC to view these microfilms, never fear – they are available through inter-library loan to your state library, academic institution or to one of the fourteen regional national archives centers (see the Appendix for a list of the regional national archives locations). You can go to the following link to see the Library of Congress's inter-library loan policy: *www.loc.gov/rr/loan/*. Books and microfilm can be borrowed for sixty days. Patrons must view them at the library to which they were loaned – you cannot take them home. Not every item in the Library of Congress catalog is actually held in the collection, and not everything in the collection can be lent or copied. Here is what the Library of Congress website says about their newspaper collection:

> The Library of Congress maintains one of the largest and most comprehensive newspaper collections in the world, comprised not only of the major papers published in all 50 states and territories of the United States, but also those published in most other countries of the world that have existed over the past three centuries. Almost all of the more than 500,000 reels of newspaper microfilm held by the Newspaper & Current Periodical, European, Asian, and African & Middle Eastern Divisions are available for inter-library loan. Only newspapers that have been microfilmed are available for loan.

In summary, if you are running into difficulties finding birth, death or marriage dates for an ancestor, consider checking out the local newspapers around the time the event in question occurred. You may find all the answers you're looking for.

Old Newspapers Checklist
____ Identify the ancestor you are researching.

____ Determine when and where your ancestor lived.

___ Determine whether or not a newspaper was published in the area your ancestor lived, while your ancestor lived there.

___ Try to determine if the newspapers published have been microfilmed. Local, county and state librarians should be helpful in your search.

___ If the newspapers were microfilmed, determine how to see them – inter-library loan, field trip, local genealogist.

Additional Resources

Arlen Ayers, *Ayers Directory of Publications*, MS Press, 1985.

Clarence S. Brigham, *History and Bibliography of American Newspapers, 1690 – 1820.*

Winifred Gregory, *Winifred Gregory's American Newspaper.*

Lubomyr R. and Anna T. Wynar, *Encylopedic Directory of Ethnic Newspapers and Periodicals in the United States.*

Anita C. Milner, *A Location and Subject Guide for Researchers.*

14. DNA RESEARCH

"We are all related because our DNA is the same with our very first mother (Eve)." – Mettrie L.

Using Deoxyribonucleic Acid (DNA) as a Research Tool
You may think it odd to read about DNA in a book on troubleshooting genealogical problems. You're probably far more likely to associate DNA with any of several 21st-century forensic detective television shows than you would with genealogy. Well, there is a connection, one that in certain circumstances may provide you assistance in your genealogical research.

You might ask, "Do you mean I can use it to identify my ancestors." No. Well, maybe. Well, not exactly, but it can be useful. Huh? Read on.

The easiest and most direct use of DNA from a genealogical perspective is if someone is adopted and has been searching for their birth parents. If an individual is located who might be the birth parent (or grandparent) of someone, then DNA could definitely be used to verify with surety the relationship between individuals.

But it is also possible to use DNA as a tool when you are climbing further back up your family tree – even many generations. Let me explain.

Using DNA in genealogical research (called genetealogy by Megan Smolenyak, a pioneer in this area) is gaining traction among scientists and genealogists alike. Following are the basics: DNA is the chemical inside the cells that make up human beings. These cells carry the genetic instructions for forming humans: their hair and eye color, height, build, tendency towards certain diseases, etc. Chromosomes are segments of DNA that contain genes, the basic unit of heredity. Each of us received one set of 23 chromosomes from each of our parents. One of those chromosomes – the 23rd one – determines our sex. Mothers contribute an X chromosome and fathers contribute either an X or a Y chromosome to the baby-building equation. If the father contributes an X chromosome to the X chromosome contributed by the mother, the child is a girl; if he contributes a Y chromosome then the child is a boy.

Scientists have discovered that a portion of the Y chromosome is passed from father to son to grandson and beyond, with little or no change. So that wee portion of the Y chromosome will be nearly identical in the son, father, grandfather, great-grandfather, etc., all the way, I suppose, to Father Adam (through Noah, of course, and assuming an unbroken paternal line!). Tests have been developed that can isolate this area and determine whether two male individuals are related, even though they are separated by many generations.

Another type of DNA, called mitochondrial DNA (mtDNA) is similarly passed identically from mothers to their sons and daughters. It stops with the sons, but continues with the daughters.

There is yet one other test that can be run on DNA that is useful for genealogists. It is a test of the Ancestral Markers of the DNA – called Single Nucleotide Polymorphisms (SNPs). This test identifies the geographic region of the world that the tested person's DNA comes from. These tests will yield a percentage: 33% South American, 60% eastern European, 7% West Africa, for example.

Several years ago I had my DNA tested (no – I wasn't a suspect in a crime…). Most of the results were hardly surprising if you know me. If you were to see me walking down the street, you would probably think, "Yeah, that guy looks like his roots are in Europe." Sure enough, my SNPs indicate my ancestry is (approximately) 69.5% western European, 21.9% eastern European, 8% Asia Minor (Turkey) and some tiny amounts of other areas.

So that all sounds fine and good, but what does that mean for you and me and our ancestral research? Let's start with the most logical and work into the more vague areas.

We mentioned earlier that DNA can be used to confirm a connection to birth parents or beyond. An example might be that you are adopted and think you may have located your birth parents. But there is a question or two that just doesn't seem right – your birth parents are both dark haired and you are blonde; they gave a child up for adoption in North Dakota, but you were adopted in Alabama. Either a DNA or mtDNA test would prove the relationship. If you are a male, you will have the same Y DNA that your father had – almost if not exactly identical. But what if your father isn't known, or passed away many years ago? Then you would turn to the mtDNA test – remember, mothers pass this identical information to their sons and daughters. If there is a match – congratulations you found your mother.

Here's another scenario: Your grandfather was adopted, and you want to research both his adopted family and his birth parents. You think you have identified his birth parents, but there are no records – just family tradition which says your grandfather was raised by a family in the same town as his birth parents. And – both of your grandfather's suspected birth parents have passed away. What to do next?

Applying your ninth-grade science knowledge (with perhaps a little brush up from this chapter), you reason that if the potential father had any brothers, and they had any male children, and they had male children, then those children would have the same Y chromosome DNA as you have (or the same DNA your mother has, if you are a woman). So you find the suspected birth father's brother (who has of course passed away long ago), and identify a grandson of his who lives in a nearby town. You contact him, explain your dilemma, and he agrees to help. You both take the Y DNA test and.....your DNA is identical – hello, cousin, mystery solved.

Another use for DNA is to determine if two individuals (fellow genealogists, no doubt) tie into a common ancestor. If you are both men, this should be a piece of cake. You both have the same surname. You are both males. If you tie into a common male ancestor, you will both have the same Y DNA results. (Remember, fathers pass the same Y DNA onto their sons, who pass it on to their sons, etc.)

Similarly, if you both have similar surnames but spelled differently, here is a way to determine if you are related. For example, I communicate with a fellow genealogist whose surname is McQuillan. My research has indicated that once upon a time, my family's surname was McQuillan. If he and I are related through a common paternal ancestor, since we are both males, our Y DNA will be identical.

Finally, let's say that as you have researched a line you have hit a brick wall. Let's further say that you find yourself at a crossroads – some research you have done indicates a possible northern European connection. But you also have some clues that your ancestors came from South America. Maybe testing your Ancestral Markers will give you a clue which direction you should forge ahead in. Several dozen specific geographic areas of the world have thus far been identified through Ancestral Markers.

Pretty exciting stuff, huh?

Okay, so I have interested you. What's next – where do you go to learn more? For starters, there is one exceptional website I have found that provides a lot of information, answers a lot of questions, and directs you to more websites to learn even more information. The website is *www.duerinck.com/surname. html*. This marvelous website features the DNA testing project for the Duerinck surname. For a list of labs providing tests, visit http://clanlindsay. com/dna_project.htm. Or you can just type "DNA Testing Labs" into your browser and voila – more labs than you can shake a Y chromosome at!

"How much will it cost?" you ask. Well, its not cheap, but neither is it unspeakably expensive. There are a variety of tests, but they run between $99 and $300, depending on the test you are requesting, whether just one or more people are being tested, etc.

Using DNA as a Research Tool Checklist
____ Do you have a situation where DNA testing and research might help?

____ Determine how the DNA would flow (father to son, mother to son/ daughter) and determine whether you can make an unbroken connection back to the person in question.

____ Check to see if the potential distant cousin is amenable to DNA testing – philosophically as well as financially. (Note: if it is really important to you, you may offer to pay all costs.)

____ Identify a DNA testing lab that performs these sorts of DNA tests.

____ Be persistent – don't get discouraged!

Additional Resources

www.sorensongenomics.com — the website for Sorenson Genomics, a testing lab that is dedicated to welding genealogical research with DNA testing.

www.oxfordancestors.com — this is the website for Oxford Ancestors, which is associated with Dr. Bryan Sykes, one of the pioneers of DNA testing for genealogical purposes.

www.familytreedna.com — the website for Family Tree DNA.

Family Chronicle magazine runs articles on using DNA and genealogical research every so often.

15. GENEALOGY SOFTWARE REVIEW

Genealogy Software

There are dozens of software packages available on the market today that will help you keep your genealogical research organized. While notebooks and file folders are fine to get you started, as you progress you'll want to begin saving and organizing your genealogy in a more readily accessible fashion, and genealogy software will help you do that. Genealogy software on the market today allows you to input critical information about your ancestors and then provides very simple ways to retrieve and display the information. Using the information you have input, it will gather your ancestors into families in a heartbeat, produce pedigree charts in the blink of an eye, and provide instant access to the 1,000s of records you may have about your ancestors.

As you begin your search for a software package that will work best for you, you'll be amazed (I am, anyway) by the many clever names of genealogy software programs out there: BirthWrite, Brother's Keeper, Family Ties, Family Tree Maker, Family Matters and Relatively Yours, to name a few.

So what should you look for when you finally decide to organize all your manual and paper records into a software program? The first and foremost thing I think is important is user friendliness. No matter how powerful your genealogy program is, or how much storage space it has, if you don't understand how to use it, it is of no real use to you. From a capacity and capability standpoint, most of the major software programs available today are pretty much the same, especially for those who are just beginning their genealogical quest.

I have one caution: be certain that whichever program you choose, whether you are a beginner or not, is capable of **GEDCOM** capability. GEDCOM is an acronym for GEnealogical Data COMmunication. It allows you to share your data with other genealogists, and also allows it to be ported (transferred) to other genealogy programs. If you choose a software program that uses proprietary formatting, you will not be able to share or transfer information except to users who use the same program as you. Fortunately, GEDCOM is a pretty standard default for the software programs on the market today, but it is wise to check to make sure.

One other caution: Be sure and check the computer system requirements before you buy. Do you have the horsepower on your computer to run the program – do you even have the space on your hard drive to install it? Once you open the box, you bought it, and as with all software - no returns allowed!

It would be really nice if you could take the various genealogy software programs on the market for a "test drive" so that you can try it out before purchasing it. Fortunately, many of the more popular genealogy programs on the market today provide a demo version of their software that you can play with on their website.

Following are some of the more popular and capable genealogy programs out there:

Personal Ancestral File, more commonly known as PAF, was produced for many years by the Church of Jesus Christ of Latter-day Saints. The LDS Church pioneered the use of software for storing and retrieving genealogy data with several early DOS versions of PAF, and in recent years moved into the Windows era with a number of versions of PAF software.

While PAF was the standard bearer of genealogy software for years, the LDS Church made the determination not to expand it beyond its current software version 5.2. That's a shame, as it has been a credible and inexpensive (free!) genealogy software option for genealogists of all experience levels for many years now. The companies marketing competing software are making huge strides in web publishing, storage, and other advanced features and the LDS Church has decided not to expend the resources to compete and expand PAF.

With that said, many of us out there will bid PAF a fond adieu, as it has served us well through these many years. Read on for other options available for genealogy software.

Family Tree Maker is one of the powerful, popular genealogy software packages on the market today. Formerly a very expensive offering, at the time of this writing, price pressures and excellent competitive products have brought the cost down to $29.99 to $59.99 for their latest packages. Family Tree Maker is available at many retail outlets as well as from its website: *www.familytreemaker.com.*

Family Tree Maker is affiliated with Ancestry.com. A rich feature set includes well-regarded charts and a strong website generation capability. You can post some of the charts that are available on the Ancestry.com website for free, thus allowing you to share your findings with others. As with the other software programs reviewed here, Family Tree Maker has the reputation of being easy to use and easy to navigate.

There are several features I like in Family Tree Maker. First of all, it has an e-mail storage capability that allows you to store the e-mail addresses of other researchers you are communicating with. Gone are the "yellow stickies" with names and e-mail addresses that plague my desktop. I also like the date calculator that allows me to determine the day of the week for any given date in any given year.

The photo capability is great in Family Tree Maker, allowing you to create electronic scrapbooks and then print directly from those scrapbooks. Photos can also be linked to specific ancestors, and source materials (birth, death and marriage certificates, wills, etc.) can be scanned and then linked to a specific event.

Ancestral Quest. Earlier versions of Ancestral Quest were once regarded as the Number 1 genealogy software on the market. Other software manufacturers have since put their development efforts in high gear and have caught and in some cases surpassed their capabilities. But they are still a strong competitor, worthy of your consideration. The website for Ancestral Quest is *www.ancquest.com.* The cost at the time of publication is $29.95-$49.90.

The documentation that accompanies the product is some of the best on the market, and for those who rely heavily on documentation to learn or feel comfortable with a software product, this is a real selling point. It is relatively easy to use software, especially for basic data entry, printing, etc. But for the more advanced features, the documentation is a huge plus.

Ancestral Quest allows you to attach photos, audio and video clips to individuals in such a manner that allow you to create a memorable multimedia keepsake scrapbook. It also has more than adequate report and charting capabilities, including the production of large (320 inch by 320 inch) wall charts.

One feature that excites many genealogists in any of their Ancestral Quest 12.x and above versions is their PAF compatibility, particularly critical now that it has been announced that PAF will not be updated or supported any longer. Ancestral Quest works directly with the data in PAF 5, without the need to convert data. And why not? Software developers from Incline Software (the developers of Ancestral Quest) assisted the LDS Church in their development of PAF. They are also one of the few programs on the market today that has TempleReady capability for LDS users.

Ancestral Quest's marketing materials say, "(Ancestral Quest's) format is perfect for the beginner and yet powerful enough for the most advanced genealogist." And I have to agree that it is more than merely marketing hype – they do seem to have been successful in blending ease of use with great power.

RootsMagic (*www.rootsmagic.com*) is currently one of the hottest genealogy software packages on the market. Their software is price competitive ($29.95) and has many of the features its main competitors have. Considered by many to be easy to learn and use, RootsMagic has gained a strong following. Comments from reviewers and users of the software include: "easy-to-use," "a well-rounded genealogy software," "intuitive navigation," "simple functions," "powerful features," etc.

It is Word 8, 7, Vista, XP, and 2000 compatible, and provides such features as a website generator, an info-sharing option that allows you to create a read-only version of RootsMagic with your family's data in it, a mapping function that displays a map with map pins for each of your family member's identified events: birth, death, marriage, etc. As with several of their competitors, RootsMagic can produce beautiful color wall charts of your family. One nice feature is a family history publishing function.

Important to many genealogists is the fact that RootsMagic can import PAF data and TempleReady.

Can you stand one more genealogy software review? Another of the powerful yet affordable genealogy software programs on the market is **Legacy Family Tree** (*www.legacyfamilytree.com*). It comes standard with many of the features its competitors have, but this software is exceptionally intuitive. I particularly like the way it lays out its various pages – they are easy to read and presented in a manner that is visually appealing and that makes sense to me. Legacy allows you to enter millions of names (provided you have the disk space), with multiple events for each person. Add photographs, sound bytes or video clips and you've got a great repository for your family records. Add to that its Internet and web page creation capabilities, along with the ability to print a family book complete with pictures and you have a versatile, powerful software package.

The standard edition is priced very attractively – it is free – and the deluxe edition is $29.95. Legacy offers slightly more expensive packages that include user's guides, and one bundle ($39.95) with video training CDs.

In recent months, Legacy software has been receiving rave reviews from users and critics alike for its power and its user friendliness.

Genealogy Software Review Checklist

____ Make sure your computer will support the software you select.

____ Make sure the software you select has the ability to share and receive files from other genealogy software packages.

____ Evaluate the software to make sure it has the features you are most likely to use.

____ Select the software package that best meets your needs and fits your budget.

____ Start loading your ancestors into the software you have selected!

Additional Resources

Family Chronicle magazine often publishes evaluations of genealogy software.

Top Ten Reviews – *www.genealogy-software-review.toptenreviews.com* – this website does reviews of software, and their reviews are updated as new versions come out for each software package.

16. SUBSCRIPTION & FREE RESEARCH SERVICES

Subscription Research Services

Okay – face it – as an experienced genealogist, you have doubtless run into subscription services for genealogical research – Ancestry.com being one of the largest out there, but also such services as Fold3.com, WorldVitalRecords. com, NewspaperArchives.com, etc. For years, I resisted subscribing to these services, just out of principle. As time went on, more and more records have become available online that were once the sole domain of these subscription services. But just as these free sites and the information they contained multiplied, so did the holdings of these subscription services.

Over time, my resistance wore down, and one-by-one I began subscribing to these genealogical research services. Initially it was just the free trials. Then it was for the smallest amount of time possible – month or quarter, usually. Finally, I realized if I was serious about being successful in my genealogical research, I would need to begin using these subscription-only services. I tried various mixes and matches of services until I found just the right mix for most of my research. Following are reviews of some of the more prominent subscription-based services.

Ancestry.com – one of the mega-subscription services out there. Seems like they have invaded so many genealogy sites and sources. Their print and television advertisements claim they have the largest collection of family-history records online (and I am sure their attorneys insist on this being a correct statement!). To be perfectly honest, there was a time I almost swore when a promising website link took me to the Ancestry.com logo / leaf icon. I have gotten past that, realizing that the service they provide is valuable, and offers me access to great resources – why shouldn't they make a buck or two for making my research easier?

As of this writing, Ancestry.com offers two area of subscriptions – US as well as world-wide, with several tiers of costs. Again, as of this writing, here are the subscription costs:

US Deluxe Membership
Monthly $19.99 per month
Six-month $16.50 per month ($99 for six months)

Worldwide Deluxe Membership
Monthly $35.00 per month
Six-month $24.83 per month ($149 for six months)

Note that while the amounts shown are based on per-month costs, you pay it all up front, so be prepared for that. Subscriptions at these levels provide access to all records and resources applicable to each area.

One of the features on Ancestry.com that is uber-impressive is the ability to create your own family tree, updating it as you find your ancestors through Ancestry.com resources, adding pictures, linking families, etc. If you are using one of several software packages (Legacy and Family Tree Maker included), Ancestry.com's family tree feature will upload your information and assimilate it onto your family tree.

Ancestry.com is far and away the leading research tool that allows users to interact with one another, request and share information, etc., through their blogs, message boards and newsletters. As you no doubt are aware, genealogists love to share their information and love to help others learn more about *their* families, especially if their families are *your* families!

A nice feature Ancestry.com offers is the **Hire an Expert** option. This allows you to engage the services of an expert to help you get past a particularly difficult research issue, photograph a gravestone in a distant city, search records in a county courthouse, etc.

From my perspective, Ancestry.com gets top marks in the areas that are important to me: the quality of their online sources are excellent (driven primarily by the quality of the original documents), features, size of collection and the value for the money place it at the top of the subscription-service hierarchy. Not only do they lead this section of reviews because of their leading role in the alphabet, they also earn the top spot because of the width, breadth, quality and value of the services they provide for the money!

One area I would like to see Ancestry work on is their internal search engine. It is terrible. I think they've become obsessed with providing you with the most possible hits for a search, but what happens is they return you an unwieldy number of hits, often seemingly ignoring the gating factors you input (date ranges, location, etc.).

Fold3.com – You might know Fold3 by the name of its predecessor company – Footnote.com. Footnote.com was one of the newer, up-and-coming subscription services and made some serious inroads in Ancestry.com's lead among subscription services. Perhaps that is why Ancestry purchased them and changed their name to Fold3, and they now focus primarily on military records.

At the time of this writing, there are two levels of service: the first is free, and it provides access to many records. However for full access to their online records, a subscription to Fold3 will run you $11.95 a month, or $79.95 for an annual subscription.

One nice feature of Fold3 is the **Footnote Page** option, which allows you to create a page to place all the information you have found on a particular individual or family. Accessible even through the free membership level, this allows you to share your findings with anyone who has access to a computer. It's relatively easy to do, and allows you to put in one place all the information you've found for one of your ancestors.

I like Fold3. However, as much as I like it, I felt they are a little weak in the ease of navigation department. Like Ancestry.com's internal search engine, I found it a little exasperating. Overall, I think Fold3 provides good value for the money. I find that most of the research I am doing is best served by a combination of Ancestry.com and Fold3.com. Between the two of those services, I am able to get great coverage of my research needs.

WorldVitalRecords.com – WorldVitalRecords was one of the first subscription research services I tested the waters with. I was frankly surprised and pleased with what I found there.

Pricing is as follows: annual $89.99 per month; one month $16.25.

Note that the annual subscription is taken as a lump-sum payment, and the monthly payments automatically renew each month. There is a seven-day trial period option.

Not as easy to navigate as some of the other services discussed in this chapter, it is nonetheless acceptable. The search capabilities are excellent, providing options to cast your genealogical net wide or narrowing it considerably in your search. Online tutorials in important genealogy and research topics, a monthly newsletter, genealogy forums and message boards offer users excellent guidance.

WorldVitalRecords is an excellent website, and is a nice toe-dipping sub-scription for those who are watching their pennies, nickels and dimes. Not as pricey as Ancestry.com (the most expensive service discussed in this section), it provides a nice mix of features, access to records and research opportunities. Its major limitation, if this is important to you, is the lack of an integrated family tree making feature. If that's not an issue for you, then this is an excellent choice.

Important Note on Subscription-Based Services
Here's a quick note on subscription-based services: if you don't want to pay for a subscription, many public libraries have subscriptions their patrons are allowed to use to Ancestry.com, Fold3.com, WorldVitalRecords.com and HeritageQuest.com. Most of those require you to have a current library card and must be used on-site at the library. However, many libraries allow you to get access from your home computer to their HeritageQuest.com subscription. Just go to your library's main website. If your local library doesn't offer this option, try your state library. You may have to search a bit for it, but if you want access and don't want to leave home to get it, it will be worth your effort.

Also, most Family History Centers have several of the subscription services available for patrons to use while visiting the center. Ancestry.com and Fold3. com are usually available, while HeritageQuest.com and WorldVitalRecords. com are sometimes available.

Free Research Services

If you just aren't ready to jump into the world of subscription-based research services, or would like to supplement your fee-based services with non-fee based services, there are myriad options. And, as has been indicated earlier in this book, it seems there are many more coming online all the time. Following are a few I have used through the years.

Cyndi's List — When you think of Cyndi's List (*www.cyndislist.com*), you should think of a mammoth card catalog in the sky — it is a gigantic index of genealogical websites. When you go to Cyndi's List, one of the first things you see will be the number of active links available through Cyndi's List. It seems that every time I log onto Cyndi's List, the number of websites grows. At the time of this writing, the number of links is more than 329,000! Now that's a lot of websites.

In addition to being an index, Cyndi's List provides links to each website listed, so once you find a website that catches your interest, you merely click on the link and you are there. It is remarkably user friendly, and provides a great service for genealogists. If there is a weakness on Cyndi's List, it is the many, many website links that are there. You'll be like a kid in a candy store, bedazzled and unsure where to turn next.

FamilySearch.org – As discussed earlier in this book, FamilySearch.org is one of the largest genealogy sites available, and since it is free, that makes it doubly valuable. Their holdings are immense, and include indexed versions of all the United States Censuses, extensive Military records, Church records and vital records from all over the world. They offer *Research Help* booklets that provide state-by-state and country-by-country research assistance. There are a number of databases you'll have access to – the Social Security Death index being one of the more popular indexes used by researchers.

FamilySearch.org is a window into the holdings of the Family History Library of the LDS Church. Many of their collections are online, but many more are currently only available on microfilm. You can identify microfilmed copies of family histories, county histories and so many more microfilmed documents, and then you can order these microfilms and view them at local Family History Centers (*see Chapter Three – Using the LDS Church*).

USGenWeb – The USGenWeb project (*www.usgenweb.org*) is a project envisioned by its founders that will provide access to genealogical records to fellow genealogists free of charge. Volunteers devote time and energy to identifying and making available valuable free websites. Their goal is to locate and publicize these sites for each county and state in the United States. They are well on the way to succeeding in their goal.

Once you hit the website, you'll discover the data is organized by state and then by county. The USGenWeb folks are also involved in a number of national projects, and the fruits of their labors are also available on this website.

I am currently doing research in an obscure county in south-central Missouri. I went to the USGenWeb site, clicked on Missouri (on a map of the United States), and then on Wright County. I was immediately presented with 36 links to genealogical information available for the county. Links included the 1850 through 1870 censuses for Wright County, funeral notices, obituaries, early marriage information (from the 1850s and 1860s), Civil War veterans (including company and regiment – important for genealogical research), tombstone transcriptions for seven cemeteries, and numerous other tidbits of genealogical data. All of this was great information from which I gleaned a great deal of genealogical information on my family and extended families.

The data contained on the USGenWeb project is all supplied by volunteers, so some counties across the US may have scant information available, while others have a ton of information. If the county you're most interested in is a little thin on information, perhaps it provides a volunteer opportunity for you. What? You live nowhere near that county? Well, you could still get involved – transcribing censuses for that county, or even for particular townships, for example, could be done from the comfort of your own home.

Ancestral Findings – *Ancestralfindings.com* is a great free website that serves as a gateway to a number of free genealogical websites. This website also provides articles on various aspects of research to help you learn more and overcome those obstacles that seem to be cropping up in your way. Recently, articles on the website covered such diverse topics as the Hamburg passenger lists, Jewish research, Native American research, immigration records, researching tax records, Welsh research, and so on.

One section of Ancestral Findings provides a state-by-state directory of genealogical resources that are available. Some of the links take you to fee-based sites, while many others take you to free sites.

Another section of the website provides free downloadable research forms, including family group sheets, research extraction logs, correspondence records, pedigree charts, census templates, etc.

Subscription & Free Research Services Checklist

____ Determine whether you are able to get the information you are seeking via free research sites.

____ If you determine that one of the subscription services may provide access to more records that you need for your research, consider first signing up for a free one- or two-week trial.

____ Put the software you choose for a free trial through a rigorous test – see what records it has available, and whether they meet your needs.

____ Select the subscription service that best meets your needs and fits your budget.

____ Determine whether or not you need more than one subscription service, based on your research needs.

17. BOOK LIST FOR SERIOUS GENEALOGISTS

"That book was made by Mr. Mark Twain and he told the truth, mainly."
— Tom Sawyer on Mark Twain's book *The Adventures of Tom Sawyer*

"I declare after all there is no enjoyment like reading! How much sooner one tires of anything than of a book!" — Jane Austen

As you are aware, there are many, many books written about genealogical research. Below are the books I think need to be in every genealogist's library. Some are somewhat pricey (like *The Source*), so you may have to wait awhile to pick them up. However, in the meantime you may be able to make use of them at your local library's genealogical section.

1. *Secrets of Tracing Your Ancestors*, 6th edition, W. Daniel Quillen (Cold Spring Press, 2013). Okay, so this may be a little self-serving, but seriously, in addition to being a genealogy guide for beginners, you will find some advanced tidbits in this book that will help you overcome some of those stumbling blocks you have come across in your research. It includes in-depth research techniques, for example, for numerous areas of ethnic research, including African American, Native American, Jewish, Hispanic, German and Irish research. Here's what one reviewer said about my book:

> "Shows those new to the hobby how to begin, while showing seasoned family historians some new tricks ... with passion and a touch of humor." – *Family Chronicle Magazine*

2. *Quillen's Essentials of Genealogy* series, Cold Spring Press. In addition to *Secrets of Tracing Your Ancestors* and this book, I have written a new series of genealogy books that offer a more focused dive into various genealogy topics. Currently, the series consists of the following books:

- Mastering Online Genealogy
- Mastering Immigration & Naturalization Records
- Mastering Census & Military Records
- Tracing Your European Roots
- Tracing Your Irish and British Roots
- Mastering Family, Library & Church Records

As with *Secrets* and *Troubleshooters*, I use members of my family to assist in illustrating various research methods, strategies and tactics. I am proud to say that all of the books in this series are now in their second or third editions.

3. *The Source – A Guidebook to American Genealogy*, Loretto Dennis Szucs and Sandra Hargreaves Luebking (editors), 3rd Edition, (Ancestry Publishing, 2006). When I think of this book, I think of the word Encyclopedic. It is a wonderful resource for genealogists, and covers most of the critical research areas in US genealogy, including censuses, tax and voting records, land records, immigration and naturalization, court house research, church records, newspapers, vital records, probate, and many other topics.

I have yet to come up empty-handed on a topic that I went to The Source to discover answers. It provides volumes of information on a score of topics.

4. *Red Book: American State, County & Town Sources*, Alice Eichholz (editor), (Ancestry Publishing, 2004). The Red Book is a great book to have handy when your research leads you to those dusty courthouses that serve as a repository of many of the nations genealogical records. It provides state-by-state information on where to go to find information on censuses, land records, cemetery records, court, tax and probate records, military records, newspapers and periodicals. It addresses immigration and naturalization records, and where you will most likely be able to find those records in each state. It provides contact information for each county courthouse and in some cases, the periods for which each courthouse has records (for example, the Las Animas County, Colorado Courthouse has birth records from 1893 to 1896, marriage records from 1868 and death records from 1893 to 1904).

If you are doing research in the United States and need to delve a little deeper than many online records will allow you, this is an invaluable book.

5. *State Census Records*, Lainhart, Ann S. (Baltimore Genealogical Publishing Co, 1992). Ann Lainhart's book on state censuses has been a great boon to me in my genealogy research. I have several families that I might not have found were it not for state censuses, and Ms. Lainhart's book helped me in my research.

State Census Records provides state-by-state information on the various non-US federal censuses that were conducted in the states through the years, and tells you how and where to access these census records. Some are county censuses, others are tax payer censuses, agriculture and livestock censuses, etc. For example, Ms. Lainhart points out that Schuyler County, Illinois, where one of my direct ancestors is from, conducted a special census in 1880, in addition to the federal census which was also conducted that year. The special census only provided the names of the heads of household, and the ages and sex of others in the household, similar to the way the US census was conducted prior to 1850. This special census, however, also provides information about the number of deaf, dumb, blind, insane and livestock. She then tells me where I can get copies of the special census, and the cost to do so.

6. *How to Do Everything with Your Genealogy*, George Morgan, (McGraw Hill, 2012). This great book covers a number of genealogical research topics from beginning through relatively advanced research. Various research strategies are discussed, and you'll be able to determine what may be the best strategy for that particularly difficult and elusive ancestor that stays just out of your reach.

Mr. Morgan takes you beyond the shores of the US, directing you to research sources in the UK, Canada and even Australia.

7. *They Came in Ships: A Guide to Finding Your Immigrant Ancestors' Arrival Record*, John A. Coletta, (Ancestry.com, 1989). This is an excellent source if you have gotten to the shores of the US and need to learn more about those immigrant ancestors of yours. Mr. Coletta helps you understand the immigration processes, and provides in-depth information on how to locate those valuable passenger lists that often contain so much genealogical information. Several chapters focus specifically on how to gain access to sometimes hard-to-find passenger lists. Ports of arrival are also covered in some depth.

8. *They Became Americans: Finding Naturalization Records and Ethnic Origins*, Loretto Dennis Szucs, (Ancestry.com, 1998). Ms. Szucs lands her second book on my list of top books for genealogists with this book about finding naturalization records. She describes the naturalization process, and points you to those places you will most likely find immigration and naturalization papers. She also discusses what your options are if the records do not appear to exist.

9. *Courthouse Research for Family Historians: Your Guide to Genealogical Treasures*, Christine Rose, (CR Publications, 2004). Ms. Rose has performed a great service to all of us who will one day need to visit courthouses to unearth the records of one or more of our ancestors. Hand-in-hand with the Red Book (mentioned above), this book is an excellent source for learning more about the treasures that are locked behind courthouse doors, and how to gain access to those records. Ms. Rose takes you a few steps further by discussing the available records and the best way to use them to maximize their genealogical value.

The author provides several valuable pointers about how to prepare for a visit to a courthouse, then discusses how to work with clerks to gain access to those documents you wish to see.

10. *The Census Book: A Genealogist's Guide to Federal Census Facts, Schedules and Indexes*, William Dollarhide, (Heritage Quest publishing, 1999). This is a great book that will help you understand the censuses and understand how to get more out of them. It provides a wealth of information about the census process and lots of interesting tidbits about these important documents.

11. Family Chronicle Magazine, *www.familychronicle.com*. Okay – so this isn't really a book, but it is a valuable resource for anyone who is working on genealogy. $25 a year gets you a great resource, delivered to your door every other month. I have found the articles to be top shelf in their quality, and each edition that comes has fresh new information that is well worth your time as a genealogist. Back issues are available on CD for $15 per year (each CD contains six issues).

Family Chronicle magazine is the only genealogy magazine that gets my subscription.

12. I would suggest that you get a good **atlas** of the United States (or the country you are researching). As you are researching a family and they disappear from the records in which you expect to find them, it is helpful to look at a map and see what other counties / town / or states they may have gone to. Many of my Quillen ancestors lived and died in the southwest corner of Virginia. However, looking at a map of that area tells me that they all lived very close to the state boundaries of four states – Virginia, Kentucky, North Carolina and Tennessee. When I couldn't find records in one state, I would just slip over the line into one of these other nearby states and was often rewarded for my knowledge of geography.

13. A good **gazetteer** (place / name dictionary) for the area you are doing your research and covering the timeframe you are doing research for is a must. For years I had a hard time locating Denver, Oklahoma. Then perusing a gazetteer from the time period of my grandmother's birth helped me locate it – at the bottom of Lake Thunderbird near Norman, Oklahoma!

Book List for Serious Genealogists Checklist

____ Determine what your research needs are.

____ Based on your research needs, select books that will meet those needs.

____ Determine whether you should purchase the books, or whether your local library has them, either in their general section or their reference section.

____ Determine whether you can afford to purchase one or more of the books that best meet your research needs.

18. TAKING YOUR RESEARCH ON THE ROAD

"On the road again — just can't wait to get on the road again."
– Willie Nelson

As many records are out in cyberspace online, sometimes you hit the proverbial brick wall and just can't seem to go any further. You reason that maybe it's time to hop in the car and go walk the ground of your ancestor, looking for clues. Before you fuel up the ol' buggy and head out on a genealogical road trip, there are a number of things you should do before you hit the road.

First and foremost, you need a plan. Where are you going? What specific information are you looking for? What resources are available – either in the place you are going, or nearby, that will help you in your research? Following are some steps and thoughts about taking your research on the road.

What Are You Trying to Accomplish?
Before leaving on a research trip, you should know exactly what you are trying to accomplish. If you don't, you may become distracted and follow genealogical threads that, while interesting, may serve only to waste your time and cause you to run out of time before you have found the information for which you were looking.

A good example will help. I was looking for my second great grandfather's grave, because I wanted to find and photograph his headstone. I was hoping it might provide me an exact birth date, which had so far successfully eluded me. Yes, I know that his tombstone inscription would be a secondary source for his birth date, but so far I had nothing better.

I decided to follow my own advice and familiarize myself with other family members, so that when I found his grave I could check to see if nearby graves were those of family members. For some reason, I remembered the maiden name of his son's wife – Coday. As I was searching through various cemeteries, I came across a whole nest of Codays! I wanted to collect all the information I could, knowing it would be awhile before I could get back to this particular cemetery. Sad to say, hours went by as I collected all this information on a line that barely connected to mine. In the meantime, I wasted precious hours which I might have spent looking for my second great grandfather's grave while I had gone to the time and expense of the trip. I did not find his grave on that trip, because I ran out of time on a tangential line.

So – identify what it is you are trying to accomplish with your research trip. You may want to list a number of activities. If you're going to drive hundreds of miles, or fly thousands of miles and rent a car, you want to maximize the value of your trip. If you identify more than one goal, you may want to prioritize your list. Maybe numbers 1, 2 and 3 are interchangeable, but maybe they all take clear priority over the other items on your list. Here's a prioritized list I came up with for a subsequent trip to find my second great grandfather's (Jonathan Baldwin Quillen) grave:

1. Find his grave
2. Find his will
3. Find when he came to the Hartville, MO area (land records)
4. Look for any other records on Quillens living and dying in the area
5. Look for any records for any lines that married into (or out of) the Quillen line:
   a. Henslee / Hensley (JB's sister Lizzie married a Henslee)
   b. Coday (JB's son Emmett married Susie Coday)
   c. Burke (JB's wife's maiden name)

Now, as I make my trip to Wright County, Missouri (a mere 15 hours by car), I have a better idea of what I want to accomplish, and in what order. I am less likely to be distracted by other tangential or lower priority tasks.

Are Online Resources Available?

Again, before you go to the time and expense of taking a road trip, determine whether there are online resources available that will enable you to further your research without having to take the trip? While road trips are exciting, even enjoyable, save your time and money for trips that will yield information that can only be gotten by being there in person.

For example, as pointed out earlier in this book, I was interested in learning about and photographing my third great grandfather's tombstone. I could have made a trip from Denver to Schuyler County, Illinois, and I may have been able to locate his cemetery and see and photograph his tombstone. But instead, I was able to find his tombstone on *www.findagrave.com*. Was I cheated out of a trip? I suppose that's one way of looking at it. But perhaps I also made it possible to find other things with my research trip; other records that might provide documents of greater genealogical value, records that could only be found by making the trip in person. If I wish to visit his grave while I am there, that is certainly an option. But it may be way down on the prioritized list of things to accomplish. Perhaps a visit to the local county courthouse will help me locate his will or other papers that may shed more light on the family.

Locate In-State Resources Before You Go

Okay – you've got your prioritized list, you've checked out all the possible online sources and have found none – are you ready to jump in the car now? Almost, but not quite. Before you leave, it is worth your while to locate each of the places you are going to visit. Locate them on a map, and if they are a government office, make sure you know the hours they are open. Let's use my search for my second great grandfather as an example.

Jonathan Baldwin Quillen settled in Hartville, Missouri sometime before his death there in 1920. A son of his was married there in 1898, so it could have been as early as that. According to an obituary I have, he was buried in Curtis cemetery eight miles south of Hartville, Missouri.

Pretty easy, huh? Well, my first stumbling block is that there is no Curtis cemetery listed in Wright County, Missouri. However, I do find a Curtis Church about 7 miles south of Hartville, near Norwood. Perhaps they had a small cemetery there?

Before heading out to Missouri (only 820 miles from my home) I will exhaust all possibilities in finding the pastor for the Curtis Church in Norwood, and see if s/he can confirm there is a cemetery associated with the Church. If not, perhaps he or she can tell me where Curtis cemetery is.

Next, I'll find out where the courthouse is for Wright County, Missouri. If I am going to stop in there to see if I can view death certificates, wills, etc.

I should know where it is. With a little effort on the Internet, I discovered that Hartville is where the County Courthouse is for Wright County – that happens to be convenient, since that's where my the object of my search lived for the last several decades of his life.

A phone call to the Wright County courthouse will enable me to find out what records they have available, and whether I will be able to have access to them. In some counties and states, records have been moved to the State Archives, or sometimes the State Library. The clerks at the courthouse will be able to tell me if the records have been moved, and where. In this case, it was easy to find information on the State Archives and Library – they are in the Appendix of this book! (Both are located in Jefferson City, MO). A quick check on Mapquest tells me that Jefferson City is about two hours north of Hartville. Not exactly convenient, but I will find out which records the county courthouse has. If they are in Jefferson City, then I may work that into my trip plans.

When you call for days and hours of operation, you may want to also determine whether they will be open on the day(s) you plan to be visiting them. Not living in the state in which you are doing research may result in arriving on a day when the county courthouse or other government offices are closed. For example, if you show up at a county courthouse in Utah on July 24th, you may find the parking lot empty and the doors closed in observance of Pioneer Day. Or Patriot's Day (the third Monday in April) in Massachusetts and Maine. Or Confederate Memorial Day in Alabama (fourth Monday in April). You get the point! Even without state holidays, some locations close for a week or two during the summer to allow employees to go on vacation, to do general cleaning / remodeling, etc. The Colorado State Archives, for example, is open on Wednesdays, but just not open to the public! It's a day for archive employees to catch up on reshelving and whatever else archive employees need to catch up on.

Don't be secretive about your visit. Let the clerk or archivist know what records you hope to see. It is possible that some records are kept at another storage facility, and must be requested ahead of time. It's possible that you will need to be accompanied by an archivist to view very old records, and if that's the case, you may need to make an appointment. I have found that records are generally more accessible to patrons in smaller locations than in state archives, state libraries or large county courthouses.

It is possible that the clerk or archivist can provide you with indexes of the available records at their location, and you can plan ahead exactly what records you want to see, and request the records ahead of time, so that they are available upon your arrival.

Finally, you may want to find out if you can photocopy records, or take digital pictures of the records you will be researching. Some organizations have very strict rules governing older records, others do not.

Gather Your Gear!

Okay – you're about ready to go. In addition to all the information you have put together above, gather all the materials you'll need: paper, notebooks, writing utensils, cell phones, computers, iPads (don't forget power cords and chargers!), etc. Check the battery on your digital camera and make sure it's fully charged, and don't forget the power cord and charger for that too.

And now you're ready to go, and climb over / bust through that genealogical brick wall that has been giving you fits for so long!

Taking Your Research on the Road Checklist

____ Before heading out on the road, determine exactly what you hope to accomplish on your research trip – be specific.

____ Exhaust all online resources before you head out on the road. Perhaps the answers you are looking for are online, and you can use your trip to further your research along your family tree by seeking information that isn't online.

____ Find out where all the in-state resources you are going to need are located – the county courthouse, where records you are liable to need are located: marriage, death, birth, wills, etc.

____ Learn the opening and closing hours of the courthouse / archives / state libraries you may be visiting. Learn what collections they have, and whether or not you will have access to them when you arrive.

____ Ask if the facility you are going to visit will be open to the public on the days you plan to be visiting. If not, you may want to reschedule your trip!

____ Find out what the organization's restrictions are on photocopying / photographing the records you are coming to see. It's good to know this ahead of time.

Additional Resources

Steven Fisher (editor), *Archival Information (How to Find It, How to Use It)*, (Greenwood Press, 2004).

Sharon DeBartalo Carmack, *The Genealogy Sourcebook*, (McGraw-Hill, 1998).

Loretto Dennis Szucs and Sandra Hargreaves Luebking (editors), *The Source – A Guidebook to American Genealogy*, 3rd Edition, (Ancestry Publishing, 2006). The Source has an extensive and very detailed chapter on Court Records.

Alice Eichholz (editor), *Red Book: American State, County & Town Sources* (Ancestry Publishing, J2004).

19. CURIOSITY AND DETECTIVE-ISM

"I seek dead people." (with apologies to The Sixth Sense!)

One of the other hats I wear is travel guide writer. When I was learning the travel writing craft, my editor once said to me: *To be a successful travel guide writer, you have to be insanely curious.* He went on to explain that I had to go beyond the obvious, to look deeper and ask more questions. "Who owned this castle?" "Why was that site selected over other sites in the area?" "Why would tourists want to stop here rather than other places?"

And so it is with genealogy: *To be a successful genealogist, you need to be insanely curious.* Look beyond the obvious. Ask questions, dig deeper and look at each source document from every possible angle. What is it telling you? What is it *not* telling you? What *might* it be telling you? Are there any hints it might be leaving to help you learn more about this particular family? Remember the will we discussed in the *Probate Records and Wills* chapter – look for all those clues that are there, and be prepared to use your best detective skills in following up on all the threads and bits and pieces of information that are there.

If you'll recall, I invited you to read over the will, and glean genealogically significant information from the will. How did you do? I got fifteen items I felt were of genealogical value. If you got fewer than that, that's okay – sometimes you just have to get in the mindset to read critically, looking for every little clue. Perhaps you did better than me; if that's the case, I definitely want to hear from you and see what I missed!

You've doubtless heard the saying, "Curiosity killed the cat, but satisfaction brought him back." I think that aptly applies to genealogical research – your curiosity will doubtless run you down many blind alleys. But when one of those blind alleys opens up into a majestic view of your ancestors – one who has been particularly elusive or a whole nest full whom you knew nothing about – the satisfaction and joy is incredible!

Remember back in the *Immigration and Naturalization Records* chapter, when we were tracking down the Peoples family? The mother and several children had emigrated from Scotland to America, coming through Ellis Island. The husband of the family, William, had apparently arrived before they did. Further research revealed that he had arrived in Philadelphia, and that his cousin William Montgomery had paid for his ticket. Later, another Montgomery, Robert James, was one of the witnesses on his naturalization papers. Without curiosity, I might not think twice about Robert James.

But I am dying to know what his relationship is, if any, to William Montgomery, who purchased William Peoples' ticket to come to America. And how exactly is William Montgomery (and by extension, Robert James Montgomery) related to William Peoples? We know he is a cousin, but whose nephew is he? William's mother's nephew, and if so, is Montgomery her maiden name, or is it her sister's son? Or could it be Annie People's mother's nephew? So many possible threads to pick up and follow, threads that might go unresolved without a healthy dollop of curiosity and a strong detective spirit.

So now you've come to the end of this *Troubleshooter's Guide* – I hope the trip has been worth your time, and that you have found some of the information to be of value in helping you overcome some of those genealogical brick walls and blind alleys that are so common in genealogical research. I have employed these tricks of the trade in my research and have found them to work well – I hope they serve you well also.

GLOSSARY

Abstract – a term commonly used with wills and deeds, where the critical information in an original document is summarized.

Ancestors – your progenitors, those from whom you descend: parents, grandparents and on up the family tree.

Ancestral File – the LDS Church's file of more than 40 million names of individuals whose genealogical information has been recorded as families. It is accessible to all who have an interest in genealogy, regardless of religious persuasion.

Bulletin Boards – this is a place where individuals can post queries about ancestors. Others read and may (hopefully) respond to these queries, providing important genealogical information. Also called Message Boards.

Census – an enumeration of the population, usually conducted by the government. It may provide only a tabulation of numbers, but may often provide the names of everyone living in the household at the time of the census.

Database – a software program that contains information that can be searched against various categories. For example, you can query a database looking for all your ancestors who were born in North Carolina, then search the same database for all ancestors named Robert.

Daughters of the American Revolution (DAR) – a well-known genealogical society for those who can prove a connection to an ancestor who fought in the Revolutionary War.

Descendants – those who descend from an individual – their children, grandchildren, etc. Each considers this person their ancestor.

Executor – the person who is responsible for seeing that the instructions in a will are carried out. Also called a personal representative. If a woman, she may be called an executrix.

Family Group Sheet — this is a document that groups a family together under their father. Included will be a man, his wife and all of their children, along with important information about each person, such as their birth, marriage and death dates and places. It is one of the main forms used in genealogy research.

Family History – this term is often used interchangeably with genealogy. It is also used to describe a narrative account of a family, typically going beyond mere statistics and usually including stories and anecdotes of the individual family members.

Family History Centers – local genealogy libraries staffed by volunteers of the LDS Church where genealogists can access the LDS Church's vast genealogical records. They are open to any genealogist, regardless of religious affiliation. Over 4,500 Family History Centers exist around the world.

Family History Library – a large genealogical research library owned and operated by the LDS Church. Staffed by volunteers, it has an enormous amount of worldwide genealogical information that is available to anyone, regardless of religious affiliation.

Gazetteer – a dictionary for places, which gives you information about places (state, county, country, etc.).

GEDCOM - a standard software format that most genealogy software uses. If you are using a genealogy program that uses GEDCOM, you will be able to share your information with others more easily. GEDCOM is an acronym for GEnealogical Data COMmunication.

Genealogy – the number one hobby in the world. It is a fascinating, scintillating hobby that involves the search for one's ancestors.

Intestate – a person who dies without a will is said to have died intestate.

Maternal - used to describe which line of the family tree you are referring to. Your maternal grandfather is your mother's father.

Message Boards - this is a place where individuals can post queries about ancestors. Others read and may (hopefully) respond to these queries. Also called Bulletin Boards.

Moveables – a term typically found in wills, indicating possessions other than land (clothing, farm implements, livestock, money, etc.).

Parish – an ecclesiastical or governmental unit where genealogical records were often kept.

Paternal - used to describe which line of the family tree you are referring to. Your paternal grandfather is your father's father.

Pedigree Chart - this is a chart the will show at a glance what your "family tree" looks like, by showing in graphic form who your parents, grandparents, great grandparents, etc., are. A limited amount of genealogical information is included. This is an important genealogical form.

Personal events – genealogical data entered into genealogy software programs; for example: birth, marriage and death dates.

Primary Source - these are genealogy records created at the time of the event. A birth certificate that was completed at the time of a birth would be considered a primary source.

Probate – The judicial procedure that investigates and then declares a will valid after a person dies. In its narrowest definition, probate requires the presence of a will, but common usage often extends it to all work settling an estate.

Probate records – Court records representing the final disposal of a person's personal and real property after s/he dies. Probate records are a summary that provides information about the person who has died – their name, birth date, death date, individuals who received property and where they lived.

Queries – from a genealogical perspective, requests for information about a particular person or family. This might be on a message board, in a genealogical publication or via e-mail.

Secondary Source—genealogy records where information is provided much later than the event. A tombstone or death certificate would be considered a primary source for death information, but a secondary source for birth information, since it is likely that the birth information was provided many years after the person's birth occurred.

Soundex – a phonetic/numeric index for various US censuses. It combines the first letter of a surname with numbers for the next three consonants to form a Soundex entry. This is then used to locate individuals in the census (it's easier to use than it sounds!).

Testator – the maker of a will; the person whose personal and real property will be disbursed as a result of the will.

Traditions – those stories that circulate around the family about great grandfather's exploits in the gold fields of California, or war stories, or how grandma and grandpa met. Besides being interesting, these stories often provide genealogical clues that help you find information on your ancestors.

Vital Records - this term is generally used to refer to genealogical records such as birth, marriage and death information. They are also called Civil Registration or Vital Statistics.

Will – A legal document witnessed by several others that represents an individual's wishes for the disbursement of his/her property after their death. It often contains information about family members.

APPENDIX

STATE LIBRARIES & ARCHIVES
Alabama
Alabama Public Library Service, Tel. 334/213-3900, 800/723-8459 (within Alabama only), *statelibrary.alabama.gov/Content/Index.aspx*

Alabama Department of Archives and History, Tel: 334/242-4435, *www.archives. state.al.us*

Alaska
Alaska State Archives, Tel. 907/465-2700, *www.library.state.ak.us/*

Alaska State Library, Tel. 907/465-2910

Arizona
Arizona State Library, Archives & Public Records, *www.lib.az.us/*

Arkansas
Arkansas State Library, Tel. 501/682-1527, *www.asl.lib.ar.us/*

California
California State Library, *www.library.ca.gov/*

California State Archives, *www.sos.ca.gov/archives*

Colorado
Colorado State Library, Tel. 303/866-6900, *www.cde.state.co.us/cdelib*

Colorado State Archives, *www.colorado.gov/archives*

Connecticut
Connecticut State Library and Archives, Tel. 860/757-6500, *www.ctstatelibrary. org/organizational-unit/state-archives*

Delaware
Delaware State Library, *www.lib.de.us/*
Delaware Public Archives, *archives.delaware.gov*

District of Columbia
District of Columbia Archives, Tel. 202/671-1105, *os.dc.gov/service/district-columbia-archives*

Florida
Florida State Library and Archives, Tel. 850/245-6600, *dlis.dos.state.fl.us/*

Georgia
Georgia Department of Archives and History, *www.sos.georgia.gov/ARCHIVES/*

Hawaii
Hawaii State Library, *www.librarieshawaii.org*

Hawaii State Archives, Tel. 808/586-0329, *ags.hawaii.gov/archives*

Idaho
Idaho State Library, Tel. 208/334-2150, *www.lili.org/portal/index.php*

Idaho State Historical Society, Tel. 208/334-2682, *www.idahohistory.net*

Illinois
Illinois State Library, Tel. 217/785-5600, *www.cyberdriveillinois.com/departments/library/*

Illinois State Archives, *www.cyberdriveillinois.com/departments/archives/home.html*

Indiana
Indiana State Library and Archives, *statearchives.us/indiana.htm*

Iowa
Iowa State Library, *www.silo.lib.ia.us/*

State Historical Society of Iowa, *www.iowahistory.org/archives/*

Kansas
Kansas State Library, Tel. 785/296-3296, 800/432-3919, *skyways.lib.ks.us/kansas/*

Kansas State Historical Society, *www.kshs.org*

Kentucky
Kentucky State Library, Tel. 502/564-8300, *www.kdla.ky.gov/*

Louisiana
Louisiana State Library, Tel. 225/342-4923, *www.state.lib.la.us/*

Louisiana State Archives, Tel. 225/922-1000, *www.sos.la.gov/HistoricalResources/ LearnAboutTheArchives/Pages/default.aspx*

Maine
Maine State Library, Tel. 207/287-5600, *www.state.me.us/msl*

Maine State Archives, Tel. 207/287-5795, *www.state.me.us/sos/arc/*

Maryland
Maryland State Library, Tel. 410/396-5430, *www.prattlibrary.org*

Maryland State Archives, Tel. 410/260-6400, *www.mdarchives.state.md.us*

Massachusetts
Massachusetts State Library, Tel. 617/727-2590, 800/952-7403 (in state), *www. state.ma.us/lib/*

Massachusetts State Archives, *www.state.ma.us/sec/arc/arcidx.htm*

Michigan
Michigan State Library and Archives, Tel. 517/373-1580, *www.sos.la.gov/Histori-calResources/LearnAboutTheArchives/Pages/default.aspx*

Minnesota
Minnesota State Library, Tel. 681/582-8722, *mn.gov/library*

Minnesota State Historical Society, Tel. 651/296-6126, *www.mnhs.org*

Mississippi
Mississippi State Library, Tel. 800/647-7542, *www.mlc.lib.ms.us/*

Mississippi State Archives, Tel. 601/359-6850, *www.mdah.state.ms.us/*

Missouri
Missouri State Library, *www.sos.mo.gov/library/*

Missouri State Archives, *www.sos.mo.gov/archives/*

Montana
Montana State Library, Tel: 406/444-3115, *home.montanastatelibrary.org/*

Montana Historical Society, Tel. 406/444-2694, *mhs.mt.gov/*

Nebraska
Nebraska State Library/Nebraska Library Commission, Tel. 402/471-2045, *www.nlc.state.ne.us/index.html*

Nebraska State Historical Society, *www.nebraskahistory.org/*

Nevada
Nevada State Library and Archives, Tel. 775/684-3360, *nsla.nevadaculture.org/*

New Hampshire
New Hampshire State Library, Tel. 603/271-2392, *www.state.nh.us/nhsl*

New Hampshire State Archives, Tel. 603/271-2236, *sos.nh.gov/Holdings.aspx*

New Jersey
New Jersey State Library and Archives, Tel. 609/292-6274, 609/292-6274, *www.njstatelib.org/*

New Mexico
New Mexico State Library, Tel. 505/476-9700, *www.nmstatelibrary.org*

New Mexico State Records Center and Archives, Tel. 505/476-9700 Tel. 505/476-9700, *www.state.nm.us*

New York
New York State Library, Tel. 518/474-5355, *www.nysl.nysed.gov/*

New York State Archives and Records, *www.archives.nysed.gov/aindex.shtml*

North Carolina
North Carolina State Library, Tel. 919/733-3270 Tel. 919/733-3270, *statelibrary.dcr.state.nc.us/*

North Carolina Division of Archives. Tel. 919/733-3952, *www.ncdcr.gov/archives/Home.aspx*

North Dakota
North Dakota State Library, Tel. 701/328-2492, *ndsl.lib.state.nd.us/*

North Dakota State Archives, Tel. 701/328-2091, *www.state.nd.us/hist*

APPENDIX

Ohio
Ohio State Library, Tel. 614/644-7061Tel. 614/644-7061, *www.library.ohio.gov*

Ohio State Archives, *www.ohiohistory.org/resource/statearc/*

Oklahoma
Oklahoma State Library, *www.odl.state.ok.us/index.html*

Oklahoma State Archives, *www.odl.state.ok.us/oar/*

Oregon
Oregon State Library, Tel. 503/378-4243, *www.osl.state.or.us/home/admin/stlib_info.html*

Oregon State Archives, Tel. 503/373-0701, *arcweb.sos.state.or.us/banners/contactus.htm*

Pennsylvania
Pennsylvania State Library, Tel. 717/783-5950

Pennsylvania State Archives, Tel. 717/783-3281

Website for both:
www.portal.state.pa.us/portal/server.pt?open=512&mode=2&objID=2887

Rhode Island
Rhode Island State Library, *www.olis.state.ri.us/*

Rhode Island State Archives, Tel. 401/222-2353, *www.state.ri.us/archives/*

Rhode Island Historical Society, Tel. 401/331-8575, *www.rihs.org*

South Carolina
South Carolina State Library, Tel. 803/734-8666, *www.statelibrary.sc.gov/*

South Carolina Archives and History Center, Tel. 803/896-6100, *scdah.sc.gov/*

South Dakota
South Dakota State Library, Tel. 605/773-3131, *www.sdstatelibrary.com/*

South Dakota State Historical Society, Tel. 605/773-3458, *www.sdhistory.org/*

Tennessee
Tennessee State Library and Archives, Tel. 615/741-2764, *www.tennessee.gov/tsla/*

Texas
Texas State Library and Archives, Tel. 512/463-5480, *www.tsl.state.tx.us/*

Utah
Utah State Library, *library.utah.gov/*

Utah State Archives, Tel. 801/538-3012, *www.archives.state.ut.us*

Vermont
Vermont State Library, Tel. 802/828-3261, *dol.state.vt.us/*

Vermont State Archives, *vermont-archives.org/*

Virginia
Virginia State Library and Archives, Tel. 804/692-3500, *www.lva.lib.va.us/*

Washington
Washington State Library, Tel. 360/704-5200, *www.sos.wa.gov/library/*

Washington State Archives, Tel. 360/902-4151, *www.secstate.wa.gov/archives/search.aspx*

Washington, D.C.
The Library of Congress, Tel. 202/707-5000, *www.loc.gov/index.html*

West Virginia
West Virginia State Library, Tel. 304/558-2041, *www.librarycommission.wv.gov/Pages/default.aspx*

West Virginia State Archives, *www.wvculture.org/history/wvsamenu.html*

Wisconsin
Wisconsin Division of Libraries, *www.dpi.state.wi.us/dpi/dlcl/index.html*

Wisconsin State Historical Society, Tel. 608/264-6400, *www.wisconsinhistory.org/index.html*

Wyoming
Wyoming State Library, Tel. 307/777-7283, *www-wsl.state.wy.us/*

Wyoming State Archives, Tel. 307/777-7826, *wyoarchives.state.wy.us/*

STATE DEPARTMENTS OF VITAL STATISTICS

Following are the mailing addresses of each state's Department of Vital Records. Also included are the rates for birth and death certificates. Address your request to the (State Name) Department of Vital Records. Note that many states are now charging additional fees – some of them nothing short of exorbitant – if you want to order either over the phone or on the internet using your credit card (one state charges $46 to use your credit card!). So, you'll have to weigh the value of getting the certificates a little sooner vs. waiting a few more days. Most of the states listed here have unfortunately caught on to the popularity of genealogy and the resultant revenues that can be gleaned from charges for certificates. In recent years, certificate costs have risen in almost every state, some of them doubling or even tripling! Still, most are within a price range that most individuals would consider reasonable.

Many states charge a non-refundable search fee, generally equal to the cost of the certificate. The search fee usually includes the cost of the first copy of the certificate found.

Alabama, Tel. 334/206-5418, *adph.org/vitalrecords/*

Alaska, Tel. 907/465-3392, *www.hss.state.ak.us/dph/bvs/*

Arizona, Tel. 602/255-3260, *vitalrec.com/az.html*

Arkansas, Tel. 501/661-2134, *www.healthy.arkansas.gov/programsServices/certificatesVitalRecords/Pages/default.aspx*

California, Tel. 916/445-2684, *www.cdph.ca.gov/programs/CHS/Pages/default.aspx*

Colorado, Tel. 303/692-2200, *www.cdphe.state.co.us*

Connecticut, Tel. 860/509-7700, *www.dph.state.ct.us/OPPE/hpvital.htm*

Delaware, Tel. 302/739-4721, *dhss.delaware.gov/dhss/dph/ss/vitalstats.html*

Florida, Tel. 904/359-6930, *www.floridahealth.gov/certificates-and-registries/certificates/birth/index.html*

Georgia, Tel. 404/656-4750, *dph.georgia.gov/VitalRecords*

Hawaii, Tel. 808/586-4533, *health.hawaii.gov/vitalrecords/*

Idaho, Tel. 208/334-5988, *www.healthandwelfare.idaho.gov/Families/BirthDeathMarriageDivorceCertificates/tabid/82/Default.aspx*

Illinois, Tel. 217/782-6554, *www.idph.state.il.us/vitalrecords/genealogicalinfo.htm*

Indiana, Tel. 317/233-2700, *www.vitalrec.com/in.html#State*

Iowa, Tel. 515/281-4944, *www.idph.state.ia.us/apl/health_statistics.asp*

Kansas, Tel. 785/296-1400, *www.kdhe.state.ks.us/vital*

Kentucky, Tel. 502/564-4212, *chfs.ky.gov/dph/vital/*

Louisiana, Tel. 504/568-5152, *www.dhh.louisiana.gov/index.cfm/subhome/21*

Maine, Tel. 207/287-3184, *www.cdc.gov/nchs/w2w/maine.htm*

Maryland, Tel. 410/764-3038, *dhmh.maryland.gov/vsa/SitePages/Home.aspx*

Massachusetts, Tel. 785/296-1400, *www.mass.gov/eohhs/gov/departments/dph/programs/health-stats/vitals/*

Michigan, Tel. 517/335-8666, *www.michigan.gov/mdch*

Minnesota, Tel. 612/676-5129, *www.health.state.mn.us/divs/chs/osr/index.html*

Mississippi, Tel. 601/576-7981, *www.msdh.state.ms.us/msdhsite/_static/31,0,109.html*

Missouri, Tel. 573/751-6400, *www.dhss.mo.gov/BirthAndDeathRecords/index.html*

Montana, Tel. 406/444-2685, *www.dphhs.mt.gov/certificates/ordercertificates.shtml*

Nebraska, Tel. 402/471-2871, *dhhs.ne.gov/publichealth/pages/vital_records.aspx*

Nevada, Tel. 800/992-0900, *health.nv.gov/VS.htm*

New Hampshire, Tel. 603/271-4650, *www.sos.nh.gov/vitalrecords/ELIGIBILITY.html*

New Jersey, Tel. 609/292-4087, *www.state.nj.us/health/vital/gen.shtml*

New Mexico, Tel. 505/827-0121, *www.vitalrecordsnm.org/birth.shtml*

New York, Tel. 518/474-3077, *www.health.state.ny.us/vital_records/*

North Carolina, Tel. 919/733-3526, *vitalrecords.nc.gov/*

North Dakota, Tel. 701/328-2360, *ndhealth.gov/vital/*

Ohio, Tel. 614/466-2531, *www.odh.ohio.gov/vs*

Oklahoma, *www.ok.gov/health/Birth_and_Death_Certificates/index.html*

Oregon, Tel. 503/731-4095, *egov.oregon.gov/DHS/ph/chs/order/faqs.shtml#rec-cost*

Pennsylvania, Tel. 724/656-3100, *www.dsf.health.state.pa.us/health/cwp/view.asp? a=168&Q=229939&healthRNavrad2F756=|#*

Rhode Island, Tel. 401/222-2811, *www.health.state.ri.us/chic/vital/index.php*

South Carolina, Tel. 803/898-3432, *www.scdhec.net/vr/*

South Dakota, Tel. 605/773-4961, *www.state.sd.us/doh/VitalRec/index.htm*

Tennessee, Tel. 615/741-1763, *health.state.tn.us/vr/*

Texas, Tel. 512/458-7111, *www.dshs.state.tx.us/VS/reqproc/certified_copy.shtm*

Utah, Tel. 801/536-6105, *health.utah.gov/vitalrecords/*

Vermont, Tel. 802/863-7275, *healthvermont.gov/research/records/vital_records.aspx*

Virginia, Tel. 804/662-6200, *www.vdh.state.va.us/vitalrec/*

Washington, Tel. 360/236-4300, *www.doh.wa.gov/EHSPHL/CHS/cert.htm*

Washington D.C., Tel. 202/671-5000, *doh.dc.gov/services/wic/index.shtm*

West Virginia, Tel. 304/558-2931, *www.wvdhhr.org/bph/hsc/vital/*

Wisconsin, Tel. 608/266-1371, *www.dhfs.state.wi.us/VitalRecords*

Wyoming, Tel. 307/777-7591, *health.wyo.gov/rfhd/vital_records/index.html*

NATIONAL ARCHIVES LOCATIONS

There are fourteen locations of the National Archives geographically dispersed around the United States. Each contains a treasure trove of genealogical information, including all the US Censuses that are available for the public to view. Following are their locations:

Alaska, Tel. 907/271-2441, E-mail: alaska.archives@nara.gov, *www.archives.gov/ pacific-alaska/anchorage/index.html*

California, Tel. 949/360-2641, E-mail: laguna.archives@nara.gov, *www.archives. gov/pacific/laguna/index.html*
or
Tel. 650/876-9009, E-mail: sanbruno.archives@nara.gov, *www.archives.gov/san-francisco/*

Colorado. Tel. 303/236-0806, E-mail: denver.archives@nara.gov, *www.archives. gov/denver/*

Georgia, Tel. 404/763-7474, E-mail: atlanta.center@nara.gov, www.archives.gov/ southeast/index.html

Illinois, Tel. 773/581-7816, E-mail: chicago.archives@nara.gov, *www.archives. gov/frc/chicago/*

Massachusetts, Tel. 781/647-8104, 866/406-2379, E-mail: waltham.center@nara. gov, *www.archives.gov/northeast/boston/*
or
Tel. 413/445-6885, E-mail: archives@pittsfield.nara.gov, *www.archives.gov/north-east/boston/*

Missouri, Tel. 816/926-6920, E-mail: kansascity.archives@nara.gov, *www.archives. gov/kansas-city*

New York, Tel. 212/337-1300, E-mail: newyork.archives@nara.gov, *www.archives. gov/nyc/*

Pennsylvania, Tel. 215/597-3000, E-mail: philadelphia.archives@nara.gov, *www. archives.gov/philadelphia/*

Texas, Tel. 817/334-5525, ext. 243, E-mail: ftworth.archives@nara.gov, *www. archives.gov/fort-worth/*

Washington, Tel. 206/526-6501, E-mail: seattle.archives@nara.gov, *www.archives. gov/seattle/*

Washington, D.C., Tel. 866/272-6272, *www.archives.gov/*

Table Index – Choose the Table that applies to the year you are seeking

2000	2001	2002	2003	2004	2005	2006	2007	2008	2009	2010
2000 - N	2001 - B	2002 - C	2003 - D	2004 - E	2005 - G	2006 - A	2007 - B	2008 - J	2009 - E	2010 - F
1990 - B	1991 - C	1992 - K	1993 - F	1994 - G	1995 - A	1996 - I	1997 - D	1998 - E	1999 - F	2000 - G
1980 - J	1981 - E	1982 - F	1983 - G	1984 - H	1985 - C	1986 - D	1987 - E	1988 - M	1989 - A	1990 - I
1970 - E	1971 - F	1972 - N	1973 - B	1974 - C	1975 - D	1976 - L	1977 - G	1978 - A	1979 - B	1980 - J
1960 - M	1961 - A	1962 - B	1963 - C	1964 - K	1965 - F	1966 - G	1967 - A	1968 - I	1969 - D	1970 - L
1950 - A	1951 - B	1952 - J	1953 - E	1954 - F	1955 - G	1956 - H	1957 - C	1958 - D	1959 - E	1960 - M
1940 - I	1941 - D	1942 - E	1943 - F	1944 - N	1945 - B	1946 - C	1947 - D	1948 - L	1949 - G	1950 - A
1930 - D	1931 - E	1932 - M	1933 - A	1934 - B	1935 - C	1936 - K	1937 - F	1938 - G	1939 - A	1940 - B
1920 - L	1921 - G	1922 - A	1923 - B	1924 - J	1925 - E	1926 - F	1927 - G	1928 - H	1929 - C	1930 - D
1910 - G	1911 - A	1912 - I	1913 - D	1914 - E	1915 - F	1916 - M	1917 - B	1918 - C	1919 - D	1920 - F
1900 - B	1901 - C	1902 - D	1903 - E	1904 - M	1905 - A	1906 - B	1907 - C	1908 - K	1909 - F	1910 - G
1890 - D	1891 - S	1892 - M	1893 - A	1894 - B	1895 - C	1896 - K	1897 - F	1898 - G	1899 - A	1900 - H
1880 - L	1881 - G	1882 - A	1883 - B	1884 - J	1885 - E	1886 - F	1887 - G	1888 - H	1889 - C	1890 - J
1870 - G	1871 - A	1872 - I	1873 - D	1874 - E	1875 - F	1876 - N	1877 - B	1878 - C	1879 - D	1880 - F
1860 - H	1861 - C	1862 - D	1863 - E	1864 - M	1865 - A	1866 - B	1867 - C	1868 - K	1869 - F	1870 - G
1850 - C	1851 - D	1852 - L	1853 - G	1854 - A	1855 - B	1856 - J	1857 - E	1858 - F	1859 - G	1860 - H
1840 - K	1841 - F	1842 - G	1843 - A	1844 - I	1845 - D	1846 - E	1847 - F	1848 - N	1849 - B	1850 - I
1830 - F	1831 - G	1832 - H	1833 - C	1834 - D	1835 - E	1836 - M	1837 - A	1838 - B	1839 - C	1840 - K
1820 - N	1821 - B	1822 - C	1823 - D	1824 - L	1825 - G	1826 - A	1827 - B	1828 - J	1829 - E	1830 - L
1810 - B	1811 - C	1812 - K	1813 - F	1814 - G	1815 - A	1816 - I	1817 - D	1818 - E	1819 - F	1820 - G
1800 - D	1801 - E	1802 - F	1803 - G	1804 - H	1805 - C	1806 - D	1807 - E	1808 - M	1809 - B	1810 - H
1790 - F	1791 - G	1792 - H	1793 - C	1794 - D	1795 - E	1796 - M	1797 - A	1798 - B	1799 - C	1800 - J
1780 - N	1781 - B	1782 - C	1783 - D	1784 - L	1785 - G	1786 - A	1787 - B	1788 - J	1789 - E	1790 - F
1770 - B	1771 - C	1772 - K	1773 - F	1774 - G	1775 - A	1776 - I	1777 - D	1778 - E	1779 - F	1780 - N
1760 - J	1761 - E	1762 - F	1763 - G	1764 - H	1765 - C	1766 - D	1767 - E	1768 - M	1769 - A	1770 - H
1750 - E	1751 - F	1752 - G	1753 - B	1754 - C	1755 - D	1756 - L	1757 - G	1758 - A	1759 - B	1760 - D
1740 - F	1741 - A	1742 - B	1743 - C	1744 - K	1745 - F	1746 - G	1747 - A	1748 - I	1749 - D	1750 - E

DAYS OF THE WEEK CALENDARS

TABLE A

January
S	M	T	W	T	F	S
1	2	3	4	5	6	7
8	9	10	11	12	13	14
15	16	17	18	19	20	21
22	23	24	25	26	27	28
29	30	31				

February
S	M	T	W	T	F	S
			1	2	3	4
5	6	7	8	9	10	11
12	13	14	15	16	17	18
19	20	21	22	23	24	25
26	27	28				

March
S	M	T	W	T	F	S
			1	2	3	4
5	6	7	8	9	10	11
12	13	14	15	16	17	18
19	20	21	22	23	24	25
26	27	28	29	30	31	

April
S	M	T	W	T	F	S
						1
2	3	4	5	6	7	8
9	10	11	12	13	14	15
16	17	18	19	20	21	22
23	24	25	26	27	28	29
30						

May
S	M	T	W	T	F	S
	1	2	3	4	5	6
7	8	9	10	11	12	13
14	15	16	17	18	19	20
21	22	23	24	25	26	27
28	29	30	31			

June
S	M	T	W	T	F	S
				1	2	3
4	5	6	7	8	9	10
11	12	13	14	15	16	17
18	19	20	21	22	23	24
25	26	27	28	29	30	

July
S	M	T	W	T	F	S
						1
2	3	4	5	6	7	8
9	10	11	12	13	14	15
16	17	18	19	20	21	22
23	24	25	26	27	28	29
30	31					

August
S	M	T	W	T	F	S
		1	2	3	4	5
6	7	8	9	10	11	12
13	14	15	16	17	18	19
20	21	22	23	24	25	26
27	28	29	30	31		

September
S	M	T	W	T	F	S
					1	2
3	4	5	6	7	8	9
10	11	12	13	14	15	16
17	18	19	20	21	22	23
24	25	26	27	28	29	30

October
S	M	T	W	T	F	S
1	2	3	4	5	6	7
8	9	10	11	12	13	14
15	16	17	18	19	20	21
22	23	24	25	26	27	28
29	30	31				

November
S	M	T	W	T	F	S
			1	2	3	4
5	6	7	8	9	10	11
12	13	14	15	16	17	18
19	20	21	22	23	24	25
26	27	28	29	30		

December
S	M	T	W	T	F	S
					1	2
3	4	5	6	7	8	9
10	11	12	13	14	15	16
17	18	19	20	21	22	23
24	25	26	27	28	29	30
31						

TABLE B

January
S	M	T	W	T	F	S
	1	2	3	4	5	6
7	8	9	10	11	12	13
14	15	16	17	18	19	20
21	22	23	24	25	26	27
28	29	30	31			

February
S	M	T	W	T	F	S
				1	2	3
4	5	6	7	8	9	10
11	12	13	14	15	16	17
18	19	20	21	22	23	24
25	26	27	28			

March
S	M	T	W	T	F	S
				1	2	3
4	5	6	7	8	9	10
11	12	13	14	15	16	17
18	19	20	21	22	23	24
25	26	27	28	29	30	31

April
S	M	T	W	T	F	S
1	2	3	4	5	6	7
8	9	10	11	12	13	14
15	16	17	18	19	20	21
22	23	24	25	26	27	28
29	30					

May
S	M	T	W	T	F	S
		1	2	3	4	5
6	7	8	9	10	11	12
13	14	15	16	17	18	19
20	21	22	23	24	25	26
27	28	29	30	31		

June
S	M	T	W	T	F	S
					1	2
3	4	5	6	7	8	9
10	11	12	13	14	15	16
17	18	19	20	21	22	23
24	25	26	27	28	29	30

July
S	M	T	W	T	F	S
1	2	3	4	5	6	7
8	9	10	11	12	13	14
15	16	17	18	19	20	21
22	23	24	25	26	27	28
29	30	31				

August
S	M	T	W	T	F	S
			1	2	3	4
5	6	7	8	9	10	11
12	13	14	15	16	17	18
19	20	21	22	23	24	25
26	27	28	29	30	31	

September
S	M	T	W	T	F	S
						1
2	3	4	5	6	7	8
9	10	11	12	13	14	15
16	17	18	19	20	21	22
23	24	25	26	27	28	29
30						

October
S	M	T	W	T	F	S
	1	2	3	4	5	6
7	8	9	10	11	12	13
14	15	16	17	18	19	20
21	22	23	24	25	26	27
28	29	30	31			

November
S	M	T	W	T	F	S
				1	2	3
4	5	6	7	8	9	10
11	12	13	14	15	16	17
18	19	20	21	22	23	24
25	26	27	28	29	30	

December
S	M	T	W	T	F	S
						1
2	3	4	5	6	7	8
9	10	11	12	13	14	15
16	17	18	19	20	21	22
23	24	25	26	27	28	29
30	31					

TABLE C

```
         January                    February                     March
 S  M  T  W  T  F  S        S  M  T  W  T  F  S         S  M  T  W  T  F  S
          1  2  3  4  5                       1  2                       1  2
 6  7  8  9 10 11 12        3  4  5  6  7  8  9         3  4  5  6  7  8  9
13 14 15 16 17 18 19       10 11 12 13 14 15 16        10 11 12 13 14 15 16
20 21 22 23 24 25 26       17 18 19 20 21 22 23        17 18 19 20 21 22 23
27 28 29 30 31             24 25 26 27 28              24 25 26 27 28 29 30
                                                       31

          April                      May                        June
 S  M  T  W  T  F  S        S  M  T  W  T  F  S         S  M  T  W  T  F  S
    1  2  3  4  5  6                 1  2  3  4                             1
 7  8  9 10 11 12 13        5  6  7  8  9 10 11         2  3  4  5  6  7  8
14 15 16 17 18 19 20       12 13 14 15 16 17 18         9 10 11 12 13 14 15
21 22 23 24 25 26 27       19 20 21 22 23 24 25        16 17 18 19 20 21 22
28 29 30                   26 27 28 29 30 31           23 24 25 26 27 28 29
                                                       30

          July                      August                    September
 S  M  T  W  T  F  S        S  M  T  W  T  F  S         S  M  T  W  T  F  S
    1  2  3  4  5  6                    1  2  3         1  2  3  4  5  6  7
 7  8  9 10 11 12 13        4  5  6  7  8  9 10         8  9 10 11 12 13 14
14 15 16 17 18 19 20       11 12 13 14 15 16 17        15 16 17 18 19 20 21
21 22 23 24 25 26 27       18 19 20 21 22 23 24        22 23 24 25 26 27 28
28 29 30 31                25 26 27 28 29 30 31        29 30

         October                   November                    December
 S  M  T  W  T  F  S        S  M  T  W  T  F  S         S  M  T  W  T  F  S
       1  2  3  4  5                          1  2      1  2  3  4  5  6  7
 6  7  8  9 10 11 12        3  4  5  6  7  8  9         8  9 10 11 12 13 14
13 14 15 16 17 18 19       10 11 12 13 14 15 16        15 16 17 18 19 20 21
20 21 22 23 24 25 26       17 18 19 20 21 22 23        22 23 24 25 26 27 28
27 28 29 30 31             24 25 26 27 28 29 30        29 30 31
```

TABLE D

```
         January                    February                     March
 S  M  T  W  T  F  S        S  M  T  W  T  F  S         S  M  T  W  T  F  S
          1  2  3  4                          1                           1
 5  6  7  8  9 10 11        2  3  4  5  6  7  8         2  3  4  5  6  7  8
12 13 14 15 16 17 18        9 10 11 12 13 14 15         9 10 11 12 13 14 15
19 20 21 22 23 24 25       16 17 18 19 20 21 22        16 17 18 19 20 21 22
26 27 28 29 30 31          23 24 25 26 27 28           23 24 25 26 27 28 29
                                                       30 31

          April                      May                        June
 S  M  T  W  T  F  S        S  M  T  W  T  F  S         S  M  T  W  T  F  S
       1  2  3  4  5                    1  2  3         1  2  3  4  5  6  7
 6  7  8  9 10 11 12        4  5  6  7  8  9 10         8  9 10 11 12 13 14
13 14 15 16 17 18 19       11 12 13 14 15 16 17        15 16 17 18 19 20 21
20 21 22 23 24 25 26       18 19 20 21 22 23 24        22 23 24 25 26 27 28
27 28 29 30                25 26 27 28 29 30 31        29 30

          July                      August                    September
 S  M  T  W  T  F  S        S  M  T  W  T  F  S         S  M  T  W  T  F  S
          1  2  3  4  5                       1  2      1  2  3  4  5  6
 6  7  8  9 10 11 12        3  4  5  6  7  8  9         7  8  9 10 11 12 13
13 14 15 16 17 18 19       10 11 12 13 14 15 16        14 15 16 17 18 19 20
20 21 22 23 24 25 26       17 18 19 20 21 22 23        21 22 23 24 25 26 27
27 28 29 30 31             24 25 26 27 28 29 30        28 29 30
                           31

         October                   November                    December
 S  M  T  W  T  F  S        S  M  T  W  T  F  S         S  M  T  W  T  F  S
          1  2  3  4                          1         1  2  3  4  5  6
 5  6  7  8  9 10 11        2  3  4  5  6  7  8         7  8  9 10 11 12 13
12 13 14 15 16 17 18        9 10 11 12 13 14 15        14 15 16 17 18 19 20
19 20 21 22 23 24 25       16 17 18 19 20 21 22        21 22 23 24 25 26 27
26 27 28 29 30 31          23 24 25 26 27 28 29        28 29 30 31
                           30
```

DAYS OF THE WEEK CALENDARS

TABLE E

January
S	M	T	W	T	F	S
				1	2	3
4	5	6	7	8	9	10
11	12	13	14	15	16	17
18	19	20	21	22	23	24
25	26	27	28	29	30	31

February
S	M	T	W	T	F	S
1	2	3	4	5	6	7
8	9	10	11	12	13	14
15	16	17	18	19	20	21
22	23	24	25	26	27	28

March
S	M	T	W	T	F	S
1	2	3	4	5	6	7
8	9	10	11	12	13	14
15	16	17	18	19	20	21
22	23	24	25	26	27	28
29	30	31				

April
S	M	T	W	T	F	S
			1	2	3	4
5	6	7	8	9	10	11
12	13	14	15	16	17	18
19	20	21	22	23	24	25
26	27	28	29	30		

May
S	M	T	W	T	F	S
					1	2
3	4	5	6	7	8	9
10	11	12	13	14	15	16
17	18	19	20	21	22	23
24	25	26	27	28	29	30
31						

June
S	M	T	W	T	F	S
	1	2	3	4	5	6
7	8	9	10	11	12	13
14	15	16	17	18	19	20
21	22	23	24	25	26	27
28	29	30				

July
S	M	T	W	T	F	S
			1	2	3	4
5	6	7	8	9	10	11
12	13	14	15	16	17	18
19	20	21	22	23	24	25
26	27	28	29	30	31	

August
S	M	T	W	T	F	S
						1
2	3	4	5	6	7	8
9	10	11	12	13	14	15
16	17	18	19	20	21	22
23	24	25	26	27	28	29
30	31					

September
S	M	T	W	T	F	S
		1	2	3	4	5
6	7	8	9	10	11	12
13	14	15	16	17	18	19
20	21	22	23	24	25	26
27	28	29	30			

October
S	M	T	W	T	F	S
				1	2	3
4	5	6	7	8	9	10
11	12	13	14	15	16	17
18	19	20	21	22	23	24
25	26	27	28	29	30	31

November
S	M	T	W	T	F	S
1	2	3	4	5	6	7
8	9	10	11	12	13	14
15	16	17	18	19	20	21
22	23	24	25	26	27	28
29	30					

December
S	M	T	W	T	F	S
		1	2	3	4	5
6	7	8	9	10	11	12
13	14	15	16	17	18	19
20	21	22	23	24	25	26
27	28	29	30	31		

TABLE F

January
S	M	T	W	T	F	S
					1	2
3	4	5	6	7	8	9
10	11	12	13	14	15	16
17	18	19	20	21	22	23
24	25	26	27	28	29	30
31						

February
S	M	T	W	T	F	S
	1	2	3	4	5	6
7	8	9	10	11	12	13
14	15	16	17	18	19	20
21	22	23	24	25	26	27
28						

March
S	M	T	W	T	F	S
	1	2	3	4	5	6
7	8	9	10	11	12	13
14	15	16	17	18	19	20
21	22	23	24	25	26	27
28	29	30	31			

April
S	M	T	W	T	F	S
				1	2	3
4	5	6	7	8	9	10
11	12	13	14	15	16	17
18	19	20	21	22	23	24
25	26	27	28	29	30	

May
S	M	T	W	T	F	S
						1
2	3	4	5	6	7	8
9	10	11	12	13	14	15
16	17	18	19	20	21	22
23	24	25	26	27	28	29
30	31					

June
S	M	T	W	T	F	S
		1	2	3	4	5
6	7	8	9	10	11	12
13	14	15	16	17	18	19
20	21	22	23	24	25	26
27	28	29	30			

July
S	M	T	W	T	F	S
				1	2	3
4	5	6	7	8	9	10
11	12	13	14	15	16	17
18	19	20	21	22	23	24
25	26	27	28	29	30	31

August
S	M	T	W	T	F	S
1	2	3	4	5	6	7
8	9	10	11	12	13	14
15	16	17	18	19	20	21
22	23	24	25	26	27	28
29	30	31				

September
S	M	T	W	T	F	S
			1	2	3	4
5	6	7	8	9	10	11
12	13	14	15	16	17	18
19	20	21	22	23	24	25
26	27	28	29	30		

October
S	M	T	W	T	F	S
					1	2
3	4	5	6	7	8	9
10	11	12	13	14	15	16
17	18	19	20	21	22	23
24	25	26	27	28	29	30
31						

November
S	M	T	W	T	F	S
	1	2	3	4	5	6
7	8	9	10	11	12	13
14	15	16	17	18	19	20
21	22	23	24	25	26	27
28	29	30				

December
S	M	T	W	T	F	S
			1	2	3	4
5	6	7	8	9	10	11
12	13	14	15	16	17	18
19	20	21	22	23	24	25
26	27	28	29	30	31	

TABLE G

January
S	M	T	W	T	F	S
						1
2	3	4	5	6	7	8
9	10	11	12	13	14	15
16	17	18	19	20	21	22
23	24	25	26	27	28	29
30	31					

February
S	M	T	W	T	F	S
		1	2	3	4	5
6	7	8	9	10	11	12
13	14	15	16	17	18	19
20	21	22	23	24	25	26
27	28					

March
S	M	T	W	T	F	S
			1	2	3	4	5
6	7	8	9	10	11	12
13	14	15	16	17	18	19
20	21	22	23	24	25	26
27	28	29	30	31		

April
S	M	T	W	T	F	S
					1	2
3	4	5	6	7	8	9
10	11	12	13	14	15	16
17	18	19	20	21	22	23
24	25	26	27	28	29	30

May
S	M	T	W	T	F	S
1	2	3	4	5	6	7
8	9	10	11	12	13	14
15	16	17	18	19	20	21
22	23	24	25	26	27	28
29	30	31				

June
S	M	T	W	T	F	S
			1	2	3	4
5	6	7	8	9	10	11
12	13	14	15	16	17	18
19	20	21	22	23	24	25
26	27	28	29	30		

July
S	M	T	W	T	F	S
					1	2
3	4	5	6	7	8	9
10	11	12	13	14	15	16
17	18	19	20	21	22	23
24	25	26	27	28	29	30
31						

August
S	M	T	W	T	F	S
	1	2	3	4	5	6
7	8	9	10	11	12	13
14	15	16	17	18	19	20
21	22	23	24	25	26	27
28	29	30	31			

September
S	M	T	W	T	F	S
				1	2	3
4	5	6	7	8	9	10
11	12	13	14	15	16	17
18	19	20	21	22	23	24
25	26	27	28	29	30	

October
S	M	T	W	T	F	S
						1
2	3	4	5	6	7	8
9	10	11	12	13	14	15
16	17	18	19	20	21	22
23	24	25	26	27	28	29
30	31					

November
S	M	T	W	T	F	S
		1	2	3	4	5
6	7	8	9	10	11	12
13	14	15	16	17	18	19
20	21	22	23	24	25	26
27	28	29	30			

December
S	M	T	W	T	F	S
				1	2	3
4	5	6	7	8	9	10
11	12	13	14	15	16	17
18	19	20	21	22	23	24
25	26	27	28	29	30	31

TABLE H

January
S	M	T	W	T	F	S
1	2	3	4	5	6	7
8	9	10	11	12	13	14
15	16	17	18	19	20	21
22	23	24	25	26	27	28
29	30	31				

February
S	M	T	W	T	F	S
			1	2	3	4
5	6	7	8	9	10	11
12	13	14	15	16	17	18
19	20	21	22	23	24	25
26	27	28	29			

March
S	M	T	W	T	F	S
				1	2	3
4	5	6	7	8	9	10
11	12	13	14	15	16	17
18	19	20	21	22	23	24
25	26	27	28	29	30	31

April
S	M	T	W	T	F	S
1	2	3	4	5	6	7
8	9	10	11	12	13	14
15	16	17	18	19	20	21
22	23	24	25	26	27	28
29	30					

May
S	M	T	W	T	F	S
		1	2	3	4	5
6	7	8	9	10	11	12
13	14	15	16	17	18	19
20	21	22	23	24	25	26
27	28	29	30	31		

June
S	M	T	W	T	F	S
					1	2
3	4	5	6	7	8	9
10	11	12	13	14	15	16
17	18	19	20	21	22	23
24	25	26	27	28	29	30

July
S	M	T	W	T	F	S
1	2	3	4	5	6	7
8	9	10	11	12	13	14
15	16	17	18	19	20	21
22	23	24	25	26	27	28
29	30	31				

August
S	M	T	W	T	F	S
				1	2	3
4	5	6	7	8	9	10
11	12	13	14	15	16	17
18	19	20	21	22	23	24
25	26	27	28	29	30	31

September
S	M	T	W	T	F	S
						1
2	3	4	5	6	7	8
9	10	11	12	13	14	15
16	17	18	19	20	21	22
23	24	25	26	27	28	29
30						

October
S	M	T	W	T	F	S
	1	2	3	4	5	6
7	8	9	10	11	12	13
14	15	16	17	18	19	20
21	22	23	24	25	26	27
28	29	30	31			

November
S	M	T	W	T	F	S
				1	2	3
4	5	6	7	8	9	10
11	12	13	14	15	16	17
18	19	20	21	22	23	24
25	26	27	28	29	30	

December
S	M	T	W	T	F	S
						1
2	3	4	5	6	7	8
9	10	11	12	13	14	15
16	17	18	19	20	21	22
23	24	25	26	27	28	29
30	31					

DAYS OF THE WEEK CALENDARS

TABLE I

January
S	M	T	W	T	F	S
	1	2	3	4	5	6
7	8	9	10	11	12	13
14	15	16	17	18	19	20
21	22	23	24	25	26	27
28	29	30	31			

February
S	M	T	W	T	F	S
				1	2	3
4	5	6	7	8	9	10
11	12	13	14	15	16	17
18	19	20	21	22	23	24
25	26	27	28	29		

March
S	M	T	W	T	F	S
					1	2
3	4	5	6	7	8	9
10	11	12	13	14	15	16
17	18	19	20	21	22	23
24	25	26	27	28	29	30
31						

April
S	M	T	W	T	F	S
	1	2	3	4	5	6
7	8	9	10	11	12	13
14	15	16	17	18	19	20
21	22	23	24	25	26	27
28	29	30				

May
S	M	T	W	T	F	S
			1	2	3	4
5	6	7	8	9	10	11
12	13	14	15	16	17	18
19	20	21	22	23	24	25
26	27	28	29	30	31	

June
S	M	T	W	T	F	S
						1
2	3	4	5	6	7	8
9	10	11	12	13	14	15
16	17	18	19	20	21	22
23	24	25	26	27	28	29
30						

July
S	M	T	W	T	F	S
	1	2	3	4	5	6
7	8	9	10	11	12	13
14	15	16	17	18	19	20
21	22	23	24	25	26	27
28	29	30	31			

August
S	M	T	W	T	F	S
				1	2	3
4	5	6	7	8	9	10
11	12	13	14	15	16	17
18	19	20	21	22	23	24
25	26	27	28	29	30	31

September
S	M	T	W	T	F	S
1	2	3	4	5	6	7
8	9	10	11	12	13	14
15	16	17	18	19	20	21
22	23	24	25	26	27	28
29	30					

October
S	M	T	W	T	F	S
	1	2	3	4	5	
6	7	8	9	10	11	12
13	14	15	16	17	18	19
20	21	22	23	24	25	26
27	28	29	30	31		

November
S	M	T	W	T	F	S
					1	2
3	4	5	6	7	8	9
10	11	12	13	14	15	16
17	18	19	20	21	22	23
24	25	26	27	28	29	30

December
S	M	T	W	T	F	S
1	2	3	4	5	6	7
8	9	10	11	12	13	14
15	16	17	18	19	20	21
22	23	24	25	26	27	28
29	30	31				

TABLE J

January
S	M	T	W	T	F	S
		1	2	3	4	5
6	7	8	9	10	11	12
13	14	15	16	17	18	19
20	21	22	23	24	25	26
27	28	29	30	31		

February
S	M	T	W	T	F	S
					1	2
3	4	5	6	7	8	9
10	11	12	13	14	15	16
17	18	19	20	21	22	23
24	25	26	27	28	29	

March
S	M	T	W	T	F	S
						1
2	3	4	5	6	7	8
9	10	11	12	13	14	15
16	17	18	19	20	21	22
23	24	25	26	27	28	29
30	31					

April
S	M	T	W	T	F	S
		1	2	3	4	5
6	7	8	9	10	11	12
13	14	15	16	17	18	19
20	21	22	23	24	25	26
27	28	29	30			

May
S	M	T	W	T	F	S
				1	2	3
4	5	6	7	8	9	10
11	12	13	14	15	16	17
18	19	20	21	22	23	24
25	26	27	28	29	30	31

June
S	M	T	W	T	F	S
1	2	3	4	5	6	7
8	9	10	11	12	13	14
15	16	17	18	19	20	21
22	23	24	25	26	27	28
29	30					

July
S	M	T	W	T	F	S
		1	2	3	4	5
6	7	8	9	10	11	12
13	14	15	16	17	18	19
20	21	22	23	24	25	26
27	28	29	30	31		

August
S	M	T	W	T	F	S
					1	2
3	4	5	6	7	8	9
10	11	12	13	14	15	16
17	18	19	20	21	22	23
24	25	26	27	28	29	30
31						

September
S	M	T	W	T	F	S
1	2	3	4	5	6	
7	8	9	10	11	12	13
14	15	16	17	18	19	20
21	22	23	24	25	26	27
28	29	30				

October
S	M	T	W	T	F	S
		1	2	3	4	
5	6	7	8	9	10	11
12	13	14	15	16	17	18
19	20	21	22	23	24	25
26	27	28	29	30	31	

November
S	M	T	W	T	F	S
						1
2	3	4	5	6	7	8
9	10	11	12	13	14	15
16	17	18	19	20	21	22
23	24	25	26	27	28	29
30						

December
S	M	T	W	T	F	S
	1	2	3	4	5	6
7	8	9	10	11	12	13
14	15	16	17	18	19	20
21	22	23	24	25	26	27
28	29	30	31			

TABLE K

January
S	M	T	W	T	F	S
			1	2	3	4
5	6	7	8	9	10	11
12	13	14	15	16	17	18
19	20	21	22	23	24	25
26	27	28	29	30	31	

February
S	M	T	W	T	F	S
						1
2	3	4	5	6	7	8
9	10	11	12	13	14	15
16	17	18	19	20	21	22
23	24	25	26	27	28	29

March
S	M	T	W	T	F	S
1	2	3	4	5	6	7
8	9	10	11	12	13	14
15	16	17	18	19	20	21
22	23	24	25	26	27	28
29	30	31				

April
S	M	T	W	T	F	S
		1	2	3	4	
5	6	7	8	9	10	11
12	13	14	15	16	17	18
19	20	21	22	23	24	25
26	27	28	29	30		

May
S	M	T	W	T	F	S
				1	2	
3	4	5	6	7	8	9
10	11	12	13	14	15	16
17	18	19	20	21	22	23
24	25	26	27	28	29	30
31						

June
S	M	T	W	T	F	S
1	2	3	4	5	6	
7	8	9	10	11	12	13
14	15	16	17	18	19	20
21	22	23	24	25	26	27
28	29	30				

July
S	M	T	W	T	F	S
		1	2	3	4	
5	6	7	8	9	10	11
12	13	14	15	16	17	18
19	20	21	22	23	24	25
26	27	28	29	30	31	

August
S	M	T	W	T	F	S
					1	
2	3	4	5	6	7	8
9	10	11	12	13	14	15
16	17	18	19	20	21	22
23	24	25	26	27	28	29
30	31					

September
S	M	T	W	T	F	S
	1	2	3	4	5	
6	7	8	9	10	11	12
13	14	15	16	17	18	19
20	21	22	23	24	25	26
27	28	29	30			

October
S	M	T	W	T	F	S
			1	2	3	
4	5	6	7	8	9	10
11	12	13	14	15	16	17
18	19	20	21	22	23	24
25	26	27	28	29	30	31

November
S	M	T	W	T	F	S
1	2	3	4	5	6	7
8	9	10	11	12	13	14
15	16	17	18	19	20	21
22	23	24	25	26	27	28
29	30					

December
S	M	T	W	T	F	S
	1	2	3	4	5	
6	7	8	9	10	11	12
13	14	15	16	17	18	19
20	21	22	23	24	25	26
27	28	29	30	31		

TABLE L

January
S	M	T	W	T	F	S
			1	2	3	
4	5	6	7	8	9	10
11	12	13	14	15	16	17
18	19	20	21	22	23	24
25	26	27	28	29	30	31

February
S	M	T	W	T	F	S
1	2	3	4	5	6	7
8	9	10	11	12	13	14
15	16	17	18	19	20	21
22	23	24	25	26	27	28
29						

March
S	M	T	W	T	F	S
1	2	3	4	5	6	
7	8	9	10	11	12	13
14	15	16	17	18	19	20
21	22	23	24	25	26	27
28	29	30	31			

April
S	M	T	W	T	F	S
			1	2	3	
4	5	6	7	8	9	10
11	12	13	14	15	16	17
18	19	20	21	22	23	24
25	26	27	28	29	30	

May
S	M	T	W	T	F	S
					1	
2	3	4	5	6	7	8
9	10	11	12	13	14	15
16	17	18	19	20	21	22
23	24	25	26	27	28	29
30	31					

June
S	M	T	W	T	F	S
	1	2	3	4	5	
6	7	8	9	10	11	12
13	14	15	16	17	18	19
20	21	22	23	24	25	26
27	28	29	30			

July
S	M	T	W	T	F	S
			1	2	3	
4	5	6	7	8	9	10
11	12	13	14	15	16	17
18	19	20	21	22	23	24
25	26	27	28	29	30	31

August
S	M	T	W	T	F	S
1	2	3	4	5	6	7
8	9	10	11	12	13	14
15	16	17	18	19	20	21
22	23	24	25	26	27	28
29	30	31				

September
S	M	T	W	T	F	S
		1	2	3	4	
5	6	7	8	9	10	11
12	13	14	15	16	17	18
19	20	21	22	23	24	25
26	27	28	29	30		

October
S	M	T	W	T	F	S
				1	2	
3	4	5	6	7	8	9
10	11	12	13	14	15	16
17	18	19	20	21	22	23
24	25	26	27	28	29	30
31						

November
S	M	T	W	T	F	S
	1	2	3	4	5	6
7	8	9	10	11	12	13
14	15	16	17	18	19	20
21	22	23	24	25	26	27
28	29	30				

December
S	M	T	W	T	F	S
		1	2	3	4	
5	6	7	8	9	10	11
12	13	14	15	16	17	18
19	20	21	22	23	24	25
26	27	28	29	30	31	

DAYS OF THE WEEK CALENDARS

TABLE M

January
S	M	T	W	T	F	S
					1	2
3	4	5	6	7	8	9
10	11	12	13	14	15	16
17	18	19	20	21	22	23
24	25	26	27	28	29	30
31						

February
S	M	T	W	T	F	S
	1	2	3	4	5	6
7	8	9	10	11	12	13
14	15	16	17	18	19	20
21	22	23	24	25	26	27
28	29					

March
S	M	T	W	T	F	S
		1	2	3	4	5
6	7	8	9	10	11	12
13	14	15	16	17	18	19
20	21	22	23	24	25	26
27	28	29	30	31		

April
S	M	T	W	T	F	S
					1	2
3	4	5	6	7	8	9
10	11	12	13	14	15	16
17	18	19	20	21	22	23
24	25	26	27	28	29	30

May
S	M	T	W	T	F	S
1	2	3	4	5	6	7
8	9	10	11	12	13	14
15	16	17	18	19	20	21
22	23	24	25	26	27	28
29	30	31				

June
S	M	T	W	T	F	S
				1	2	3	4
5	6	7	8	9	10	11
12	13	14	15	16	17	18
19	20	21	22	23	24	25
26	27	28	29	30		

July
S	M	T	W	T	F	S
					1	2
3	4	5	6	7	8	9
10	11	12	13	14	15	16
17	18	19	20	21	22	23
24	25	26	27	28	29	30
31						

August
S	M	T	W	T	F	S
	1	2	3	4	5	6
7	8	9	10	11	12	13
14	15	16	17	18	19	20
21	22	23	24	25	26	27
28	29	30	31			

September
S	M	T	W	T	F	S
				1	2	3
4	5	6	7	8	9	10
11	12	13	14	15	16	17
18	19	20	21	22	23	24
25	26	27	28	29	30	

October
S	M	T	W	T	F	S
						1
2	3	4	5	6	7	8
9	10	11	12	13	14	15
16	17	18	19	20	21	22
23	24	25	26	27	28	29
30	31					

November
S	M	T	W	T	F	S
		1	2	3	4	5
6	7	8	9	10	11	12
13	14	15	16	17	18	19
20	21	22	23	24	25	26
27	28	29	30			

December
S	M	T	W	T	F	S
				1	2	3
4	5	6	7	8	9	10
11	12	13	14	15	16	17
18	19	20	21	22	23	24
25	26	27	28	29	30	31

TABLE N

January
S	M	T	W	T	F	S
						1
2	3	4	5	6	7	8
9	10	11	12	13	14	15
16	17	18	19	20	21	22
23	24	25	26	27	28	29
30	31					

February
S	M	T	W	T	F	S
		1	2	3	4	5
6	7	8	9	10	11	12
13	14	15	16	17	18	19
20	21	22	23	24	25	26
27	28	29				

March
S	M	T	W	T	F	S
				1	2	3	4
5	6	7	8	9	10	11
12	13	14	15	16	17	18
19	20	21	22	23	24	25
26	27	28	29	30	31	

April
S	M	T	W	T	F	S
						1
2	3	4	5	6	7	8
9	10	11	12	13	14	15
16	17	18	19	20	21	22
23	24	25	26	27	28	29
30						

May
S	M	T	W	T	F	S
		1	2	3	4	5	6
7	8	9	10	11	12	13
14	15	16	17	18	19	20
21	22	23	24	25	26	27
28	29	30	31			

June
S	M	T	W	T	F	S
				1	2	3
4	5	6	7	8	9	10
11	12	13	14	15	16	17
18	19	20	21	22	23	24
25	26	27	28	29	30	

July
S	M	T	W	T	F	S
						1
2	3	4	5	6	7	8
9	10	11	12	13	14	15
16	17	18	19	20	21	22
23	24	25	26	27	28	29
30	31					

August
S	M	T	W	T	F	S
		1	2	3	4	5
6	7	8	9	10	11	12
13	14	15	16	17	18	19
20	21	22	23	24	25	26
27	28	29	30	31		

September
S	M	T	W	T	F	S
					1	2
3	4	5	6	7	8	9
10	11	12	13	14	15	16
17	18	19	20	21	22	23
24	25	26	27	28	29	30

October
S	M	T	W	T	F	S
1	2	3	4	5	6	7
8	9	10	11	12	13	14
15	16	17	18	19	20	21
22	23	24	25	26	27	28
29	30	31				

November
S	M	T	W	T	F	S
				1	2	3	4
5	6	7	8	9	10	11
12	13	14	15	16	17	18
19	20	21	22	23	24	25
26	27	28	29	30		

December
S	M	T	W	T	F	S
					1	2
3	4	5	6	7	8	9
10	11	12	13	14	15	16
17	18	19	20	21	22	23
24	25	26	27	28	29	30
31						

INDEX

I'd love to get your feedback, no matter how small. Please e-mail me at wdanielquillen@gmail.com with your comments.

Cold Spring Press Genealogy

If you are interested in buying additional copies of this book or any of our other genealogy titles, go to *www.essentialgenealogy.com* and order through our site at a great discount.

Secrets to Tracing Your Ancestors, 7th Edition
The Troubleshooter's Guide to Do-It-Yourself Genealogy,
3rd Edition

Quillen's Essentials of Genealogy series offers the following books, all now in revised editions:
• *Mastering Online Genealogy*
• *Mastering Immigration & Naturalization Records*
• *Mastering Census & Military Records*
• *Mastering Family, Library & Church Records*
• *Tracing Your European Roots*
• *Tracing Your Irish & British Roots*

Author W. Daniel Quillen is working on still more books in this indispensable series. All our books available in major bookstores, online booksellers, or through our website, where you will find all sorts of genealogical info, our books, Dan's blog, and much more!

_ML_   4-14